Edward de Vere, Seventeenth Earl of Oxford. (Miniature by Nicholas Hilliard in the Collection of His Grace, the Duke of Buccleuch. Reproduced by courtesy of the owner.)

OXFORD

AND HIS

ELIZABETHAN LADIES

by

Eleanor Brewster

DORRANCE & COMPANY
Philadelphia

ISBN 0-8059-1700-4
Library of Congress Catalog Card Number: 72-78246
Printed in the United States of America

To Helen and Genevieve, Loretta and Hester.

"I count myself in nothing else so happy
As in a soul remembering my good friends."

NOTE

I have taken the liberty of putting sixteenth century quotations into modern spelling, except in a very few instances. I believe this will make it easier for the reader to understand. However, inevitably, something is lost in this change which is why I have kept a few quotations in contemporary spelling.

CONTENTS

LIST OF ILLUSTRATIONS

ACKNOWLEDGMENTS

So many people have helped me in the preparation of this little book that it is impossible to name them all; I believe they know my gratitude. The list includes the staffs of the following: the British Museum, the London Museum and the Guildhall Library, in London; the New York Public Library, and the Trinity College Library in Hartford.

My interest in the Earl of Oxford was first aroused by the books of the Ogburns, Dorothy and the late Charlton Ogburn, who wrote: *This Star of England,* and Charlton Ogburn, Jr., who collaborated with his mother in *Shakespeare, The Man Behind the Name.* The Ogburns have not only permitted me to quote from their works, but Dorothy Ogburn in particular has given me invaluable help by suggestions in letters and in personal conversations. Miss G. M. Bowen, Hon. Secretary of the Shakespeare Authorship Society in London, and Miss R. M. D. Wainewright, Hon. Librarian of the same Society, have given me scholarly help many times, both in allowing me to quote from their own researches, and also in conversations. I have been given kind permission to quote from H. Amphlett's *Who Was Shakespeare?;* from the Rev. Ian Dunlop, to quote from *The Palaces and Progresses of Elizabeth I;* and from a lineal descendant of Edward de Vere's sister Mary, Thomas Goff, to quote from the books of his mother, Lady Cecilie Goff: *A Woman of the Tudor Age,* and *Four Generations of a Loyal House,* and many other courtesies. I wish to extend my gratitude to Dr. A. L. Rowse, who has not only allowed me to quote, but, through his magnificent books, has imbued me with the spirit of Elizabethan England.

And finally I want to write of my gratitude to another distinguished member of the de Veres who is not now living, who allowed me the rare privilege of quoting from notes he had compiled about them for his own family, and who also took time from his busy life to answer my questions both by letter and in conversations. He, and recently his widow, have shown many courtesies to me, which I appreciate.

The National Gallery, London, has allowed me to reproduce the painting in their collection, *Queen Elizabeth with Feather Fan*; the Victoria and Albert Museum has allowed reproduction of the drawing, *Queen Elizabeth Hawking*; the National Gallery, Washington, has given permission to reproduce the Constable painting, *Wivenhoe Meadow*. To all of these I am grateful.

The Hon. Simon Wingfield Digby, M. P., has kindly allowed me to reproduce the painting in his collection: *Queen Elizabeth in Procession*, a privilege I appreciate. Finally I extend my profound gratitude to his Grace the Duke of Portland, for allowing me to reproduce the Welbeck Portrait of Lord Oxford; to his Grace the Duke of Buccleuch for giving me permission to use as frontispiece the Hilliard Miniature of Lord Oxford; and my very special thanks go to his Grace the Duke of St. Albans, another de Vere descendant, not only for allowing me to reproduce the Gheeraedts Portrait of Lord Oxford, but also for his courteous encouragement and many kindnesses to me.

INTRODUCTION

Lord Oxford

Every word doth almost tell my name.[1]

Sonnet 76

A mysterious enigma surrounds the person of Edward de Vere, Seventeenth Earl of Oxford. Fascinating he was to his contemporaries, and fascinating he is to us today. Could the mystery be part of the fascination?

But the truth must out some day; that was our hero's great desire. This little book is an attempt to sort out his story with the help of the nine charming ladies he knew best.

The Elizabethans were indefatigable letter writers. They wrote to each other from the city, from the country, from the Court, from foreign lands and even from the wars. It might be said that these loquacious and articulate English of the Sixteenth and early Seventeenth Centuries wrote to one another as we moderns telephone today. There are in existence letters from Lord Oxford in Hackney to his brother-in-law in Westminster, each suburb contiguous to London, though on opposite sides of the city. Distances seemed greater then as transportation was more difficult than it is now and more hazardous (although this last statement might be open to question).

Indeed, many a noble family in England today can count its riches not only in its gold or silver plate protected behind iron bars in the dungeon, but also in a hoard of even greater riches in its library. There may be found the collection of letters written to and from its own ancestral members. The Elizabethans wrote to one another about great events and small, from the Massacre of St. Bartholomew to such trivia as the Queen's toothache. Some of the letters are dull reading, but from others one is able to reconstruct life in the reign of England's Virgin Queen, the very minutiae lending a vivid touch. It is as though we were learning the family news from a near relative. This hoard of letters is one of the chief sources of research for a biographer writing about this literate and entertaining age.

True, there are other sources, i.e., state papers, legal documents, publisher's records and even receipted bills. All these must be studied; but they give only the bare facts without contemporary embellishments.

A few diaries have been carefully preserved. Lord Burghley's notebooks immediately come to mind, for he was conscientious about writing down not only the daily happenings in the realm but also what was pertinent to his family. He even wrote down the precepts he gave to his younger son, Robert. These precepts are actually repeated in *Hamlet*, in the scene in which Polonius bids farewell to his son, Laertes.[2] Lord Burghley also notes in his diary that he bought some scales and weighed in not only each member of his family, but his household staff as well, recording the exact weight of each. But few Elizabethans kept as meticulous notes as he.

There are, however, inherent difficulties in attempting to reconstruct history from personal letters. The letter writer gives, naturally, his own understanding of what he describes, which in some instances may be prejudiced. Unless another person's account can be compared, the reader today has a distorted view of what actually happened. As an example one might attempt to describe that famous tennis court quarrel between Lord Oxford and young Philip Sidney. Fulke Greville, Sidney's earliest biographer, reports that Sidney was on the court when Lord Oxford appeared. But then, forgetting that he had said that, he goes on to tell that "Oxford continued his game." Now if he *continued*, it is obvious that he must have been playing on the court when *Sidney* interrupted the game. Greville then proceeds to tell that Lord Oxford challenged Sidney to a duel. But Sidney himself had written to his friend in Germany, Hubert Languet, that *he*,

Sidney, had sent the challenge to Lord Oxford, having considered himself insulted when Oxford called him "Puppy!"[3]

Another problem implicit in using private letters in a search for historic truth is that both spelling and punctuation were haphazard in those early days when our language was new. That is one reason why Elizabethan letters are such fun to read. But a copyist attempting to correct a mistake may actually change the meaning of what he is copying; his mistake is then repeated and perhaps exaggerated by generations of biographers, until by repetition the wrong interpretation comes to be accepted as the true.

There is an even more fundamental danger of misinterpreting history from available documents in that the historian is dependent upon the sources which the Elizabethans have chosen to preserve. Would it not be possible to change the future reputation of a Courtier, for instance, by keeping only accounts of the less flattering episodes in his life, while destroying all reference to his triumphs? This it is feared was the ill fortune which befell the lasting reputation of the Seventeenth Earl of Oxford.

Why is it that in so many histories of the age this noble peer has been maligned as a wastrel, spendthrift and even "a little mad"? One explanation might be that Lord Burghley and his son, Sir Robert Cecil, kept in their files the correspondence derogatory to this kinsman of theirs by marriage, while preserving all too little to show to future generations his magnificent gifts and accomplishments. The Cecils, to be sure, had excellent reasons for down-grading the Earl. In this story some of them may be indicated.

There is still one more source of information which scholars are only beginning to tap, and that is Elizabethan literature. In those days giants walked the earth: Sackville, Marlowe, Spenser, Sidney, Nashe, Lyly, Lodge, Peele, Jonson and, the greatest of them all, whom we know as Shakespeare. It is true that many of these writers lifted their themes from the classics, or from history which was just beginning to be widely read. But when the Elizabethans came to draw the characters in their plays and other works of literature they drew the men and women whom they knew, often retelling episodes which had occurred in their own or their contemporaries' lives. Hamlet recognised this tendency when he referred to the plays as "the abstract and brief chronicles of the time."

And now comes our crucial question: Whose name is given as the dramatist of the greatest plays in the English language? William Shakespeare. From earliest school days we have been taught that *Shakespeare* is the foremost name in all our literature. Why, then, should there be so much interest in the Earl of Oxford?

This biographer speaking personally believes that there was indeed a William Shakespeare, born at Stratford-upon-Avon, that he married Anne Hathaway, fathered three children and ran away to seek his fortune in London. There he was undoubtedly associated with the theatre, and one tradition is that when he first came to the city he supported himself by holding the reins of the horses of the gentry as they dismounted to enter the playhouse.

To tell why the present writer cannot believe William Shakespeare of Stratford to be the author, poet and dramatist we have been taught that he was, would take a tome in itself. Here is offered only one argument against his claim. Shakespeare's will has beeen preserved, and can be seen by any interested scholar today. From this document it is deduced that William Shakespeare had risen to the status of country gentleman in Stratford, that he had a coat of arms, and that he had acquired some wealth indicated by his bequests of rings and bedsteads. Yet this gentleman of wealth, position and property does not mention in his will *a single book*, although the will was drawn in the age of the Stuarts when books were coming to be as commonplace as spoons. One hears of Shakespeare's "well-thumbed Holinshed." But he didn't leave it in his will! Nor did he leave any book of Plutarch, or Ovid, or even Chaucer. If he had owned one, would he not have bequeathed it as a cherished possession to one of his dear ones? Neither does he mention any plays of his own either finished or unfinished. Reader, does this sound to you like the will of a cultured author of profound learning?

Doubt as to the identity of the famous dramatist has been prevalent ever since the middle of the seventeenth century. A number of well-educated Elizabethans have been suggested as the probable author, i.e., Kit Marlowe, Francis Bacon, Lord Derby and even Queen Elizabeth.

It was not until 1920 that the claim of Edward de Vere was seriously put forward. In that year a schoolmaster by the name of Lunei, or Looney, published a book called *Shakespeare Identified*. Years of laborious effort had preceded this publication. Looney, doubting as other scholars had that the actor from Stratford had composed the plays attributed to him, used a detective's method to try to discover the true author. Being an English literature professor, he was thoroughly familiar with the Shakespeare plays and poems. Looney made a long list of characteristics derived, let us repeat, from most painstaking reading of the plays and poems. Looney said the author must be:

a mature man of recognised genius;
of intense sensitivity;
unconventional;
of pronounced and well-known literary tastes;
an enthusiast for the world of drama;
a lyric poet of recognised talent;
of superior education—classical—the habitual associate of educated and cultured people;
a member of the aristocracy, more likely the nobility;
belonging to a family with Lancastrian leanings;
familiar with Continental cities, especially Italian cities;
a follower of sport, including falconry, the sport of nobility;
a lover of music;
doubtful and somewhat ambiguous in his attitude toward women.[4]

The last characteristic might prove to be the most tell-tale of all.

To Looney's list of characteristics of the mysterious author, we might emphasize this important note: the man was definitely stage-struck. Not only his dramas, but even his poems mention plays and players countless times; they must have been constantly on his mind. The most noteworthy examples, of course, are the familiar scenes from *Hamlet.* But here is a lesser-known passage from *The Taming of the Shrew,* referring to the strolling players who were so much a part of Elizabethan England:

> *A Lord:* How now! who is it?
> *Servingman:* An it please your honour,
> Players that offer service to your lordship.
> *Lord.* Bid them come near.
> *Enter Players.*
> Now, fellows, you are welcome.
> *Players.* We thank your honour.
> *Lord.* Do you intend to stay with me to-night?
> *A Player.* So please your lordship to accept our duty.
> *Lord.* With all my heart. This fellow I remember,
> Since once he play'd a farmer's eldest son:
> 'Twas where you woo'd the gentlewoman so well.
> I have forgot your name; but, sure that part
> Was aptly fitted and naturally perform'd.

After some talk between the Lord and the Players the Lord continues:

> Well, you are come to me in happy time,

and he proceeds to tell the leading Player just what he wants them to do. When he believes his instructions are clearly understood, he calls one of his servants:

> Go, sirrah, take them to the buttery,
> And give them friendly welcome every one:
> Let them want nothing that my house affords.

Here are a few random references to actors. In *King Henry IV,*

Part I, (Act II, sc. 4, line 435) the Hostess retorts to a protestation of Falstaff, with:

> O Jesu, he doth it as like one of these harlotry players as ever I see!

And here is a cry of anguish from the depths of despair (*Macbeth*, Act V, sc. 3, lines 24-28)

> Life's but a walking shadow, a poor player
> That struts and frets his hour upon the stage
> And then is heard no more: it is a tale
> Told by an idiot, full of sound and fury
> Signifying nothing.

Finally there is Jacques' stimulating yet humorous passage in *As You Like It*, presenting his own, and also the dramatist's view of life; beginning:

> All the world's a stage,
> And all the men and women merely players:
> They have their exits and their entrances;
> And one man in his time plays many parts,
> His acts being seven ages.
> (Act II, sc. 7, ll. 139-143.)

It may be significant that these brief quotations represent the viewpoint of the spectator, the audience, and not that of the player himself.

Now let us return to Looney, since it is he who has been most responsible in following up clues in regard to the life and works of Edward de Vere, Lord Oxford.

He made serious studies to find out which of the Elizabethans could best fit the description he had in mind, using the list of attributes he had drawn up. The long search narrowed down to one man: the Seventeenth Earl of Oxford. So Looney studied extensively to find out more about this elusive nobleman. His first enquiry was, What did his contemporaries think of him? This is part of what he found:

In 1586 William Webbe published *A Discourse on English Poetry,* in which he wrote:

> I may not omit the deserved commendations of many honourable and noble Lords and Gentlemen in her Majesty's Court, which in the rare devices of poetry have been and yet are most skillful; among whom the Right Honourable the Earl of Oxford may challenge to himself the title of the most excellent among the rest.

The Art of English Poesie was published in 1589, written, it is supposed, by Lord Lumley. In it we find:

> But in these days (although some learned Princes may take delight in Poets) yet universally it is not so . For as well Poets as Poesie are despised and the name become of honourable infamous, subject to scorn and derision and rather a reproach than a praise to any that use it.

Is this not pertinent? But Lord Lumley wrote further:

> And in Her Majesty's time that now is are sprung up another crew of Courtly Makers [poets], Noblemen and Gentlemen of Her Majesty's own servants, who have written excellent well as it would appear if their doings could be found out and made public with the rest, of which number is first that noble gentleman Edward, Earl of Oxford.

The reader is asked to note the phrase "as it would appear if their doings could be found out and made public." The verb *could* indicates that there is some reason why Lord Oxford's poetry *could not* "be found out and made public," meaning perhaps that, while the poetry might be published, the name of the poet could not be.

In 1590 Edmund Spenser published the first books of *The Faerie Queen*, prefaced by *Verses addressed by the Author . . . to Several Nobleman & C.* Among these dedicatory verses may be found a most significant poem addressed

To the Right Honourable the Earl of Oxford,
Lord High Chamberlain of England, & c.

Receive, most noble Lord, in gentle gree,
The unripe fruit of an unready wit,
Which, by thy countenance, doth crave to be
Defended from foul Envy's pois'nous bit.
Which so to do may thee right well befit,
Sith th'antique glory of thine ancestry
Under a shady veil is therein writ,
And eke thine own long living memory
Succeeding them in true nobility:
And also for the love which thou dost bear
To th'Heliconian ymps, and they to thee:
They unto thee, and thou to them most dear:
Dear as thou art unto thyself, so love
That loves and honours thee; as doth behove.[5]

Without going into too many particulars in regard to how and when this poem was written, it is obvious that it contains unmistakable references to Lord Oxford's life and character. Spenser writes with deep respect to this "most noble lord," asking him to accept "in gentle gree" (favor) that which he modestly calls "the unripe fruit of an unready wit." Then he refers to the glory of the old aristocratic family of de Vere. Note the phrase "shady veil," which could be significant. Spenser goes on to write of "thine own long living memory," suggesting that generations to come would venerate the noble peer who had succeeded to his noble forbears. He then writes, again significantly, of the love of Lord Oxford for the Muses—"th' Heliconian ymps," and further than that, of the love the Muses bear to *him*, Oxford. He ends the poem with a warm and affectionate greeting to the Peer:

> . . . so love[s]
> That [him that] loves and honours thee.

So this is what Edmund Spenser thought of Lord Oxford!

Later in the decade of the 1590s, in 1598 to be exact, Frances Meres had this to say: "The best for Comedy among us be Edward Earl of Oxford." Yet by this year a number of plays attributed to Shakespeare had appeared in print, including several of the comedies.[6]

Next, Looney sought out the early signed poems of Lord Oxford and compared them with the poems we know as Shakespeare's. Here he found such striking similarities that he felt he could proclaim to the world that Edward de Vere, Seventeenth Earl of Oxford, was in truth the long-sought author. Yet let it be understood that Looney did not assert that Lord Oxford had written every word attributed to William Shakespeare. He believed that Edward de Vere had been the presiding genius, that he was indeed the dramatist and poet of the glorious literature known to posterity as Shakespeare's work.

However, implicit in this belief are again many mysteries. Some of them have been cleared away already. Others may never be solved to a lawyer's satisfaction. Let it be said here that many scholars since 1920 have been examining Lord Oxford's claim assiduously, and that while complete proof of his authorship has never been established, neither has positive disproof ever been found.

The inquisitive reader may then ask: But why did not Lord Oxford sign his true name to his work? Let us explore this problem.

For one thing, "it wasn't done." A nobleman just didn't write dramas and poetry, and Lord Oxford was the Premier Earl of the realm. Then Lord Lumley's words should be recalled: "Poets," he said, "are despised and the name become a reproach than a praise to any that useth it." We today may not understand this attitude, but the Elizabethans did. However, there were more important reasons for Lord Oxford's identity to remain unknown.

The first time the name *William Shakespeare* appeared in print was as the author of *Venus and Adonis* published in 1593. It is our belief that this courtly poem tells the thinly veiled love story of the Queen of England for her young and handsome courtier, Oxford, and in particular of his extreme distaste for her amorous attentions. At the time of publication the fiction of the *Virgin* Queen had become a matter of state policy for England. The unwise love affair of Elizabeth Tudor with a mere subject was reason enough for shielding the identity of the poet. Later, as the famous plays began to appear on the stage and in print, stories of Court scandal were recognised in them only thinly disguised. Undoubtedly there were people especially at Court who were well aware of the identity of "William Shakespeare," and knew also the poet of those "sugar'd sonnets" mentioned by Francis Meres. But the public at large, and even future generations, must not be given a clue to the true stories behind the beautiful and innocent-seeming plays and poems.

Then there were other reasons for this author to remain anonymous. He was married to the daughter of the great Lord Burghley, and that august personage would have gone to great length to protect the reputation of his favorite child.

Even beyond these personal considerations, the Principal Secretary to the Queen who was later to become Lord Treasurer of England would have seen it his clear duty to protect the personal reputation of her gracious Majesty.

Granted Edward de Vere had to remain anonymous as an author, there was good reason for his choosing the name *Shakespeare*, since besides holding title to the earldom of Oxford, he held a lesser title of Viscount Bolebec whose crest consisted of a lion brandishing a broken spear.

By coincidence the lives of these two Elizabethans, Lord Oxford and William Shakespeare, so widely diverse, have curiously one factor in common, a birthday. It is a matter of historic truth that Edward de Vere was born on April 23rd, 1550.[7] The record is in the parish church at Castle Hedingham. It is only a matter of conjecture, however, that William Shakespeare was born on April 23rd, 1564. He was christened April 26th, so it was thought that he probably was born on April 22nd, or 23rd, and the 23rd is now accepted as his birthday. Both of these men died in their fifties. It was considered a goodly age then, but it seems today that each of them was cut off in his prime.

There have been other biographies of Lord Oxford. This writer has chosen to tell his story by considering what is now known about the ladies most intimately connected with his life, and also, rather daringly, to relate the ladies to heroines in the famous plays. This approach has been most interesting to develop, yet the very title of the story inhibits the telling of much about this distinguished Earl that is important, as, for example, his relations with the other literary geniuses of the time, and again, his own growth as poet and dramatist.

The Age

> Aurea nunc vere sunt saecula.
> Truly now is the golden age.
>
> *Ovid: Ars Amat,* Book II, 277.

> These most brisk and giddy-paced times.
>
> *Twelfth Night,* Act II, sc. 4.

In presenting these vignettes of nine ladies an attempt has been made not only to throw a new light upon the life of Edward de Vere, Seventeenth Earl of Oxford, but also to reflect something of the glory of "the spacious times of great Elizabeth." This was an age of change, perhaps of greater change than in any time of history until our day.

Before the Tudors came to the throne England had been a medieval country, beset by war within her borders as well as without. Her culture was largely French, as reflected in her language, and in the architecture of many of her cathedrals, most notably Westminster Abbey.[23] The cult of nationality, of being English as opposed to European, reached its height in the days of Elizabeth the Queen, who more than any of her statesmen, drew her people together into one united family.

This was an age of religious and cultural upheaval. The reformation of religion was dividing the English people into dissident groups from the High Church Anglicans to the Puritans; these differences were bound to cause dissension within the kingdom.

The Queen herself remained true to much of the doctrine of the old faith. She had an oratory in each of her palaces and she sought the consolation of confession and the blessing of the Church. What she could not stomach was the supremacy of the Pope! Yet while she stormed against the Catholics who from time to time were a very real threat to her throne, she raged equally against the psalm-singing Puritans who were trying among other things to crush the drama then bursting into flower.

The reformation of culture was almost as pervasive as the reformation of religion. Following the Turks' capture of Constantiople in 1453, the revival of the classics of Greece and Rome opened up new avenues of thought to the Western world. But the Renaissance in England took a course peculiarly *English*, in art, in music, and in literature, particularly in the drama which reached its zenith in the Shakespeare plays.

The renaissance of learning appealed to Lord Oxford far more than the reformation of religion. He determined to travel to the Continent, especially to Italy where the new learning was burgeoning. To the English writers Italy was the fount, and to that exotic land came a procession including Sir Philip Sidney, John

Lyly, Thomas Chapman and others, as well as Lord Oxford himself.

But what he absorbed in Italy Edward de Vere made quite his own. His work frequently reflects the classics, but the reflection is tinged with a glow luminous only in England.

Change was perhaps most noticeable in the way men lived. Domestic architecture before the Tudors had consisted largely of castles for defense, surrounded by clusters of thatched hovels. But with the dissolution of the monasteries by King Henry VIII many of the former church estates were apportioned to the nobility, as, for instance, Woburn Abbey. Gracious manor houses rose up all across the land, with tapestries on the walls to keep out the cold and dampness, open fireplaces with chimneys instead of a hole in the roof, and rushes on the floor[24] changed often, even the top layer. There were still Kenilworth and Arundel Castles, but there was also Hatfield House, Theobalds and Penshurst Place. Sometimes the country house was added onto the still existing fortress, as at Castle Hedingham and Knole, and at the great royal Castle of Windsor. Everywhere the accent was on luxury, with beautiful wooden cabinets for clothes and fine linen, carved tables and chairs, and warm quilts on the great carved oak beds.

It was not uncommon for a nobleman to have a country seat as well as a town house, even as Lord Burghley lived on the Strand when the Court was at Whitehall, but went out to Theobalds, his estate in Hertfordshire whenever he could get away. This lovely place started as a small house, but with each visitation of the Queen and her Court a new addition had to be added, until Theobalds became one of the great country houses of the land.

The important rooms in these new Tudor houses were the chapel and the great hall,[25] even as Elizabethan social life revolved around religious ceremony and ceremonial dining, with endless arguments and disputations parlayed across long tables.

Music was an important part of this life, and many a noble family sponsored trained "musicyons" who performed in the minstrel gallery overlooking the great hall. Frequently members of the family made their own music, playing upon the lute, the Viola di Gamba, the recorder or the virginals, either separately or in a small chamber orchestra.

Another form of music dear to the Elizabethans was the singing of madrigals. There is a pretty picture of the aristocratic family having supper usually at half past five in the afternoon, followed by a long winter evening when the great hall would be lighted by homemade candles on wooden coronas suspended from the ceiling. After supper the lady of the manor "was wont to serve out the part-books and call upon her guests to join with the family in singing madrigals."[26] Indeed, the guests and family were so well trained in music that they could read at sight the most difficult motets. Such was the setting which made "all England a nest of singing birds!"[27] John Farmer published his *First set of English Madrigals for Four Voices* in 1599, dedicating the volume to the Earl of Oxford with these words:

> As a recreation your Lordship have overgrown most of them that make it [music] a profession.[28]

Even the commoners now lived in houses instead of hovels, with glass window panes instead of horn which had let only faint streaks of daylight filter through.[29] And with the new architecture came a new demand for domestic comfort. It is surprising to learn that water was piped into cisterns in London streets as early as in the reign of King Henry VII.[30] However, running water was rare until about 1582.

Sir John Harington, the Queen's godson, is credited with having the first water-closet in England, although he installed it only in his own house in the country.[31] The pollution of streams of which we are today so conscious had aready begun.

It is, therefore, not unexpected to learn that in Queen Elizabeth's day Thames water was unpotable and fresh water had to be brought in to her palaces from some distance. It took 250 tons of lead pipe to bring fresh water to Hampton Court from Coombe Hill three miles away.[32] In Whitehall and in Richmond there was installed next to her Majesty's sleeping chamber "the Queen's bathroom."[33] What this consisted of, or how often the Queen bathed here, is not told, but it is significant that she even had such a room.

With the softening of living conditions came a new interest in clothes for both men and women. After the introduction of starch from the Continent, elaborate ruffs began to appear. Styles were copied from those of Italy, as noted in *King Richard II*, Act II, sc. 1:

> Report of fashion in proud Italy,
> Whose manners still our tardy apish nation
> Limps after in base imitation.

Indeed, after the Earl of Oxford came home from Italy bringing gorgeous apparel including rich capes and feathered caps, he was called half-mockingly, half-enviously, "the Italianate nobleman." He brought the Queen a present of "a pair of perfumed gloves trimmed only with four tufts of roses of coloured silk," which pleased her Majesty so much that she had her portrait painted wearing them.[34] John Stow, the tailor's son who became the chronicler of Elizabethan London, writes that after this, Italian gloves and girdles embroidered with silk and gold thread began to be stocked in the London shops and were in great demand.[35] Gloves are mentioned a number of times in the famous plays; here are two references:

> The gloves the Count sent me; they are an excellent perfume.
>
> *Much Ado About Nothing*. Act III, sc. 4.

> Gloves as sweet as damask roses.
>
> *Winter's Tale*. Act IV, sc. 4.

Undergarments were not common in Elizabethan England, although the museums of London do show some shifts dating from this period. One piece of gossip rumored about Queen

Elizabeth was that she had appeared after keeping a rendezvous with Simier, the French emissary of the Duc d'Alençon. Just as she stood there she was confronted with the Duc himself, "at the door of her bedchamber with *only her shift and nightgown on* [Italics mine]."

In the great hall the nobility still dined on a raised dais, while their retainers in descending order of social degree[36] sat upon benches at long tables at right angles to the head table. This arrangement is still found in most English college dining halls today, and indeed in many in America. Glass goblets were coming into use for wine and ale.[37] It is recalled that Mistress Quickly complained to Falstaff that because he would not pay his bill to her she "must fain pawn both my plate and the tapestry of my dining-chamber." But he rudely retorts: "Glass, glass, is the only drinking," trying to convince her that glasses are more fashionable and pleasanter to drink from than silver goblets. In some of the great houses china plates were to be found, and gold and silver spoons and knives with gold or silver handles, in contrast to the bone utensils common before the Tudors. But the more usual setting would have been wooden trenchers.[38] We are reminded that *Beatrice* remarks that *Benedict* "is a very valiant trencherman." (*Much Ado*, Act I, sc. 1). There is in the Victoria and Albert Museum a set of wooden trenchers which could be turned over for dessert, and on this dessert side were delightful little verses, each one different.

Most people used pewter vessels, though pitchers have been found of beautifully ornamented glass.[39] Forks were in use at this time in Italy and in parts of France, but the English stubbornly resisted this new-fangled gadget.[40] The custom of eating meat with the fingers gave rise to the Office of the Ewery, a hereditary prerogative of the Earls of Oxford in the royal Court. On ceremonial occasions it was the noble Edward de Vere who, on bended knee, held the basin of warm water into which her Majesty could dip her lovely hands after eating her chicken or chop, and then wipe them on the clean linen towel he held out to her.

Toward the middle of Queen Elizabeth's reign the coach

appeared; after this the nobility could travel in comfort instead of by litter or horseback. It was said that one of the reasons the Queen was so ragingly jealous of Lettice Knollys was not only that Lettice had had the temerity to marry Elizabeth's own "sweet Robin," but that she splurged about London in a finer coach than the Queen's. There is mention of a coach in *The Second Part of King Henry the Sixth,* Act II, sc. 4, in the tragic scene in which the Duke of Gloucester sees his Duchess trudging through the "flinty" streets of London led by her guard on her way to banishment on the Isle of Man. The Citizens of London are jeering at her. The Duke speaks:

> Sweet Nell, ill can thy noble mind abrook
> The abject people, gazing on thy face
> With envious looks still laughing at thy shame
> That erst did follow thy proud chariot wheels
> When thou didst ride in triumph through the streets.

Actually this scene is anachronistic, as are many other scenes in the Shakespeare plays, for there were no "chariots" in London in the time of King Henry VI. The dramatist is suggesting a picture of Elizabethan London, the nobility riding by in state while the "abject people," gaze up to their faces with envious looks.

It was the women who benefited most from the changes sweeping across England. The woman of the Tudor age reached a status never before attained by earlier women in that country. While marriages were still arranged by parents in the old mercenary manner, there were now romantic marriages, too. Emancipation from drudgery was the Elizabethan woman's greatest gain. Proficiency at the spinning wheel was still expected of the daughter in families of both high and low degree, yet the fast-growing weaving industry brought to England by the Flemings released her from much of the hard labor she had known before. This release provided the leisure time which she could then spend in the study of music and art and language, luxuries heretofore reserved only for her brothers.

The Queen was said to be the best educated English woman of her day, having been tutored with her brother by the most learned scholars in the land engaged by King Henry VIII to teach his children. Among these scholars was Sir Anthony Coke[41] of Cambridge University.

Queen Elizabeth was justly proud of her learning and frequently astounded the foreign ambassadors accredited to her Court by lecturing them in Latin or Greek. It was said that she could turn from French to Italian, "Scotch or Dutch," with equal facility.

Of the ladies at her Court most noted for knowledge of the classics, Lady Burghley and Lady Bacon, daughters of Sir Anthony Coke mentioned above, were outstanding. Toward the latter part of the Queen's reign the most distinguished intellectual lady was Mary Sidney, Countess of Pembroke, the sister of Sir Philip Sidney.

The Palaces

The cloud-capp'd towers, the gorgeous palaces . . .
The Tempest, Act III, sc. 3.

Since the Earl of Oxford was best known to his contemporaries as a courtier to the Queen, and since all his ladies were deeply concerned with the Court, it seems appropriate to describe the royal palaces, which are the flamboyant setting for the stories to follow.

The first scene is, of course, at Whitehall, that heterogeneous group of buildings, courts, gardens and orchards situated between St. James Park[8] and the river. The Thames in those days was wider than it is today, for there was no Embankment and the palace extended down to the pebbled shore. Whitehall comprised more than 2,000 rooms; it was, according to a contemporary account of a Frenchman, more commodious than the Louvre.[9] The principal entrance was from the river, and the Queen's privy chambers also had steps leading to a dock.

When Henry VIII had seized the palace from the fallen Wolsey, he changed the name from York Place to "the King's Manor of Westminster," though it was generally known as Whitehall. The dramatist of the play *King Henry the Eighth* refers to this change of name in Act IV, sc. 2, ll. 95-7:

> You must no more call it York-place, that's past;
> For since the cardinal fell, that title's lost:
> 'Tis now the king's, and call'd Whitehall.

Henry VIII had given Hans Holbein a free hand in decorating his new residence and the artist had made it one of the great royal palaces of the time. Astride King Street there were two gates, one called the Holbein Gate similar to the Holbein Gate at St. James Palace. Holbein did not design the gate over King Street, but he may have had an apartment over it, for it was known for sometime afterward as "Hance's House."

The palace buildings were on both sides of King Street. A visitor riding down from Charing Cross would pass first the royal orchards on the river or left side of the road, with the tilt-yard on the other side, about where the Horse Guards are today. Next to the tilt-yard would be the royal tennis courts, two of them outdoors and one enclosed. On the river side would be the gardens and then the buildings of the royal palace itself, with its great halls overlooking the river, the Queen's privy chambers also on the river. Across King Street would be the accommodations for the lesser nobility and all the servants and royal retinue.

Across the river, the Queen's barge would be moored on the Surrey side, ready to take her on a royal progress to one of the other palaces, or perhaps for just a restful afternoon on the Thames.

Travelling by river was the Queen's favorite means of moving between palaces. Also when the weather was balmy she loved to sit in her barge floating lazily on the water, sometimes bringing her musicians along to entertain her guests, sometimes playing herself upon her lute. Are we not reminded of another queen reclining in state in her barge as it floated on the Cydnus River?

Whenever the Queen set forth upon the Thames, she was attended by a flock of white swans. A visitor writes that they lived "in great security, nobody daring to molest them." Once a year their feathers were plucked to repair the upholstery in the royal residences.[10]

Skimming along the river past Westminster where Parliament met and the Law Courts held their sessions, the Queen must have had a real sense of speed. Soon the barge would come to open country with green meadows and sluggish backwaters. Herons and kingfishers would rise up with a whirr of wings startled by the voices of the courtiers chatting and laughing together. . . .

At Syon House the river turns south by the island of Islesworth Eyot, and the Palace of Richmond would be in sight. First along the shore would be the orchards, and then the group of buildings of brick and half timber, the jakes. This is why the palaces were built beside rivers, and also why the Thames water was unsafe to drink even in Elizabethan days.[11]

The Queen loved Richmond; she enjoyed especially riding and hunting in the Great Park. The palace had been built by her grandfather, Henry VII, soon after he became king, and he had given it the name of his former dukedom.

A foreign diplomat has drawn a delightful word picture of the Queen in this palace. Soon after her arrival, he wrote, as her Majesty looked down from her window in the gallery, all her retinue fell to their knees. Truly moved, she called down to them: "God bless my people!" to which they all responded with a shout: "God save the Queen!" The people remained kneeling until she gave them the sign to rise.[12]

Hampton Court was the most beautiful of the royal residences. Yet an Italian diplomat wrote that "as for the rooms, there is no imaginable order,as the English merely look to convenience."[13] In Hampton Court garden were roses, violets, sweet William, gilliver slips and primroses, and country women were employed at tuppence a day to keep it weeded.[14] Yet after 1562 this palace was the least attractive to the Queen, since she had been very ill there with smallpox.

Greenwich, where Elizabeth was born, was down river from London. It was a favorite for summetime, with fresh breezes blowing off the Thames, and wharves and ships seen from the windows of Her Majesty's privy chamber. Later in the reign, Drake's *Golden Hind* would be anchored offshore. Frequently there were military reviews on the vast green lawns of Greenwich. Tradition has it that this was where the country lad from Devon spread his cloak over the mud puddle so that the Queen might walk over it dryshod.[15]

Oatlands was one of the hunting lodges, with a view over the meandering river between Staines and Shepperton, Windsor Castle looming up like a great mountain of gray stone in the distance. When hunting in the country hereabouts, the Queen was awaited at the chase by fifty archers in scarlet boots and yellow caps, and armed with gilded bows. The Queen's own arrows were headed with silver and "flighted with peacock feathers."[16]

Newhall Palace the Queen used only until 1573, when she granted it to Thomas Radcliffe, Earl of Sussex, the friend of Lord Oxford's father. Edward de Vere must have visited often at Newhall.

Nonsuch, like its name, was the most bizarre of the palaces, and also the smallest. When the Court was in residence there, many of the nobility and most of the retainers had to live in tents.[17]

The oldest and most imposing of all the royal residences was Windsor Castle. Frequently it was used for entertaining foreign diplomats, who never failed to be impressed by its magnificence.[18] There was hunting at Windsor in the Great Park. And here the Queen came every year for St. George's Day, June 18th, when the young noblemen to be created Knights of the Garter would ride out from London in splendid array with their attendants in the family livery, to be invested with the Order in the beautiful Royal Chapel of St. George. At Windsor the Queen built a great wide esplanade overlooking the Thames valley and Eton College, so that her ladies might take the air without soiling their fine apparel.

The Queen's palaces often figured in negotiations in regard to her marriage, and foreign diplomats were wont to be taken on a tour of them, or on a royal progress from one to another. One negotiator wrote home to his master: "Hence she is well worth the trouble." Another wrote in his report: "Never have I seen so much splendour and such rich clothes."[19]

To move the Court by land on a progress from one palace to another took three hundred baggage carts and two thousand four hundred horses. Burghley and Walsingham usually rode first in the long procession. Then "the Queen sitting all alone in her splendid coach, appeared like a goddess."[20] Sometimes she would have by her side the particular foreign emissary or courtier she wished at the moment to impress, never failing to call the attention of the guest to the tumultuous adulation of her people. Following her coach would come the courtiers and twenty-four Maids of Honour, mounted and beautifully attired; then fifty of the Queen's Guard. Two empty coaches and baggage carts brought up the rear, the extra coaches brought along in case the main coach broke down. A progress was accompanied by the ringing of church bells; indeed, it was the bells of St. Margaret's, Westminster, that announced to the people that the royal progress had begun.[21] Wherever the Queen would go, by land or by river, her people would stop work and come running out to see her, their sovereign liege lady for whom they prayed each Sunday in the Litany.

Her Majesty is pictured most frequently at Whitehall, where she felt most at home, with the busy highway, King Street, running through the midst of the palace buildings to Charing Cross and beyond. Elizabeth Tudor was a true Londoner, loving all the clamor and clatter of the city streets, the tolling and chimes of the city churchbells. To Whitehall the Queen always came for Accession Day, November 17th. It is tempting to linger over descriptions of her Majesty and her glittering Court here in the pomp and magnificence of her London home. For instance, a German visitor, Platter, has written that her Courtiers always knelt when addressing her, even when playing cards with her.[22]

Now let us turn to the ladies. And let us look to the players, too, remembering Prince Hamlet's words:

The players cannot keep counsel; they'll tell all.

NOTES TO INTRODUCTION

1. The words *ever, every* and *very* appear frequently in the works we know as Shakespeare's. It will be noted that each contains the name of *Vere. Ever* and *every* might be considered the hidden signature of Lord Oxford: *E. Vere.* He often used these same words so.

2. A. L. Rowse, *William Shakespeare: A Biography.*

3. H. Amphlett, *Who Was Shakespeare?* p. 107.

4. J. T. Looney, *Shakespeare Identified.*

5. Francis J. Child, ed., *The Poetical Works of Edmund Spenser.*

6. According to *A Companion to Shakespeare Studies,* edited by Harley Granville-Barker and G. B. Harrison, *The Merchant of Venice* and *Love's Labour's Lost* had already appeared in print by 1598. Meres would also have known the comedies which were being acted on the London stage at this time, i.e., *The Taming of the Shrew, The Comedy of Errors, Two Gentlemen of Verona, Midsummer Night's Dream,* and *Much Ado About Nothing.* This list also taken from *A Companion to Shakespeare Studies.*

7. According to the "New Calendar."

8. This marshland was a royal hunting preserve, known even in Tudor times for its wild water fowl.

9. Ian Dunlop, *The Palaces and Progresses of Elizabeth I*

10. Ibid.

11. Ibid.

12. Ibid.

13. Ibid.

14. Ibid.

15. Ibid.

16. Ibid.

17. Ibid.

18. Ibid.

19. Ibid.

20. Ibid.

21. Ibid.

22. Ibid. The Elizabethans enjoyed playing practical jokes. In the privy garden of Whitehall there was a trap; loiterers found themselves drenched by water forced by a gardener operating a wheel "plentifully sprinkling those that are standing around."

23. *Official Guide* to *Westminster Abbey.*

24. Suppose the singing birds musicians;
The grass whereon thou tread'st, the presence strew'd.
King Richard II, Act I, sc. 3.

A relic of this custom of spreading rushes or "hay" upon the floor is found in our modern word *threshold—the rush hold.*

25. Ian Dunlop, *The Palaces and Progresses of Elizabeth I*

26. Edmund H. Fellowes, *The English Madrigal.*

27. Ibid.

28. Ibid.

29. H. V. Morton, *In Search of London.*

30. Dunlop.

31. Ibid.

32. Ibid.

33. Ibid.

34. John Stow in his *Survey of London* tells that starch was

brought over to England by a Flemish refugee lady who in 1564 set herself up as "a starcher."

35. Ibid.

36. The less important diners were seated as was customary in ancient Rome, "below the salt."

37. See *Notes* by Professor Samuel B. Hemingway in the Yale edition of *King Henry IV, Part II* (New Haven: Yale University Press, 1921).

38. Dunlop.

39. In London in the summer of 1968 there was a loan exhibit of priceless glass at the Victoria and Albert Museum, which included an exquisite glass pitcher which had belonged to Lord Burghley.

40. Forks appeared in London in 1582 but were not in general use until 1611. In 1582 Queen Elizabeth was given a New Year's present of "a fork of coral," and in 1588 "a spoon and fork of gold." These forks had only two tines. M. St. Clare Byrnes, *Elizabethan Life in town and Country.*

41. Other spellings of the name are *Cook* or *Cooke.*

OXFORD AND HIS ELIZABETHAN LADIES

Chapter I
HIS MOTHER

Whose infancy from the beginning was ever sacred to the Muses.

Angel Day, in an *Address to the Earl of Oxford* in 1586

The first woman to influence a hero is usually his mother. Was this true of Lord Oxford's mother? And if so, was her influence benign or malign? It is hard to write of her as the heroine of this first chapter in his story, for there seems to have been little love lost between Margery Golding de Vere and her only son.

It may be worth noting that, although the Shakespeare plays dramatize nearly every other human relationship, the first and most direct of all, the gentle, protecting love of a mother for her son is hardly touched upon. To be sure, the dramatist portrays a mother who is fiercely loyal and prepared to fight for the rights of her son. Queen Margaret immediately comes to mind. But she who wore a "tiger's heart wrapp'd in a woman's hide"—what did she know of warm maternal love? Another "tiger-hearted" woman is Volumnia, mother of Coriolanus, who gloried in her boy's prowess as a soldier, boasting that "when he was but tender-bodied and the only son of my womb . . . to a cruel war I sent him," later greeting his return from battle with: "O! he is wounded, I thank the gods for 't." Neither of these ladies can be said to have been blessed with tender mother love.

It is perhaps not too much to conclude from evidence in the plays that the dramatist himself had never experienced the love of his mother.

Margery Golding was born in the county of Essex, that green corner of rural England that is still unspoiled. Its tiny thatch-roofed villages, each with fieldstone church all out of proportion to the meager population, must look today about as they did when Margery was a little girl. This is a sheep-grazing country, its landscape familiar to us from the paintings of the artist Constable.

The Goldings were an ancient family of considerable means. The name is found in Essex even before the Norman Conquest, spelled variously as Goding, Goldinc, Godinc and Goulding. Their seat was Paul's Hall, Belchamp St. Paul, pronounced "Belcham," as perhaps it was in Margery's day.

Margery was the daughter of John Golding by his first wife, Elizabeth Worthy, an heiress who died leaving four small children. John Golding married again and seven more children were born into the family, the youngest of whom was the brilliant little boy, Arthur.

The tomb of Margery's mother lies directly under the square tower of the old parish church, with a beautifully preserved brass portrayal of the lady in early Tudor costume, her children represented in small brasses about her.

A wing of Margery's birthplace, the Manor House (see page 40 a), is still standing behind the church from which it is separated by a wide green lawn with trees old enough to have sheltered the young Goldings in their play. In spring the Manor House garden is fragrant with roses, sweet William and old-fashioned pinks. One can imagine the Golding children at play there, or under the great trees in the park.

According to the parish record, on August 5th, 1548, Margery was married in this church of Belchamp St. Paul to John de Vere, Sixteenth Earl of Oxford, lord of the great Castle of Hedingham eighteen miles away. With so many children in the family, her father and step-mother must have been relieved to have Margery taken off their hands, especially since she was marrying so illustrious a husband.

John de Vere, a widower with one daughter, was both aristocatic and wealthy, and he held title to the oldest earldom in England.

Once in his younger day, this Earl John while visiting in France, slew a boar single-handed, "attired as when he walked in his own bedchamber, only a dancing rapier at his side." To the cries of wondering admiration from the Frenchmen, he retorted:

> What have I done? Is it the killing of the English pig? Why every boy of my nation would have performed it.[1]

Something of the pomp and style to which this nobleman was accustomed may be gleaned from Stow's description of his entry into London from his Essex home. "He rode," Stow writes,

> to his house by London Stone with eighty gentlemen in livery of Reading tawny and chains of gold about their necks, and one hundred tall yeomen in the like livery to follow him without chains but all having his cognizance of the blue boar embroidered on their left shoulders.[2]

Many were the ladies who aspired to be Lord Oxford's new countess, not only ladies in Essex but in London town as well, for the de Veres were blessed with irresistible charm and magnetism as well as wealth and prestige. Indeed, it was rumored that more than one fine lady thought she had captured the noble widower for her daughter, only to learn of his marriage to Margery Golding.

A somewhat surprising contender for the honor of becoming Countess of Oxford had been a "Mrs. Dorothy, a Waiting woman" to his only child, Catherine. John de Vere must have carried the affair with Mrs. Dorothy pretty far, because twice the marriage banns were read in church.

The reason why Earl John did not marry Mrs. Dorothy, at least the reason given out, was that "the Protector Somerset prevented it." Behind this gossip lurked some court intrigue not pertinent to this story. Could it not have been that the Earl had deeper personal reasons for preferring Margery Golding? She must have been a very pretty girl; her son was noted for his handsome face. And there was another reason for John de Vere to seek his bride from the Golding fcamily. The Earl was an intellectual, his sister a poetess married to the Earl of Surrey, foremost poet in the land. It would have been natural that Lord John should be drawn to a personable young lady whose family were cultured aristocrats, even as his own.

In due time after their marriage the young Countess accomplished her foremost duty by providing the longed-for son and heir to the earldom. He was born April 23rd, 1550, and christened in the little church of St. Nicholas at Castle Hedingham. He was given the name Edward, which does not appear earlier in the de Vere family, suggesting that he might have been named for the boy king, Edward VI.

In 1558 John de Vere, Earl of Oxford, was accorded a signal honor. He was one of five Peers of the Realm to accompany the young Princess Elizabeth from Hatfield to London to be crowned. Thus began the friendship between the Queen, Elizabeth Tudor, and the de Veres, father and son, a friendship which was to last—with variations—for her lifetime.

Early in the new reign John de Vere, as Premier Earl, was chosen "to entertain" the heir to the King of Sweden, first of the long line of suitors for the hand of the beautiful young Queen.

While the Earl was fulfilling his duties at Court, his Countess joined him there upon her appointment as Lady in Waiting. Her finest hour would have been presiding as hostess to the Queen when her Majesty with her entire Court made the famous five-day visit to Castle Hedingham in 1561. For the occasion her eleven-year-old son, the Viscount Bolebec, heir to the Earldom, would have been brought home from Cambridge University where he had been a student at Queen's College since he was nine years old. His sister, Mary, would have been present, too, and possibly his older step-sister, Catherine, though at about this time Catherine married the Baron Winsor, and neither she nor her husband seem to have been very friendly with Margery's family.

In 1561 the new Queen was young, beautiful and vivacious,

with golden hair inherited from her Welsh ancestors. She had a lovely clear complexion, the pointed chin of her mother, Anne Boleyn, and dark sparkling bright eyes. All her portraits show her beautiful tapering hands with the long fingers. Elizabeth Tudor had a quick tongue, and she liked nothing better than witty repartee. There would have been plenty of that on this visit, for the de Veres were noted not only for their cultured charm, but also for their stimulating conversation.

It would have been during this royal visit that the Queen and her future Lord Great Chamberlain met one another for the first time. Summer in the verdant county of Essex would have been the ideal setting for so portentous an encounter. It would be interesting to know whether the Queen paid any special attention to the young Viscount Bolebec. He must have been a fascinating little boy, with curly auburn hair, bright mischievous eyes, and by all accounts possessed of the irresistible Vere charm. Both the the Queen and the youth were fond of learning. They could have found much in common even at this time when the diversity in their ages was most apparent.

Unfortunately the record merely notes the visit, so imagination must be called upon to fill in the scenes in that gracious Tudor country house, which must have been as large as a palace to accommodate all the courtiers and retainers visiting with the Queen.

Earl John and the Countess Margery would have invited all the distinguished members of their two respective families, to be present. There would have been the Earl's sister Frances, mentioned before, who, after the death of the Earl of Surrey, married another member of the Howard clan. A younger sister of the Earl was married to Baron Sheffield, composer of music as well as sonnets; they would surely have been invited. And almost certainly it may be said that the Countess of Oxford's young brother, Arthur Golding, was there, for he seems to have been close to the de Veres ever since his sister married.

There is one pertinent item of historical interest in regard to this visit. Before the Queen came to Castle Hedingham Earl John had had a stage erected in the Great Hall upon which the company of actors he sponsored could "show their cunning." Their plays had been honed to a finish by frequent appearance in the country villages before the actors dared to perform before royalty. Both the Queen and the de Veres were enthusiastic lovers of theatre; the stage productions would have been high-lights of the royal visit.

It would be fascinating to have a detailed account of the daily happenings during this five-day royal visitation! All we know is that there was undoubtedly riding, hunting, hawking, dining and dancing[3] and conversing.

The Queen on each occasion would be dressed appropriately in the latest London style. She would honor for special attention first one and then another of the guests on the houseparty. Or perhaps she would draw to herself a small group for some special talks, or exchanging of the latest jokes, or for just pleasant chatter. Always she would be the center of the gay throng, gesturing with her lovely hands, her bright eyes dancing, or grave or shrewd.

There would have been music on this house party, plenty of it; music by the trained "musycians" in the minstrel gallery overlooking the great hall. And more than likely there would have been music performed by the nobility, even by the Queen herself, for she played upon the virginals, and she was never timid about showing off her accomplishments . . .

Those five days of summer must have flown by all too quickly. But before leaving the houseparty it should be mentioned that the Earl's steward noted that the Queen's visit had cost her host "£ 558, 1 s and 11 d," a prodigious amount, although a sum which Earl John could well afford.

But Margery's days as hostess to the Premier Earl in the great Castle of Hedingham were numbered. For the year after the Queen's visit, i.e., in 1562, the Sixteenth Earl of Oxford died. His death brought about many changes.

Margery's son Edward, now the new Earl of Oxford, being a Royal Ward and only twelve years old, was sent to London, to the household of Sir William Cecil to be educated to bear the responsibilities of a Peer of the Realm. The young lad seems to have been broken-hearted at the death of his beloved father. In later years the dramatist known as Shakespeare many times extolled the love and admiration of a son for his father, the most notable example, of course, being in *Hamlet*. However, here are some lines from *All's Well That Ends Well*, the King speaking of Bertram's father:

> . . . It much repairs me
> To talk of your good father. . . .
> . . . .
> . . . Such a man
> Might be a copy to these younger times
> Act I, Sc. 2

The lines may have echoed words of Queen Elizabeth to the young earl just beginning his attendance at her Court.

Most fortunately for the lad his uncle, Margery's brother, Arthur Golding, was appointed one of his tutors. At that time Golding was translating *Ovid's Metamorphoses* into English verse. Young Edward de Vere would have been thoroughly familiar with this classic.

Another courtier helpful to the lad should be mentioned at this time: the Earl of Sussex, his father's old friend, a wise and never failing source of advice. The older courtier became almost a second father to the younger, helping him to deal with the multiple problems and intrigues of Court life. The affectionate relationship between them lasted for the life-time of Lord Sussex. He contracted tuberculosis, and finally died. But his apotheosis came about when his character was drawn as "old John of Gaunt, time-honour'd Lancaster." His portrait can be seen in the Tower; the description is most apt.

Not long after the new Lord Oxford went to Cecil House to live, his mother wrote a letter saying that in her husband's life-time she had been allowed to have no care of money at all. In this letter there is no mention of her young son, no warmth or enquiries about his welfare.

Then in what appeared to be unseemly haste after her noble husband's death, Margery married Sir Charles Tyrrel, who may have been a retainer in the household of the late Earl. There was rumor that he had been her lover.

It is not hard to sympathize with the pretty young widow who soon found it necessary to leave Castle Hedingham, turning for advice and comfort to the first man who would help her, Charles Tyrrel. But her son at his studies in London could not be expected to understand his mother's plight. To him she had married in undue haste after the death of his beloved father and that distressing fact left an unhealed scar on the personality of young Edward de Vere. While at Cecil House Edward wrote a number of letters to various people; they have been preserved to this day. But not one letter to his mother has been found....

Now let us turn to the plays.

The dramas of Shakespeare are full of warm father-to-son and son-to-father relationships, as has been noted. The history plays show an unusual father-son love between Henry IV and Prince Hal. Even when the zestful Prince is roistering with Falstaff, his father, though disappointed in him, still speaks lovingly of him. Later in the play the Prince actually saves his father's life in battle. Still later the son is deeply moved when the King is ill.

Is there a corresponding evidence of mother love? As noted before, Shakespeare mothers are tiger-hearted like Queen Margaret; or ambitious like Queen Eleanor. But the natural love of a son for his father so beautifully portrayed in *King Henry IV* seems to have no counterpart in the love of a son for his mother, or the mother for her son. As suggested earlier, this may be because the dramatist never really knew the love of his own mother.

The year after the death of the Sixteenth Earl of Oxford, that is, in 1563, Arthur Golding was made "receiver" for the estate of the Seventeenth Earl. Exactly what that means is not clear, but it must have concerned the ever-widening debts of the de Veres.

That same year Edward's half-sister, Catherine, now Baroness Winsor, claimed that Margery Golding and John de Vere had never married, and that therefore their children, being "bastards," should not inherit the properties of the late Earl of Oxford, which were rightfully hers. Why the Baroness had waited so long to bring the claim is not known, but probably "Mrs. Dorothy" was behind the scheme. Indeed, Catherine cites the twice-reading of the banns in church of Lord John's intended marriage to "Mrs. Dorothy" to support her charge of bigamy.

And who was it who defended Edward and his sister Mary de Vere when this monstrous charge of bigamy compounded with bastardy was made? Not Sir William Cecil, Edward's guardian. It was young Arthur Golding, Margery's twenty-seven-year-old brother who took full responsibility for refuting the charge. Edward de Vere and his sister had good reason to love and respect their uncle Arthur.

Just how deeply hurt young Edward had been by this baseless charge may be guessed by reading the first poem he ever wrote to which he signed his initials. Refuting the wretched claim had been, indeed, a bitter experience for the thirteen-year-old Courtier to the Queen, steeped as he was in the tradition of chivalry and honor of the ancient family of de Vere, whose motto was *Vero nil Verius*, "Nothing is truer than truth." *Truth* in this context is almost synonymous with *honor*. Here is the poem:

The Loss of My Good Name

Fram'd in the front of forlorn hope past all recovery
I stayless stand to abide the shock of shame and infamy,
My life, though ling'ring long, is lodg'd in lair of loathsome ways;
My death delay'd to keep from life the harm of hapless days.

My sprites, my heart, my wit and force, in deep distress
are drown'd;
The only loss of my good name is of these griefs the
ground.

And since my mind, my wit, my head, my voice and tongue
are weak,
To utter, move, devise, conceive, sound forth, declare and
speak
Such piercing plaints as answer might, or would my woe-
ful case;
Help crave I must, and crave I will with tears upon my
face,
To wail with me this loss of mine, and of these griefs the
ground.

Help God, help saints, help sprites and powers that in
the heaven do dwell,
Help man, help beasts, help birds and worms, that on the
earth do toil,
Help fish, help fowl, that flock and feed upon the salt sea
soil,
Help echo that in air doth flee, shrill voices to resound,
To wail this loss of my good name, as of these griefs the
ground.

E. O.

This is hardly a great poem, but it does show promise.[3] It shows, too, Edward de Vere's familiarity with his uncle Arthur Golding's translation of the *Metamorphoses* in its rhythm and metre and in many of its phrases. It suggests, also, young Edward's religious training in his calling upon God and the saints and "sprites" and powers of heaven. The "fowl that feed upon the salt sea soil" phrase is reminiscent of the county of Essex, for example, Wivenhoe by the sea, where the Earls of Oxford had a country seat. Interesting, too, is the reference to "echo that in air doth flee,"[4] another borrowing from Golding (*Meta.*, Book III, beginning at line 474). Later the poet-dramatist will use the *echo* simile many times.

A careful reading of Arthur Golding's translation shows how frequently his nephew borrows from this work. It has been said[5] that the author known as Shakespeare has "drawn on every book of the *Metamorphoses*, and there is scarcely a play untouched by its influence." By his repetition of Golding's very words and phrasing, we know that it was this translation of *Ovid* which the dramatist knew and seemed to care for deeply.

The Countess Margery and her lover Tyrrel drift out of this story and out of the life of her famous son, Edward de Vere. Yet the hurt of her hasty marriage remained with him most of his life. Years afterward the author of *Hamlet* tells of a mother's hasty marriage and of the heartbreak it had brought to the son:

> . . . Frailty, thy name is woman.
> A little month; or ere those shoes were old
> With which she follow'd my poor father's body,
> Like Niobe, all tears; why she, . . . —
> O God! a beast, that wants discourse of reason,
> Would have mourn'd longer . . .
> . . . .
> . . . Within a month,
> E're yet the salt of most unrighteous tears
> Had left the flushing in her galled eyes,
> She married. O most wicked speed . . .
> . . . .
> But break, my heart, for I must hold my tongue.
> Act I, sc. 2.

Later in the play there is the searing scene between Hamlet and his mother. It cannot be read, much less seen on the stage, without an instinctive feeling that the words were torn out of the very soul of the dramatist. Could it be the remembrance of a mature man brooding still upon the bitter anguish he experienced when only twelve, upon hearing that his mother had married again in undue haste after the death of his adored father? Here is the scene:

Hamlet. Come, come, and sit you down; you shall not budge;
You go not till I set you up a glass
Where you may see the inmost part of you.
. . . .

Queen. What have I done, that thou dar'st wag thy tongue
In noise so rude against me?

Hamlet. Such an act
That blurs the grace and blush of modesty;
Calls virtue hypocrite; takes off the rose
From the fair forehead of an innocent love,
And sets a blister there; makes marriage-vows
As false as dicer's oath: O such a deed
As from the body of contraction plucks
The very soul, and sweet religion makes
A rhapsody of words; heaven's face doth glow;
Yea, this solidity and compound mass,
With tristful visage, as against the doom,
Is thought-sick at the act.

Queen. Ah, me, what act,
That roars so loud, and thunders in the index?

Hamlet. Look here upon this picture and on this,—
. . . .
See what a grace was seated on this brow;
Hyperion's curls; the front of Jove himself;
An eye like Mars, to threaten and command;
A station like the herald Mercury
New-lighted on a heaven-kissing hill;
A combination and a form, indeed,
Where every god did seem to set his seal,

To give the world assurance of a man:
This was your husband. —Look you now, what follows:
Here is your husband, like a mildew'd ear
. . . Have you eyes?
Could you on this fair mountain leave to feed,
And batten on the moor? Ha! have you eyes:
You cannot call it love: for at your age
The hey-dey in the blood is tame, it's humble,
And waits upon the judgment: And what judgment
Would step from this to this? Sense, sure, you have,
Else could you not have motion: but sure that sense
Is apoplex'd: for madness would not err;
. . . .
But it reserv'd some quantity of choice
To serve in such a difference. What devil was't
That thus cozen'd you at Hoodman-blind?
Eyes without feeling, feeling without sight,
Ears without hands or eyes, smelling sans all,
Or but sickly part of one true sense
Could not so mope.
O, shame! where is thy blush? Rebellious hell,
If thou canst mutine in a matron's bones,
To flaming youth let virtue be as wax
And melt in her own fire: proclaim no shame
When the compulsive ardor gives the charge,
Since frost itself as actively doth burn,
And reason pandors will.

Queen. O Hamlet, speak no more:
Thou turn'st mine eyes into my very soul:
And there I see such black and grained spots
As will not leave their tinct.

. . . .

O, speak to me no more:
No more sweet Hamlet.

Act III, Sc.4

There follows the scene with Hamlet's father's ghost.

The Queen is distraught by Hamlet's words. In anguish she cries out:

O Hamlet, thou hast cleft my heart in twain.

Notes To Chapter I

1. Col. B. M. Ward, pp. 81-2, quoting Gervase Markham, *Honour in his perfection.*

2. John Stow, *Survey of London.*

3. ". . . to utter forth his mind," *Metamorphoses,* Golding Translation, Book III, l. 478.

4. ". . . the salt sea soil," and "of this my grief the ground," *Meta.,* Book XIII, l. 19. ". . . or in the Earth do dwell," Book VII, l. 326.

5. In *Shakespeare, the Man Behind the Name,* Dorothy and Charlton Ogburn, Jr., point out that an early play, *Locrine,* attributed on the title page to "W. S." begins:

Fram'd in the front of forlorn misery.

There is concern for the poet's "good name" in the Sonnets, and in many of the Shakespeare plays. Iago in *Othello,* Act III, sc. 3, (ll. 157-161):

But he that filches from me my good name
Robs me of that which not enriches him,
And makes me poor indeed.

Again, the Ogburns recall Hamlet's anguished cry for his "wounded name" as he lies dying, Act V, sc. 2, (l. 347).

6. John Frederick Nims, in his Introduction to the 1965 re-issue of Golding's *Translation of Ovid's Metamorphoses,* page xx, quoting L. F. Wilkinson.

Chapter II
HIS SISTER

Gremio: But will you woo this wild-cat?
Petruchio: Will I live?
The Taming of the Shrew, Act I, sc. 2, ll. 199-200

Castle Hedingham, seat of the Earls of Oxford since the Eleventh Century, crowns a little hill in the gently rolling countryside of Essex. From the ramparts of its Norman Keep in springtime there is a view of green fields broken only by furrows of new-turned red earth, while in another direction one can see the leafy woods of what was once the Forest of Essex. This country has been overrun by Roman legions and Saxon invaders, and was chosen by the conquering Normans to be one of their strongholds.

The story of young Edward de Vere, Viscount Bolebec, and his sister, the Lady Mary, begins here in the early 1550s. As recounted earlier Edward and his sister were the only children of John, the Sixteenth Earl of Oxford and his second wife, Margery Golding.

It is tempting to imagine the little siblings playing their childish games at the great estate. And after their games, they would have heard stories of what had happened on this very land. They would have heard tales told by their father about their illustrious ancestors, whose stories were the history of England itself. They would have heard of Aubrey,[1] founder of the family, who came over to England even before the Conqueror, from Ver in France. Later William the Norman presented Aubrey with the Manor of Kensington near London, because of his services during the Conquest.

It was this Aubrey's son who was granted extensive acres in

Essex. He built Castle Hedingham and planted the vineyard nearby. From that time the castle had been a favorite for sovereigns to visit while on royal progresses through the kingdom.

Little Edward and Mary would have heard about the Earl of Oxford who was a Crusader and of how, one night as it was "waxing dark," he and his companions were confronted by the Saracens. But "God willing [their] safety" showed a white star over the Christian host "there shining excessively." Ever since then the Mullet, or five-pointed star, has been the cognizance of the de Veres. It is to be seen today on the square tower of the flint stone church at Earl's Colne, in Essex, within which are the tombs of members of this noble family.

During the Wars of the Roses, Earl John would have told his children, it was the confusion of this "radiant star" of the de Veres with the badge of the "sun with rays" borne by the followers of Edward IV which brought about the decisive defeat of the Lancastrians at Barnet in 1471. The children would have listened spell-bound to the story of the Thirteenth Earl, a Lancastrian, fighting all through this terrible battle in the cold damp fog when enemies were mistaken for friends and friends for enemies.[2]

The dramatist of *King Henry VI, Part III,* has taken liberties with history in his description of this battle in Act V, sc. 2 and 3. But it should be noted that in this play and again in its sequel, *King Richard III,* a prominent part is given to the Earl of Oxford.

The eager listening children would have learned that, although the powerful "kingmaker," the Earl of Warwick, was slain in the Battle of Barnet, their ancestor, the Thirteenth Earl of Oxford, escaped. Being a Lancastrian, he had to flee for his life, seeking refuge first in France, where he was captured and imprisoned. Later he escaped to Cornwall, trudging up St. Michael's Mount as a pilgrim. There the family was forced to remain during the period when the Yorkists were in power.

Opportunity to return to favor came with the advent of Henry

Tudor, Duke of Richmond. The noble Earl of Oxford fought by his side at the Battle of Bosworth Field (1485), when the battle crown of the fallen Richard was snatched from a hawthorn bush where it had been left hanging, and placed upon the head of the conquering duke. Thus began the close association of the House of de Vere with the House of Tudor.

However, after Henry became king as Henry VII, he was entertained so sumptuously by the Earl of Oxford that before his Grace left Castle Hedingham he fined his host £10,000 for his overlavish display. The new king could not afford to allow a mere vassal to live more luxuriously than he did himself, especially since the family of de Vere was older and nobler than his own. Besides, the king needed the money.

These stories, the very fiber of English history, were learned by Edward de Vere and his sister Mary not from school books but from hearing about their own forefathers who had lived in the very castle where the children were now growing up. No wonder that Edward's tutor reported that his young charge excelled in English history.

On rainy days the youngsters might have gone exploring of the Norman Keep, the walls of which were twelve feet thick at ground level. They would see where in earlier times the retainers had huddled around the central wood fire at night, sleeping on the cold stone floor with logs for bolsters. The children would climb the winding stone stairs to the former great hall where so many English sovereigns had been entertained.

The Keep was old when the children were young, but adjacent to it was the new Tudor country house, one of the finest in the land. Here they lived in the style becoming to the family of the Premier Earl of the Realm, with servants and horses and spaniels[3] and all the appurtenances wealth and prestige can bring.

The Great Park and the Little Park gave ample space for the young boy and girl to gallop their horses and later to learn to hunt. Something about another aspect of their childhood training is learned from the fact that the open space in the center of the tiny village of Castle Hedingham hard by the parish church is called Falcon Square. Here would have been the mews where the trained hawks were kept. There are many allusions to falconry in the Shakespeare plays.

> O for a falconer's voice,
> To lure this hassle-gentle back again!

writes the author of *Romeo and Juliet,* Act II, sc. 2. And

> A falcon, towering in her pride of place,
> Was by a mousing owl hawk'd at and kill'd.
> *Macbeth,* Act II, sc. 4

And here are two more references to hawking:

> If I do find her haggard,
> Though that her jesses were my dear heart strings
> I'd whistle her off, and let her fly down the wind
> To play at fortune.
> *Othello,* Act III, sc. 1

> My falcon now is sharp, and passing empty;
> And till she stoop, she must not be full-gorg'd,
> For then she never looks upon her lure.
> Another way I have to man my haggard
> To make her come and know her keeper's call.
> *Taming of the Shrew,* Act IV, sc, 1

How familiar is the dramatist with the termininology of this sport of kings!

The story of the Lady Mary de Vere is important only because it weaves in and out of that of her distinguished brother. They were very close to one another all their lives.

But the carefree days of play and story-telling came to an end when the little boy was sent away to Queen's College, Cambridge, when he was nine years old. That left his sister to wander through the echoing halls of the great estate alone.

The year after the Queen's visit to Castle Hedingham, their father died. There is a description of the funeral of this Sixteenth Earl of Oxford. It was attended by "three Heralds of Arms,[4] with a standard and a great banner of arms and eight banner rolls, crest, target, sword and coat of armour, and a hearse with velvet and a dozen of scutcheons, and with many mourners in black; and a great moan was made for him."[5]

What a frightening experience for a little girl to endure! But hardest of all for her must have been parting with her brother, seeing him ride off to London at the head of a procession of secretaries and retainers, the entire group dressed in mourning black. The titles of his father now descended to Edward; he was the Seventeenth Earl of Oxford, Lord Great Chamberlain of England, and Officer of the Ewery, as well as being the Premier Earl of the Realm.

Mary seems to have stayed on in Essex County with her mother, though life with the Tyrrels could not have been pleasant for her. With her step-father to cope with and no imaginative brother to play with, it must have been a hard and lonely life for little Mary. It is not surprising to learn that she had a reputation for being irritable, with a rasping temper. The inheritance which in her brother came out in vivacious wit, showed only as hurting bursts of anger in his sister.

Before she was twenty Mary was appointed to be a Lady-in-Waiting to the Queen at the Court where her brother was already cutting quite a dashing figure. Eleanor Bridges writes to the Earl of Rutland: "The Lady Mary de Vere is sworn one of the Privy Chamber," adding caustically that "The Court is full of malice, and spite, as when you left it."[6]

This was the Court to which the little country girl from Essex came to serve the Queen, and where her brother was already in a position of prominence.

The Court of Queen Elizabeth was one of the most regal in all Europe. For most of the winter months, from Accession Day, November 18th, until spring, the Court was in residence at Whitehall, where the Queen loved to be, close to London and near St. Stephen's Palace where Parliament met and the law courts held their sessions.

Whitehall Palace comprised that heterogeneous group of buildings between St. James Park[7] and the river. The Thames in those days was wider than it is today, for there was no Embankment and the palace extended right down to the pebbled shore.

Whitehall contained the most luxurious great hall in any private residence in England. It had a ceiling painted by Holbein. The palace had a chapel with a choir famous throughout the land, for Queen Elizabeth loved music and would have only the best. Also there was an outdoor pulpit, from which more than one droning preacher had been harangued by the impatient Queen, who not infrequently found the sermon too long. "Stick to your text, Mr. Dean! Stick to your text!" she is known to have cried out.[9]

Henry VIII had seen to it that there was plenty of opportunity for sports in the vicinity. He built a tiltyard about where the Horseguards go through their colorful manoeuvres today. And he built three tennis courts, two of them open to the sky. There was also a cockpit on the site of Downing Street; near it a bowling alley, and "a ball-house where they play at featherballs" (badminton).

When the Queen was in residence at Whitehall her barge would be moored across the river on the Surrey side near Paris Garden. The central cabin of the barge was covered with an awning of red satin, the interior hung with coats of arms, while the floor was always strewn with fresh sweet-smelling flowers. The Queen reclined on a cushion of cloth of gold, a crimson velvet rug across her knees in chilly weather. It took twenty-two lusty bargemen rowing in the forward boat to pull the barge.[10]

Such was the setting for the debut of Lady Mary de Vere into the social life of Tudor England at the very highest level. As a de Vere, daughter of one Premier Earl of the land and sister of another, she was soon found to be a desirable matrimonial choice.

A short time after her coming to Court a match was being considered between the young Maid in Waiting and "Lord Garrat." Nobody seems to be quite sure who this nobleman was, but that is of no concern because he doesn't stay long in the story.

Mary did not marry "Lord Garrat" and the reason was not hard to find in a twenty-two-year-old lad who, it is surmised, had been introduced to her at the home of Sir William Cecil, his guardian. It will be recalled that this was the household where Mary's brother was being brought up as a Royal Ward.

The young gentleman Mary fancied was Peregrine Bertie (pronounced Bartie in the English way), and he was the only child of the Duchess of Suffolk[11] by her second husband. The Duchess had more than once admitted that Peregrine's father, formerly her "gentleman usher," had been "meanly born," while trying at the same time to procure a title for him. But they had lived through many vicissitudes together, and from all that is known about them it would seem that Peregrine's parents were genuinely fond of one another.

Peregrine Bertie was born in Wesel while his parents were refugees[12] on the Continent because of their religious belief, they being staunch Protestants in the reign of Queen Mary Tudor. When Elizabeth came to the throne, the Duchess and her "gentleman usher" felt that they could bring their young child home to their own country. Once they were established in England, their properties were recovered and they lived in much the same style which they had known before, although the Duchess never forgave Queen Elizabeth for withholding a title from her second husband.

Peregrine became a ward of Sir William Cecil, living in his household on the Strand. He was a personable young man, and his guardian had said that he "made great progress in learning and courtly accomplishments."[13] But later it was said of Peregrine:

> I have heard it spoken that had he not slighted the Court but applied himself to the Queen, he might have enjoyed a plentiful portion of her grace: it was his saying, and it did him no good, that he was none of the Reptilia: intimating that he could not creep upon the ground; and that a Court became a soldier of good skill as a bed of down would one of the Tower lions.[14]

The quotation gives evidence of the independent character of this young man, of which there is proof in the following story.

When Peregrine was seventeen there was a question of his marrying Elizabeth Cavendish, second daughter of the Countess of Shrewsbury, better known as Bess of Hardwick. Although Peregrine's father may have been "meanly born," the young gentleman was considered a good matrimonial match for the daughter of an earl.

That engagement was suddenly broken, however, and soon after Elizabeth Cavendish was affianced to the young Earl of Lennox, brother to Lord Darnley, who had married Mary Queen of Scots. This proposed marriage displeased Queen Elizabeth, who did not want any more Lennox cousins having babies. The young lady's father was hard put to it to explain the matter to her. Finally he gave this excuse:

> I must confess to your Majesty, as true is, it was dealt in suddenly, without my knowledge, but as I dare undertake to add insure to your Majesty, for my wife, finding her daughter disappointed of young Barté, where she had hoped, and the other young gentleman being inclined to love with a few days acquaintance. . . .[15]

The circumstances of "young Barte's" disentanglement from marriage to Elizabeth Cavendish are not clear, but one is inclined to believe that he had come under the spell of the irresistible Vere charm of the Lady Mary.

The young people were very much in love, but it was almost a Montague-Capulet affair, for both families were opposed to their marriage and so was the Queen.

This is what Peregrine's mother, the Duchess, wrote to Sir William Cecil, her son's guardian, though her letter is too long and too discursive to quote in full:

> It is very true that my wise son has gone very far with my Lady Mary Vere, I fear too far to turn. I must say to you in counsel what I have said to her plainly, that I had rather he had matched in any other place. . . . Our religions agree not, and I cannot tell what more. . . . She said that she could not rule her brother's tongue, nor help the rest of his faults, but for herself she trusted so to use her as I should have no cause to mislike her, she desired my good will and asked no more. . . . She told me how Lord Sussex and Master Hatton had promised to speak for her to the Queen. I told her her brother used you and your daughter so evil that I could not require you to [speak for her.] . . . Within this fortnight there was one spoke to me for one Mistress Gaymege, an heiress to a thousand marks land, which had been a meeter match for my son.[16]

In that last sentence the old lady has shown her hand. The dwindling of the inheritance of the de Veres would have been common gossip at Court.

There is a letter to the Earl of Rutland dated November 11, 1577, advising him that

> . . . the marriage of the Lady Mary Vere is deferred until Christmas, for as yet neither has Her Majesty given license, nor has the Earl of Oxford wholly assented thereto.[17]

But Peregrine Bertie was deeply in love; he was also a very determined young man. This is one of the letters he wrote Mary; it is undated but written obviously during the time of their courtship:

> My own good Lady, I am not a little grieved, that I have not, ere this time, resolved the doubt I left you in, and so much the more as I fear it hath caused you unquietness, of which I make more account than of myself or of life; therefore resolve yourself that if I had fit time, I would not have so slightly overpassed it. But the truth is, by other troubles, I have yet heard nothing of that matter worth the sending. Yet did I think not to lose so much occasion since I know not when to recover it again, as to let you know how uncourteously I am dealt with by my Lord your brother, who, as I hear, bandeth against me, and sweareth my death, which I fear not, nor force not, but lest his displeasure withdraw your affections from me. Otherwise, I think no way to be so offended as I can not defend, and thus, good lady, persuade yourself no less that you shall find me. I will give cause, or perform above all things, if you wish me well; let nothing grieve you whatsoever you hear do hap. For my own part, my good or evil fortune dependeth only on you, whom I must request as well this scribbled well meaning as better eloquence, excusing my imperfections which, owing to my troubled mind, are locked up so fast I can scarce get pens and paper to be the poor messenger of my poor good will. And thus end a wilful man, having now received new occasion at this instant by your letter, to trouble you no more hereafter.
>
> From Willoughby House
> Yours more than his own,
> and so till the end[18]

There is no doubt about that lover's affections. It is not known why Mary's brother should have been so opposed to the match, but being close to his sister he may have been jealous. Also there may have been extenuating circumstances unknown today. However, Edward de Vere was not one to hold grudges.

By December the Duchess had grown so fond of her future daughter-in-law that she sought her connivance in a scheme to bring together the Earl and Countess of Oxford.[19]

Peregrine and his beloved were finally united in marriage early in 1578. The Duchess writes to Lord Burghley asking him

> to grant her daughter Mary and her husband a bill of impost for two tuns of wine to be taken at Boston or Hull.[20]

The Duchess was magnanimous in arranging not only for her son and his bride to enjoy imported wine, but also in giving them the ancestral seat of Grimsthorpe in Lincolnshire. And soon there are these notations in her accounts:

> For a lute for Mr. Peregrine...............46 S.
> To Roes, when he mended Mr. Peregrine's lute.8 s. 3d.[21]

The notations are interesting not only because they tell that "Mr. Peregrine" had a musical propensity, but also because they suggest something of the home life of this young Elizabethan couple.

However, it was not long before the ardent bridegroom was coming to realize what a sharp tongue his beloved possessed. Later in the year of their marriage *The Taming of the Shrew* was presented at Court. It should be noted that the Shrew's name was Katherine, the name of Lady Mary's meddlesome mother-in-law.

Sir Thomas Cecil writes to his father, Peregrine's former guardian, before visiting the Berties at Grimsthorpe:

> As touching such disaggreements that have fallen out there, I shall better satisfy your Lordship by my next letter, after that I have been there, than now I can; but at

> this far, I understand that my Lady of Suffolk's coming from London was to appease certain unkindnesses grown between her son and his wife. More particularly I cannot write at this time, but I think my Lady Mary will be beaten with the rod, which heretofore, she prepared for others. For it is an old saying, "in peccateir eadem puniter."[22]

Does this not sound to you, dear reader, like *The Taming of the Shrew?*

Let us look into this play. The heroine is "renowned in Padua [London] for her scolding tongue." Again, she is referred to as

> Katherine, the curst!
> A title for a maid of all titles the worst.
> Act I, sc. 2, ll. 129-30

Petrucchio, the intended lover, remarks:

> I know she is an irksome, brawling scold.
> Act I, sc. 2, l. 188

To which Gremio retorts:

> O, sir, such a life with such a wife, were strange!
> But if you have a stomach to't, i' God's name:
> You shall have me assisting you in all.

Petrucchio: Will I live?

> . . . .
> Think you a little din can daunt mine ears?
> Have I not in my time heard lions roar?
> Have I not heard the sea, puff'd up with winds,
> Rage like an angry boar chafed with sweat?
> Have I not heard great ordnance in the field,

And heaven's artillery thunder in the skies:
Have I not in a pitched battle heard
Loud larums, neighing steeds, and trumpets' clang?
And do you tell me of a woman's tongue,
That gives not half so great a blow to hear
As will a chestnut in a farmer's fire?
Tush, tush!

Act I, sc. 2, ll. 196-8, 213.

How the Queen and her courtiers at Richmond would have laughed at this comedy, many scenes of which they might have witnessed in real life when Peregrine Bertie was courting the shrewish Lady Mary!

Still, even allowing for Mary's well-publicized temper, it is hard not to take her side as opposed to that of the Duchess, who seems to have been a rather suspicious and interfering mother-in-law. This is part of a letter she wrote to the Earl of Leicester, dated March 1579:

> To the Right honorable, and very good lord, the Earl of Leicester; I am very sorry that my evil fortune to be troublesome to any of my friends, specially being brought to the same evil hap of my dear Son's marriage by whom I had hope to have comfort in my old days, which, by any deserts towards me, I have found no other cause of grief than by his unadvised and unlucky choice of a fair lady.[23]

The Duchess rambles on and then proceeds to accuse Mary of accusing *her* of treason. She begs Leicester to intervene with the Queen in her behalf, writing:

> . . . there is no cause to part my head from my body . . . and I thank God I am not the beginner of complaints. . . . But I lament that I have deserved no better of such good lady. . . . And so I commit you to Him, from my

> little unwholesome house in Hampstead, whither I flyed [have fled] to seek quiet from these brawls. . . .[24]

"My little unwholesome house in Hampstead!" How this self-pity betrays the Duchess!

Fortunately for Mary her unhappy mother-in-law died in September of 1580, and the "gentleman usher" soon after, so the young matron was saved further trouble from them. The Willoughby title descended to Peregrine Bertie, together with the estates of Grimsthorpe and Eresby in Lincolnshire and Willoughby House on the Barbican in the City of London.

Peregrine must have been something of a Petrucchio, for the Lady Mary was later known as a devoted and pliant wife to her distinguished husband.

Bertie, now Lord Willoughby, became a famous soldier best known for his victories in the Netherlands. He accompanied the Earl of Leicester and Sir Philip Sidney to the Low Countries on the ill-fated expedition following Lord Oxford's service there. It must have been something of an embarrassment to Edward de Vere that his sister's husband succeeded brilliantly on this mission in which he had signally failed, although the failure was through no fault of his own.[25]

In the Battle of Zutphen Lord Willoughby was rescued in the thick of the fighting by Sir Philip. It was this deed of gallantry which cost Sir Philip his fatal wound.[26]

While on this mission Lord Willoughby came to know and greatly to admire the Earl of Essex, a devotion which lasted many years. In writing to Essex from the battlefield, Willoughby calls him "the man I love and honour above all men."[27]

By Christmas of 1586 the Earls of Leicester, Essex, and Lord Willoughby returned to London, and together they attended the state funeral of Sir Philip Sidney at St. Paul's. Sir Philip left his best sword to his uncle, the Earl of Leicester, and his second best to his friend, Lord Willoughby.[28] Shortly after this, Lord Willoughby replaced Sir Philip as governor of Bergen-op-Zoom, serving against immense odds, which he describes vividly in letters still in existence.[29]

While the doughty Peregrine was fighting for his Queen and country in the "pays bas," his wife was busy travelling back and forth from England to be with him in the war zone as much as she could. She presented her husband with no less than six children, five boys and a girl. The sons were Robert, Peregrine, Henry, Vere and Roger;[30] the name of the little daughter is not known. Mary Lady Willoughby must have been a strong, healthy lady, because not only did she have the children to bring up, and her husband to care for in the Netherlands, but she took on the management of the estates of Grimsthorpe and Eresby, and had the care of their London house on the Barbican as well.

To show the esteem in which this family was held, an account of the first son's christening is here quoted:

> Queen Elizabeth would needs be god-mother to the young General, as she called him, and the Earls of Essex and Leicester being his god-fathers, christening him Robert a name she [the Queen] observed "happy in soldiers and statesmen. . ."[31]

Now turn to *Twelfth Night*, and consider for a moment Sir Toby Belch and Maria. Are they not recognizable counterparts of Lord and Lady Willoughby? Like many another soldier-man Lord Willoughby seems to have been at times over-fond of his sack, as the name given him in *Twelfth Night* implies, while Maria appears to be scarcely a disguise for the Lady Mary. Sir Andrew Aguecheek's first greeting to her is:

> Bless you, fair shrew.
>
> Act I, sc. 3, l. 48

recalling Mary's shrewish temper. Then the Clown later teasing her, says:

> Well, go thy way: if Sir Toby would leave drinking, thou wert as witty a piece of Eve's flesh as any in Illyria.
>
> Act I, sc. 5, ll. 28-30

An example of Maria's mischief-making is the practical joke she plays on Malvolio, persuading him to wear the yellow stockings cross gartered which Olivia—and evidently the Queen, too—"abhorred."

Now Malvolio, the Evil-Wisher, seems to be a rather cruel lampoon of Sir Christopher Hatton, an affected dandy at Queen Elizabeth's court, a rival to Lord Oxford for her favor. Hatton was a Puritan. In Act II, sc. 3, Maria describes Malvolio in line 151:

> Marry, sir, sometimes he is a kind of puritan.[32]

Sir Toby Belch and Sir Andrew Aguecheek discuss this playfully, and Maria chimes in, adding:

> The devil a puritan that he is, or anything constantly but a time-pleaser. ll. 161-3

However, an even more significant clue to the identity of Malvolio is the signature that Maria signs to the forged letter: THE FORTUNATE-UNHAPPY. This is a play on the posy which Hatton used to sign his poems in the Elizabethan anthologies: *Felix Infortunatus*. Maria is trying to make Malvolio think that Olivia is a Fortunate Unhappy like himself. The analogy may be carried further by supposing that Olivia represents the Queen. Sir Christopher fancied himself in love with her; indeed, he was said to have been one of her lovers, though this seems impossible to believe. Anyway, he would have been deeply impressed by a love letter he *thought* had been written to him by his Queen.

Maria is a wicked little tease and given to puns, as in this scene in which she responds to Sir Andrew's remark:

> And your horse now would make him an ass,

with

> Ass, I doubt not.
>
> Act II, sc. 4, ll. 85-6

Here is perhaps the most telltale line of all: Sir Toby is describing his wife:

> She's a beagle, true bred, and one that adores me. l. 98

Once again the dramatist is punning on the family name of Vere, *true*, which he does so many times in the plays and also in his poetry. There is another version of the pun when Sir Toby refers to the scheme that he and Maria are hatching, as "our *very* pastime."

Note Sir Toby's reply to his wife's: "Follow me":

> To the gates of tartar, thou most excellent devil of wit!
> Act III, sc. 1, ll. 226-28

This delightful comedy is full of clues and allusions to courtiers and court ladies, but only one more will be mentioned. Near the beginning of the play Sir Toby, Sir Andrew and the Clown are carousing. Maria comes in attempting to quiet them, but the "caterwauling" continues. Finally Sir Toby roars out the popular song:

> O! the twelfth day of December, —

and is hushed up by Maria.

Now this song he is bellowing is definitely a parody of the ballad of *The Brave Lord Willoughby*, which was set to music by William Byrd, the composer of madrigals and church music. It is one of the ironies of history that Bertie, the brilliant scholar, should be known to future generations best not as a scholar, but as a soldier.

Here is the version of *The Brave Lord Willoughby* parodied in *Twelfth Night*, to which Byrd wrote the music:

> The fifteenth day of July,
> With glistening spear and shield,
> A famous fight in Flanders
> Was foughten in the field:

The most courageous officers
Were English captains three;
But the bravest man in Battle
Was the brave Lord Willoughby.[33]

Another version of the ballad is as follows:

The brave Lord Willoughby,
Of courage fierce and fell,
Who would not give an inch of way
For all the devils in hell.

And then the fearful enemy
Was quickly put to flight;
Our men pursued courageously,
And rout their forces quite.

And at last they gave a shout,
Which echoed through the sky,
God and St. George for England!
The Conquerors did cry.

The news was brought to England,
With all the speed might be,
And told unto our gracious Queen,
Of this same victory.

O this is brave Lord Willoughby,
My love hath ever won;
Of all the Lords of Honour
'Tis he great deeds hath done.

For soldiers that were maimed
And wounded in the fray,
The Queen allowed a pension
Of eighteen pence a day.

Besides all costs and charges
She quit and set them free;
And this she did all for the sake
Of brave Lord Willoughby.

Then courage, noble Englishmen,
And never be dismay'd;
If that we be but one to ten,
We will not be afraid.

We fight with foreign enemies,
And set our country free;
And thus I end this bloody bout
Of brave Lord Willoughby.[34]

The lampoon in *Twelfth Night* including the parody appears to have been taken in good fun by Lord Willoughby and his Mary. No one could long harbor resentment against the irrepressible Lord Oxford.

Returning to Lord Peregrine, there is an old saying that a man may be judged by the friends he keeps. It might be worthwhile to mention a few of the famous Elizabethans with whom Lord Willoughby corresponded. He seemed to be on intimate terms with Dr. Ruy Lopez, a Christian of Jewish birth, the Director of St. Thomas's Hospital, London. Lopez was described by a contemporary as "being in great favor with the Queen, and all the great Lords and Ladies."[35]

Another correspondent was Captain Martin Frobisher, who, in a letter to Willoughby dated July 30, 1586, regrets that

> my departure from Court was so sudden that I could not stay to bring you any message. We had but an hour's warning. . . . I see sometimes and am sore troubled for so honourable a mind to be tied to so base a people as these be, for here can nothing profit nor honour come to satisfy your expectations.

What bitterness! And what a picture Frobisher paints of the Court as he proceeds:

> Mr. Raleigh stands others under the cloth of estate; my Lord of Essex is all in all, but upon Thursday last he was gone in a fume from the Court as far as Margate and was stayed from coming over. I fear it was such a toy as will do him no good. . . . Your children are in health, God be praised. . . . Thus leaving your Honour to God till I see you,
>
> Your honours most humble and loving
> Martin Frobisher.[36]

It may have been through his brother-in-law that Lord Oxford was persuaded to invest so lavishly in Frobisher's Third Expedition. Oxford had wanted to accompany the explorer himself, but when this seemed impossible (doubtless because the Queen refused her permission), the Earl invested several thousand pounds, a prodigious sum compared to the £167. 10 s. invested by Sir Philip Sidney, or the £33. 15 s. by his sister,the Countess of Pembroke. But Lord Oxford was noted for being generous with money, especially when the project fired his imagination.

Upon the recall of the Earl of Leicester as Commander in Chief of her Majesty's forces in the Low Countries, Lord Willoughby succeeded him. As related above, Lady Willoughby visited her husband frequently, sharing his privations in the field. Each time she came over she brought with her some of her own jewels and silver plate, possibly even some of the de Vere silver and family jewels from Castle Hedingham. These it became necessary to sell in order to pay the troops and to buy provisions for them to eat, for the Queen gave her soldiers insufficient funds to support themselves even while they were fighting England's battles. Lord Willoughby complained bitterly about this in a letter to the Lord Treasurer. The lack of financial support seems especially ironic considering that the battles Lord Willoughby and his troops were fighting so brilliantly in the Netherlands were the final coup to the Spanish forces following the victory over the Armada in 1588.

When his tour of duty ended and he was finally allowed to return to England a hero, Lord Willoughby found himself a poor man.[36] having provided from his own pocket £ 900 for the siege of Bergen alone. He ran into debt to the sum of £ 4,000 and was forced to mortgage his estates in Norfolk.[37] There is no record to prove that Lord Oxford helped his sister and brother-in-law at this time, yet because he was so close to them he probably would have assisted them financially. This might have been one of the reasons his own finances became so badly depleted.

Somewhat later Sir Francis Drake urged Lord Willoughby to take supreme command of the projected Portuguese Expedition. But Peregrine Bertie, the heroic soldier, wrote back to him:

> My long service in the Low Countries . . . has so exhausted me that I could not undertake the charge of the voyage out of my own purse. My bodily ailments and infirmities also render me unmeet to be employed in such service.[38]

And now must be told the most interesting link between Lord Oxford and his brother-in-law. It consists of a signal honor conferred on Lord Willoughby by the Queen.

In 1583 her Majesty commissioned Lord Willoughby d'Eresby to go to Denmark to invest the Danish king with the Order of the Garter. Lord Willoughby's account of the ceremony written in his own hand has fortunately been preserved.

The excited interest of the family when Willoughby returned to tell of his visit to the Danish court can readily be imagined. Lord Oxford had always taken a keen interest in foreign lands and people. He would have been most interested of all in learning from his brother-in-law about Denmark's history, and of what Peregrine could tell him of the *Historica Danica* of Saxo Grammaticus, the Danish chronicler who lived at the end of the twelfth century. This is, of course, the history from which the bare facts of the *Hamlet* story were taken.

The prominent Dane, Jan Steffanson, has written that the author of *Hamlet* has shown "a local knowledge of the royal Castle of Elsinore which he could not have derived from books." Steffanson also claims that the dramatist had a remarkably accurate knowledge of "Danish names, words and customs of his time." He mentions the fact that in *Hamlet* the playwright uses the word *Dansker* for *Dane*. Polonius asks: "Inquire me first what *Danskers* are in Paris." Now *Dansker* is the Danish word for *Dane*, but curiously, until the play of *Hamlet* appeared, it had nowhere else been found in English literature. English writers had been using the form *Dansk*, or *Danske*, but both forms are incorrect.

But Steffanson writes still further of the playwright's familiarity with the Danish custom of drinking "cannon healths," which means that every time the king drinks, guns are fired from the battlements.[30]

Look closely at the text of *Hamlet:*

No jocund health that Denmark drinks today
But the great cannon to the clouds shall tell.
Act I, sc. 2, ll. 125-6

Hamlet. The King doth wake tonight and takes his rouse,
Keeps wassail and the swaggering up-spring reels;
The kettle-drum and trumpet thus bray out
The triumph of his pledge.
Act I, sc. 4, ll. 7-11

King. Give me the cups;
The trumpet to the cannoneer without,
The cannons to the heavens, the heavens to earth,
"Now the king drinks to Hamlet!"
Act V, sc. 2, ll. 274-8

Lord Willoughby in his written description mentions the feast and then: "... a whole volley of all the great shot of the castle discharged."

If Peregrine Bertie did nothing more for his brother-in-law than to whet his interest in Danish history, there is good reason to be grateful to him.

The subsequent history of Lord and Lady Willoughby is the history of England and England's wars in the last of the sixteenth and the beginning of the seventeenth centuries. Lord Willoughby died on June 25th, 1601, after a short illness contracted while doing his duty to his sovereign. It had been a year of bitter disillusionment to him, with wrangling and jealousies at court. Especially hard to bear must have been the testimony that came out at the trial of his former hero, the Earl of Essex.

The Lady Mary Willoughby d'Eresby will come into this story again.

Upon the death of his father, Robert Bertie, oldest son of Peregrine and Mary, succeeded to the title of Baron Willoughby d'Eresby. Much later he succeeded his cousin, the Eighteenth Earl of Oxford, as Keeper of Havering Castle and Park.

Robert like his father became a famous soldier. It is interesting to Americans to note in passing that one of his special friends was John Smith.[40] son of one of his tenant farmers in Lincolnshire, but better known as the founder of the State of Virginia.[41]

Notes To Chapter II

1. Some biographers of the Earl of Oxford assert that Aubrey had Danish blood, giving as evidence another version of his name, Alberic. This is refuted by the correct ancestry for

Aubrey de Vere to be found in *The Complete Peerage* (edition of 1951). A distinguished descendant of the family tells me that this is the authoritative account of the early de Veres. Confusion seems to have arisen by mistaking the name *Veer* for *de Vere.* The de Veres were definitely Norman. Yet Denmark and Normandy were so close geographically that it may well have been possible for a Danish ancestor to have slipped into the family in the dim dark ages. No explanation has yet been given for the presence of the harpy as supporter of the de Vere arms. This monstrous creature, half-woman, half-vulture, signifies rapacity, and sometimes divine vengeance. (*The Oxford Dictionary*). H. Amphlett notes that the harpy is found on Danish treasure chests of the eighth and ninth centuries in the counties along the east and southeast coast of England which had been raided by the Danes. See her book, *Who Was Shakespeare?*, p. 53.

2. This description is taken from a private notebook in the possession of a descendant of the de Veres.

3. There are numerous references to spaniels in the plays. In *Midsummer Night's Dream*, Helena, following the spurning Demetrius, calls out to him:

> I am your spaniel.
>
> Act II, sc. 1, l. 204

4. Bannerol or bannerole, a banner one yard square borne at funerals of great men and placed over their tombs (*Oxford Dictionary*).

5. From *Machyn's Diary*, quoted by H. Amphlett in *Who Was Shakespeare*?

6. *Rutland MSS.*, Cal. p. 95.

7. This marshland, as mentioned earlier, was a royal hunting preserve, known even in Tudor times for its wild water fowl.

8. Ian Dunlop, *The Palaces and Progresses of Elizabeth I.*

9. Dunlop.

10. David Piper, *The Companion Guide to London*, p. 96.

11. Surely the Duchess of Suffolk is worthy of a footnote, even

though she is in this story only a minor character. Peregrine's mother is actually one of the most forceful and dynamic women of the Tudor age. Her parents were the Tenth Lord Willoughby d'Eresby of Grimsthorpe, Lincolnshire, and his wife, nee Maria de Salinas, a Castilian Lady in Waiting to Queen Katherine of Aragon. The only child of this marriage, she was naturally named Katherine after her mother's beloved mistress. After her father's death, her wardship was sold for £ 2,266 13 s. and 4 d. to Charles Brandon, Duke of Suffolk, who had previously been married to Mary Tudor, widow of the French king Louis XII. Six weeks after his first wife's death the Duke, then forty-nine, married his sixteen-year-old ward, Katherine Willoughby d'Eresby. By the Duke, Katherine had two sons who died young. Much later when she was a widow of thirty-three, she married her "Gentleman usher," Richard Bertie, who seems to have been both her lawyer and man of business. Peregrine was their only child. The story of the Duchess of Suffolk is taken from the fascinating book by Lady Cecilie Goff, *A Woman of the Tudor Age*, privately printed in London.

12. We in New England are reminded of another Peregrine, whose last name was White, born to parents while they were refugees from England because of religious persecution, about two generations later.

13. Lady Cecilie Goff, *Three Generations of a Loyal House.*

14. Ibid.

15. Shrewsbury MSS. Vol. F, I Fol., No. 663, ibid.

16. Ibid.

17. Shrewsbury MSS., Cal. xiii, No. 146, in ibid.

18. Ancaster MSS., p. 4, quoted in Goff, p. 15.

19. Chapter V.

20. Goff, *A Woman of the Tudor Age.*

22. Ibid.

23. Ibid.

24. Ibid.

25. The story will be told in Chapter III.

26. John Buxton, in *Sir Philip Sidney and the English Renais-*

sance, quotes the writer Carleton, who "gives a most vivid and circumstantial account of Sidney's exploit in rescuing Willoughby d'Eresby which was the occasion of his fatal wound.

27. Goff, ibid.

28. Ibid.

30. Ibid.

31. Ibid.

32. The Ogburns in *This Star of England,* p. 180, in writing of another play, tell us: "Hatton the (psalm-singing) Puritan is lightly jibed at. Oxford could no more keep his wit off Hatton than he was able to keep it off Burghley."

33. Dorothy and Charlton Ogburn, *This Star of England.*

34. Goff, ibid.

35. From the Ancaster MSS, p. 48, ibid.

36. Ibid.

37. Ibid.

38. In *The Contemporary Review,* January, 1896. Quoted by Eva Turner Clark, *Hidden Allusions in Shakespeare's Plays.*

39. Chapter IX.

40. Philip L. Barbour, *The Three Worlds of Captain John Smith.*

41. Additional notes to Chapter Two: The story of Lord Willoughby's visit to Denmark and the linking of the tales he brought home to the play of *Hamlet* is told most convincingly in *This Star of England,* Dorothy and Charlton Ogburn, p. 640-641.

Other suggestions relating Lord Oxford's sister and brother-in-law to characters in the Shakespeare plays are taken from Eva Turner Clark's *Hidden Allusions in Shakespeare's Plays.*

Part of the Manor House, Belchamp St. Paul, Essex. *Photograph by the author.*

Castle Hedingham, Essex. *Photograph by the author.*

De Vere houses, Falcon Square, village of Castle Hedingham, Essex. *Photograph by the author.*

Lord Oxford, aged twenty-four. The Welbeck Portrait. *Painted in Paris by an unknown Flemish Artist. National Portrait Gallery, London, on loan from His Grace, the Duke of Portland. Reproduced by courtesy of the owner.*

Queen Elizabeth with Feather Fan. *Painted by an unknown artist, c. 1575. Reproduced by courtesy of the National Portrait Gallery, London.*

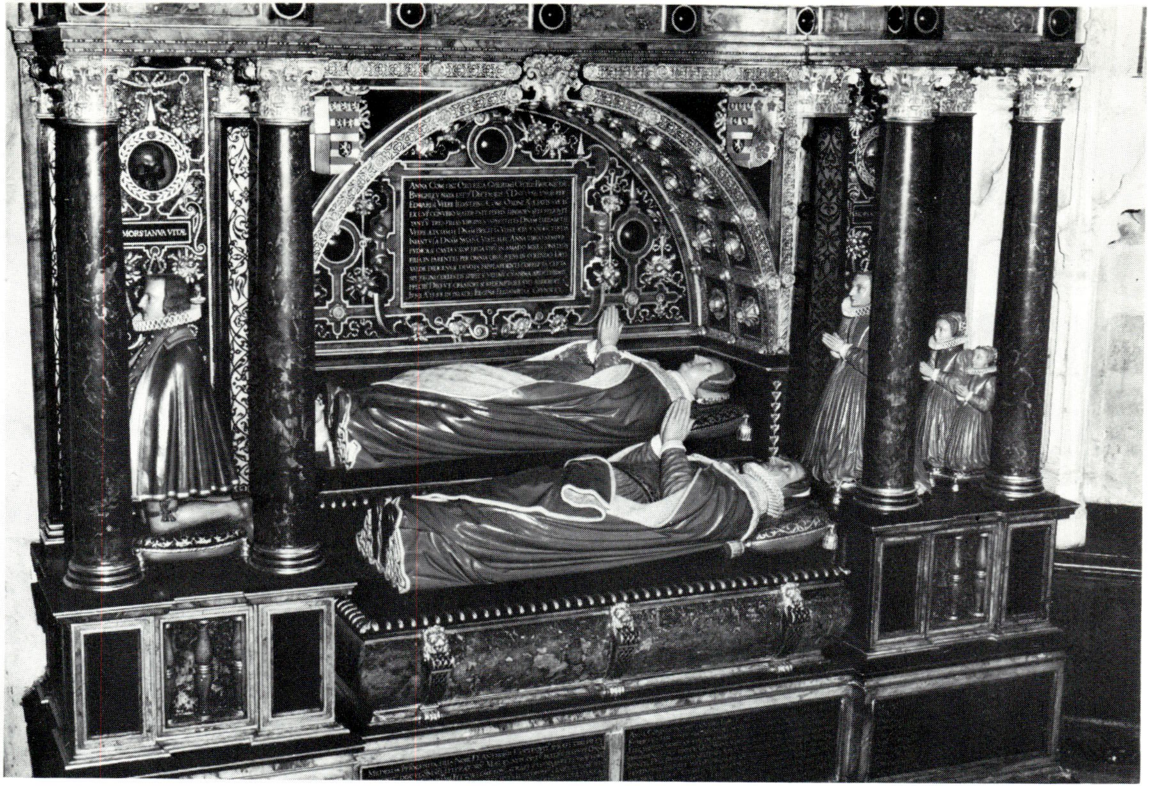

Tomb of Lady Burghley and Lady Oxford, Westminster Abbey. *By courtesy of the Church Information Office.*

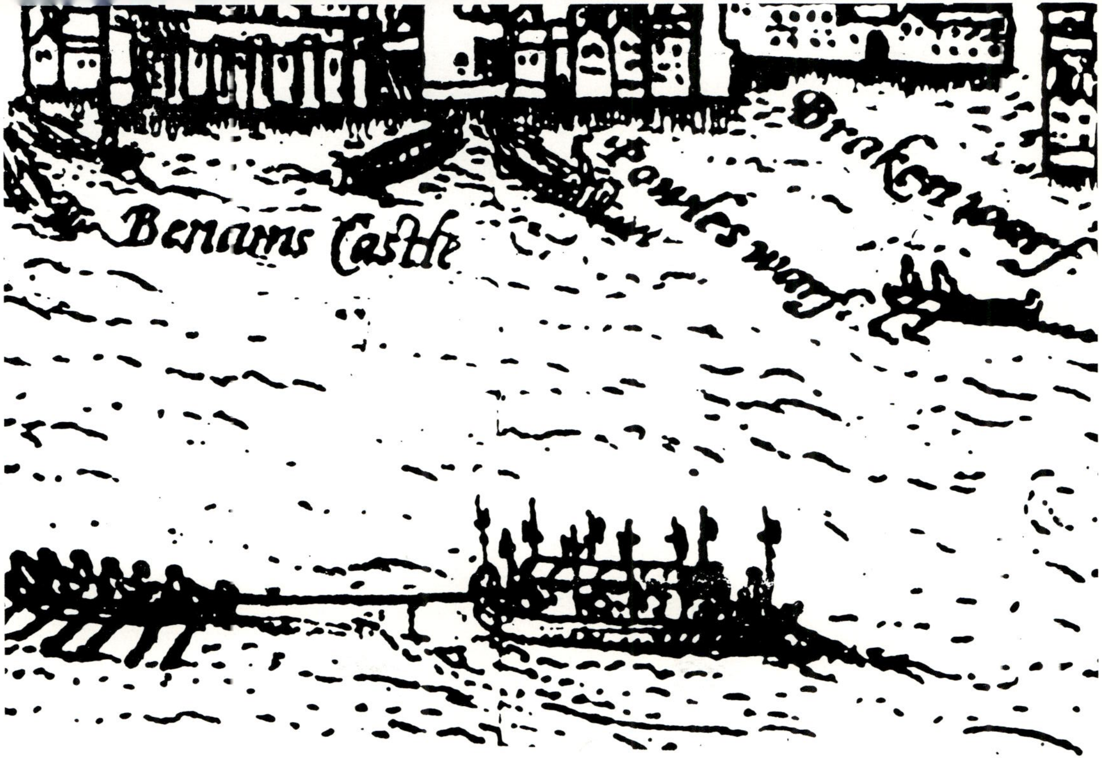

The Royal Barge on the Thames: detail from the *Civitates* map. *London Museum.*

Anne Vavasor. Portrait by an unknown artist.
Reproduced by courtesy of the Courtauld Institute of Art.

Lord Oxford, a portrait by Marcus Gheeraedts c. 1586. *In the collection of His Grace, the Duke of St. Albans, and reproduced by courtesy of the owner.*

Queen Elizabeth Hawking. *By courtesy of the Victoria and Albert Museum. Crown Copyright.*

Wivenhoe Park, Essex. *Painted by John Constable. Reproduced by courtesy of the National Gallery of Art, Washington, D.C. Widener Collection.*

Queen Elizabeth in Procession. *Attributed to Robert Peake the Elder. Reproduced by courtesy of Simon Wingfield Digby, M.P., Sherborne Castle.*

Chapter III

HIS WIFE

I am from humble, he from honour'd name:
No note upon my parents, his all noble,
My master, my dear lord he is; and I
His servant live and will his vassal die.
All's Well That Ends Well, Act I, sc. 3, ll. 164-67.

"Natus est Anna Cecil." This was the entry in the diary of Sir William Cecil for December 5th, 1556, recording the birth of his older daughter, one of the most appealing heroines in all history. Ann Cecil should have had a happy, rewarding life, for she was born into one of the most distinguished and influential families in all England, although it could boast no aristocratic blood. Her father, Sir William, was principal secretary to the Queen, holding the most important post in her Majesty's government. Her mother, born Mildred Coke, was the daughter of Sir Anthony Coke, who had been tutor to the children of King Henry VIII, and Lady Cecil herself was one of the intellectual women of her age.

Ann had a younger sister, Elizabeth; a brilliant young brother, Robert, a little hunchback; and an older half-brother, Thomas Cecil. Anthony and Francis Bacon were her first cousins.

There were always charming and aristocratic young lads in the Cecil household, for Sir William was Master of the Wards. This meant that any fatherless heir to a noble lord would probably be placed in his care until the ward attained his majority. There were even lads there with both parents living, for the honor of being brought up in Sir William's household was considered an education in itself and was much coveted.

Cecil House on the Strand had originally belonged to West-

Minster Abbey. Sir William had recently bought the monastic buildings and added to them considerably until his mansion was one of the great houses in this fashionable suburb of the City of London.

A contemporary has drawn for us a word picture of the house, which he describes as standing on the north side of the Strand. It was, he writes "raised with bricks proportionably adorned with four turrets" on the four corners of the house. It was "curiously beautified within with rare devises and especially by the oratory placed in the angle of the great chamber." Moreover, it contained the finest private collection of books in London.

The Secretary employed eighty persons as retainers in this palatial home, their wages amounting to upwards of £40 a week when the family was in residence and even £30 when it was not. Sir William notes in his expense account that his table alone cost him over one thousand marks a year. This was because he was a most generous host to all the great and near-great personages of the time. The Queen particularly enjoyed dining with him, dropping in unexpectedly, he notes in his diary, even before the house was ready for company.

There was a famous garden behind Cecil House covering many acres, up to and including Covent Garden; in fact it was more extensive than any other private garden in the environs of London.

Sir William had brought over from the Netherlands the gardener, John Gerard. Gerard was justly famed for his rose culture; indeed, many of the roses we enjoy today were developed by him for the garden of Cecil House. He was noted, too, for growing herbs in his own garden in Holborn, and he wrote a book, *Herbal,* about the special plants which would grow in the English climate, mentioning the potato, recently brought over from the New World. This was the first time that humble vegetable has been mentioned in print in Europe.[1] The following year, after publication of his first book, he wrote a whole treatise on growing potatoes.

Cecil House across from the river side of the Strand was only a few hundred yards from the public wharf at the bottom of Ivy Lane. Here the watermen waited to be hired, a noisy, raucous lot. A customer at the wharf would hail a boatman by calling out: "Westward *ho*!" or "Eastward *ho*!" depending on the direction he wanted to be taken. For the River Thames was the busy highway between the City and Westminster, and competition for passengers was intense. Ann Cecil would have been familiar with the watermen's loud harsh cries.

Sir William had a country estate also, Theobalds, in Hertfordshire, where the Queen was equally delighted to visit him, coming to stay for weeks at a time with all her retinue, so that it became necessary to add on rooms each time she elected to visit. Twelve times she stayed at Theobalds, even using this private residence for receiving foreign diplomats, causing considerable strain on the resources of her host. But he most generously welcomed her and appeared to be happy to have his sovereign use his house so freely. The Cecils also owned an estate in Stamford, where Sir William had been brought up.

Such was the background for the story of little Ann, who should have had one of the happiest of childhoods and adult lives. Yet the cruel fates doomed this girl to a bitterly tragic life, with longings unfulfilled, with rejection, and finally with an early death.

It seemed that Ann never learned how to cope with life. She is always referred to as "sweet" and "gentle" and "little." This may have been in contrast to her mother, who was a most formidable lady, to judge by her portrait at Hatfield House. Ann was the darling of her father; Sir William doted on her all her life.

Turning to the plays, it is interesting to find how many father-daughter themes there are in "Shakespeare." There is the Shylock-Jessica theme in *The Merchant of Venice*, though Shylock loved not only his daughter but also his ducats. Olivia in *Twelfth Night* mourns her father rather more passionately than most daughters would. Juliet defies her father, it is true, but it is surprising to both her parents when she does. Polonius-Ophelia is, of course the classic example. "She will be rul'd by me!" Polonius confidently declared. And Ophelia obeyed him in her response to Hamlet even though she was in love with the Prince. Again, note that it is not her lover's rejection which drives Ophelia mad, but the death of her beloved father.

When Ann Cecil was six years old, an event occurred which was destined to change the whole course of her life. It was the coming to Cecil House of the recently bereaved young Earl of Oxford. Henry Machyn has written in his diary a vivid description of the arrival of this twelve-year-old boy, the newest Royal Ward, who was now the Premier Earl of the kingdom:

> The third day of September, 1562, came riding out of Essex from the funeral of the Earl of Oxford's father the young Earl of Oxford with seven score horse all in black through London and Cheap and Ludgate and so to Temple Bar . . . between five and six of the clock at afternoon.[2]

Would little Ann ever forget that picture! From down the Strand she would have heard the clatter of the horses' hoofs on the stone pavement[3] as the procession approached. Then she would have caught her first glimpse of the new Lord Oxford, only a boy, riding so nobly at the head of his retainers, one hundred and forty strong, both the retainers and the horses caparisoned in mourning black. "The young Earl" must have been downcast and sorrowful as he walked his horse sedately toward the fine mansion which was to be his home, for he mourned his father deeply. He may also have been a little frightened, though trying not to show it, wondering what this new experience of city life would mean after the quiet countryside of Castle Hedingham and the scholarly seclusion of Cambridge.

By the time a daily routine had been established Ann could not have had much chance to see the new ward, for her father had planned a full schedule for him, a copy of which has been preserved: "Orders for the Earl of Oxford's exercise."[4]

The day began at 7 A.M. with dancing as soon as he was dressed; from 7:30 to 8, breakfast; then French and Latin studies with short periods for writing and drawing. Then Family Prayers, to which the entire household staff would come. This was one time when Ann could have seen the new earl, though she would have been sternly told by Lady Mildred to keep her mind on higher thoughts than little boys. After this came dinner at noon. And then again the Earl would be closeted with his tutors in study of cosmography, more Latin and French and writing till 4:30, when the family met for prayers and then supper.

On holy days the strenuous schedule relaxed to allow reading of the Epistle and Gospel before dinner, and the young ward could then spend "the rest of the day in riding, shooting, dancing, walking, and other commendable exercises."[5]

Ann would have been taken into the great hall to be presented to the Queen when her Majesty came to visit. One year while the family was in residence at Theobalds, Ann caught smallpox and was desperately ill. There is a record of this in Sir William's diary, which notes that the Queen was visiting at the time and that she had to leave hurriedly to avoid contracting the disease. This seems to have made things hard for everybody concerned, serving men and women, and the carters and baggage men. No mention is made again of little Ann, of who took care of her, whether she was ill for long, or whether she was in any way disfigured.

The curtain of mystery surrounding Ann's childhood rises once again on New Year's Day of her thirteenth year, when her father writes to her this gently paternal poem:

To Mistress Ann Cecil,
upon Making her a New Year's Gift.
Written in 1568.

As years do grow, so cares increase;
  And time will move to look to thrift:
Though years in me work nothing less,

Yet, for your years, and New Year's gift,
This house wife's toy is now my shift!
  To set you on work, some thrift to feel,
  I send you now a spinning wheel.

But one thing first, I wish and pray,
  Lest thirst of thrift might soon you tire,
Only spin one pound a day,
  And play the rest, as time require:
  Sweat not! (oh fie!) fling rocks in fire!
    God send, who send'th all thrift and wealth,
    You long years: and your father, health![6]

The last line refers to Sir William's gout, which plagued him all his life.

Meanwhile Ann and the young Lord Oxford were being brought up in the same household, though not quite as brother and sister. Edward would have found Ann not nearly as much fun as his own sister, Mary de Vere.

Sir William had chosen for Edward's tutors Sir Thomas Smith, the English scholar; Lawrence Nowell, brother of the dean of St. Paul's; and Edward's uncle, Arthur Golding, the classicist.

Sir Thomas Smith had been a classmate of Cecil at St. John's College, Cambridge. Eventually he became a noted lawyer who was to have a lasting and beneficial influence on English law. Among other suggestions for correcting existing abuses, he wrote that putting pressure on a jury was "accounted very violent, tyrannical and contrary to the liberty and customs of the realm of England." He insisted that the liberty of the meanest subject was something precious, an inalienable possession of the Englishman.[7] It is apparent that his reforms and his convictions strike at the very heart of English law.

Lawrence Nowell was regarded in his time as the chief reviver of the Anglo-Saxon language and learning. In the Bodleian Library, Oxford, there is a manuscript of an Old English dictionary that he compiled. Nowell had an intense curiosity about every aspect of the land of Britain. In 1563 he made a proposal to Sir William for help in making maps of the entire country and each of its counties. Only a few exquisitely finished maps of his have been preserved, but it is interesting that one of them seems to have been carried about by Sir William, even with notations in his hand. Nowell's map of Scotland was said to be "in advance of that of the great Mercator."[8]

Lawrence Nowell also made transcripts from the works of the Venerable Bede, Giraldus Cambrensis and Matthew Paris, and he wrote a description of Ireland. He also attempted to codify the laws of the Anglo-Saxons. But he never published any of his work, and it is unfortunate that much of it is now lost.[9]

Arthur Golding has been mentioned before. But it should be recalled that it was at this time while he was tutoring his young nephew at Cecil House, that Golding was translating Ovid's *Metamorphoses* into English verse.

Sir William had chosen well, in appointing tutors for Edward de Vere. We believe that much of their teaching is evident in the famous plays.

From his earliest days Lord Oxford had had a special flair and style of his own. He wanted fine clothes and expensive luxuries even when he was a school boy, and he seems to have persuaded his guardian to allow him to spend £200 a year for his "personal effects." There is in the *Chester Herald*'s account a notation[10] of how some of this money was spent:

To John Spark, draper, for fine black cloth for a cape and riding cloak £6 5 0.

To Myles Spilsby, tailor, for one doublet of cambric, one of canvas and one of black satin: and the furniture for a riding cloak £12 13 0.

To John Martin, hosier, for one pair of velvet hose—black, £10 9 0.

And here is a most significant notation, not for apparel, but for something even more important to the young earl:

> To William Sears, stationer, for a Geneva bible, gilt, a Chaucer, Plutarch's works in French, with other books and papers. £ 2 7 10.

How many times in the plays are found expressions culled from the Bible, from Plutarch, and even from Chaucer!

And then there is this item:

> To George Hill, saddler, for collars and girths for my lord's horse, £5 s. 0.
>
> And for board and diet of my lord with his tutors and servants at Cecil House for 14 days of this quarter at £3 a week, £60 0 0.

Finally may be noted the earl's penchant for caps. He paid his "capper":

> £4 6 0 for one hat of velvet, one of taffeta, two velvet caps together with a scarf, two pairs of garters with silver at the ends, a plume of feathers for the hat, etc. etc.[11]

Is it not amazing that the diminishing capital held out?

The year after Edward de Vere's arrival at Cecil House, Lawrence Nowell told Sir William that he felt his services to the young lord "were no longer required." Edward's guardian consequently decided that he should return to Cambridge University, only this time instead of going back to Queen's College where he had been before his father died, he was entered at St. John's, which was Sir William's own alma mater. It was while he was at Cambridge that Edward incurred the wrath of his guardian for the first time, for overspending his wardrobe allowance.

The curriculum of the University consisted of lectures,

athletics and discipline. But on Saturday and Sunday evenings plays were presented. The plays were not always by classical dramatists; a student might be honored by having one of his own plays presented, provided it was in Latin.

It is thought that possibly—or even probably—Lord Oxford's first plays were written while he was a Cambridge student, though what the plays were and whether he ever wrote any in English while there is not known.

The year that Lord Oxford received his degree, the Queen paid a state visit to Cambridge, which included a round of academic exercises, preachings and plays, and perhaps a little extra ceremony because Sir William Cecil, her Principal Secretary, was at that time Lord Chancellor of the University. There was a special presentation of the *Aulularia* of Plautus. This was in 1564, when Lord Oxford was fourteen and a half.[12]

He spent the next two years at Christchurch, Oxford, the University awarding him a degree of Master of Arts in 1566.[13]

After that, Gray's Inn was chosen for his legal and courtly training, because Sir William himself had matriculated there.[14] Legal instruction was given in a method which was a combination of debate, tutorial classes and lectures, and during the season when the law courts were in session members of the Inn were allowed to attend. Students were also allowed to practise law as solicitors.[15] Gray's Inn gave excellent and intensive training for a young man who was about to be a courtier.

It was while Edward was at Gray's Inn that he first met young Philip Sidney, a fellow student from Penshurst, Kent.

It is true that Edward de Vere was given an excellent education for the time in which he lived. Yet we know from the plays that it was life, itself, which interested him far more than books. Listen to Berowne in *Love's Labours' Lost:* (Act I, sc. 1, lines 71-94).

> . . . all delights are vain; but that most vain
> Which, with pain purchas'd, doth inherit pain:
> As, painfully to pore upon a book,

To seek the light of truth; which truth the while
Doth falsely blind the eyesight of his look,
Light seeking light doth light of light beguile....
So, ere you find where light in darkness lies,
Your light grows dark by losing of your eyes.
Study is like the heaven's glorious sun,
That will not be deep-search'd with saucy looks:
Small have continual plodders ever won,
Save base authority from others' books.
These earthly godfathers of heaven's lights,
That give a name to every fixed star,
Have no more profit of their shining nights
Than those that walk and wot not what they are.
Too much to know is to know nought but fame;
And every godfather can give a name.

King. How well he's read, to reason against reading!

Exactly when Lord Oxford first came to be a courtier to the Queen is not recorded. Certainly he was giving full time to his Court duties upon leaving Gray's Inn, and it is known that he had appeared at Court several times before that.

To Ann Cecil, brought up in the protected atmosphere of a little Elizabethan lady, he must have seemed a glamorous creature inhabiting a world about which she could only dream. She would have heard her father tell that Lord Oxford was rapidly coming to be the favorite of the Queen.

When Ann was approaching marriageable age, her hand was sought by Sir Henry Sidney for his son, Philip. Whether Ann and Philip ever had a chance to meet is not known; usually marriages were planned by parental negotiation in those days. Ann being the daughter of the powerful Secretary to the Queen, Sir Henry Sidney would have thought her a good match for his son.[16]

But the marriage offer was not accepted, as hoped by Sir Henry. Sir William Cecil had higher ambitions for this, his favorite daughter. One of the Royal Wards, the Lord Oxford, held title to the oldest and proudest earldom in England. To enable his daughter even to be considered as Lord Oxford's bride, it would be necessary for Sir William himself to be elevated to a baronetcy. This the Queen was most willing to do, and on February 25th, 1571,[17] she created him Baron Burghley. Queen Elizabeth seems to have been anxious that this marriage go through, although it was well known at Court that she had carried on an outrageous flirtation with the young nobleman herself.

Ann's feeling about her intended bridegroom can only be surmised. He was young, handsome, scholarly, accomplished, a beautiful dancer, a passable poet, and a musician who also composed music. He was, indeed, the most eligible bachelor in the land, and, need it be added, possessed of that beguiling magnetism which has been described in various ways by contemporaries who knew him. Could little Ann's emotions be doubted? It is possible that she answered the proposal, speaking of "their faithful love's vow":

> I gave thee mine before thou didst request it.
>
> *Romeo and Juliet,* Act III, sc. 3

Indeed, all the Cecil family seemed to think that this marriage was eminently right. We can almost hear Lady Burghley clucking with Juliet's mother: "Well, well, thou hast a careful father."[18] Lord Burghley himself wrote to the Earl of Rutland in regard to his future son-in-law:

> I confess to your Lordship, I do honour him so dearly from my heart as I do my own son, and in any case that may touch him for his honour and weal, I shall think his mine own interest therein. And surely, my Lord, by dealing with him, I find that which I often heard of your Lordship, that there is much more in him of understanding than any stranger to him would think. And for my part I find that whereof I take comfort in his wit and knowledge, grown by good observation.[19]

But what might the young bridegroom's reaction have been to these negotiations which moved so rapidly to a climax? He couldn't very well thwart the well-laid plan of his guardian by refusing to marry his daughter. Yet it is clear that this simple girl, so eager to give herself to him, was hardly one to appeal to his urbane, sophisticated taste.

The ceremony was planned to take place at Theobalds in September, but for some reason it was postponed. One story is that the prospective bridegroom ran away to the Continent. Careful research proves that this story is not true, that Edward did once run away to the Continent and was brought back by Bedingfield, but this was at a later date. It is suggested that the wedding was postponed in order to wait until the Court returned from the summer progresses.

The wedding finally took place on December 19th, 1571, in Westminster Abbey, in the presence of the Queen and Court.

It is indeed tempting to the imagination to try to picture this great fashionable wedding in the beautiful old Abbey. Anyone familiar with its lofty pointed arches can see in his mind's eye the festive scene; the Queen resplendent in the regalia she so loved to wear; the Court in gorgeous costumes of costly silk and velvet; the handsome, graceful and aristocratic bridegroom, twenty-one, glamorous in his Court apparel, the faint suggestion of a moustache adding manliness to his youthful appearance; the bride, just fifteen, trembling on her father's arm. The newly-created Baron would be wearing his furred robe and Ann would look very little beside him; she would probably be both happy and frightened.

Lord St. John wrote to the Earl of Rutland:

> The Earl of Oxford hath gotten him a wife—or at least, a wife hath caught him; this is Mistress Anne Cecil, whereunto the Queen hath given her consent, and the which has caused great weeping, wailing, and sorrowful cheer of those that had hoped to have had that golden day.[20]

The evening of the wedding Lord Burghley wrote a long letter to his friend, Francis Walsingham, then English ambassador at Paris—a typical father-of-the-bride letter, saying in part:

> I can write no more for lack of leisure, being occasioned to write at this time divers ways, and not unoccupied with feasting my friends at the marriage of my daughter who is this day married to the Earl of Oxford, to my comfort, by reason of the Queen's Majesty, who hath very honourably with her presence and great favor accompanied it.[21]

The young couple spent their honeymoon at Wivenhoe[22] (see page 40 k), one of Lord Oxford's estates in Essex, not far from his country seat of Castle Hedingham. Wivenhoe was a pleasant rural village on the sea, where Lord Oxford chose to build a new brick house back from the water front, with a view of gently rolling meadows where cows were lazily grazing, the sparkling sea with white sails in the distance. Lord Oxford must have known happiness there with Ann for a time, because one of his letters is signed "from my new country Muses of Wivenghole."

But it is not long before the bridegroom is back in London alone, and the reason is mother-in-law trouble. Lord Oxford charged that Lady Burghley "at Wivenhoe caused a division" in the house. The bridegroom decided to take up bachelor quarters on returning to the city, renting an apartment in the old Savoy Palace[23] on the Strand. Here he was able to entertain his growing circle of literary friends, many of whom seem to have been rather bibulous young men. The Countess Ann would not have enjoyed being hostess to these young blades.

It is only fair to suggest that another reason why Lord Oxford left Wivenhoe might have been because the Queen had summoned him to Court. Edward de Vere had become such a favorite by this time that she wanted him always by her side, or at her feet, to converse with her, to flatter and amuse her. He was proficient in all the accomplishments expected of a courtier; he could dance, sing, or compose poetry and frequently did. Best of all, he could talk beguilingly or listen attentively. The Queen found it pleasant to while away many a weary hour in the diverting company of this charming young man after wrestling with affairs of state with her learned but elderly Secretaries. One can understand though hardly condone the demands she made upon his time, heedlessly ignoring the dreadful loneliness, not to say jealousy, of the new little bride left behind in Wivenhoe.

But soon Lord Oxford found himself in real trouble. Concurrently with his marriage and honeymoon in Wivenhoe were his ever-present troubles with and on behalf of his Howard cousins. Thomas Howard, Duke of Norfolk, inclined toward Catholicism though he was not a Catholic himself.[24] Indeed, religion seems to have been the least of his interests at this time. Norfolk was possessed of a "vaulting ambition" and he felt himself slighted and unappreciated at the Court of his cousin, Queen Elizabeth. This nobleman was found to be the central figure in a plot promoted by the Catholics on the Continent to usurp the throne of England and place upon it Mary Queen of Scots. Mary was the young and beautiful widow of the French king, Francis II, her mother a member of the powerful family of Guise. Norfolk had never met the lady, so could not claim that he had fallen in love with her. But there is no doubt that he aspired to marry her and to reign over England and Scotland jointly with her.[25] According to the Catholics Mary was the rightful heiress to the English throne by her descent from King Henry VII, because, they claimed, Henry VIII and Ann Boleyn, Elizabeth Tudor's parents, had never really been married.

Fortunately this treacherous plot was discovered and Norfolk imprisoned in the Tower. Edward de Vere, who also was a cousin, tried in every way he could to get the Duke released, although he, Oxford, had not been in any way involved in the plot against the throne. He appealed to his powerful father-in-law; then, failing to enlist his sympathy, he appealed directly to the Queen. When neither of them would release Norfolk, Edward himself impulsively attempted to break into the Tower and rescue his cousin. This plot was foiled and to nobody's surprise, the favorite, Oxford, escaped imprisonment, though he received a blistering lecture from his sovereign. After a trial before the Peers in Westminster Hall at which Lord Oxford was present, the Duke of Norfolk was found guilty, and in 1572 he was executed.

In spite of Lord Oxford's machinations on behalf of his cousin, Thomas Howard, which could not have endeared him to his father-in-law, there is no sign of hostility between the two courtiers at this time. August 24th, 1572, Lord Oxford wrote to the Secretary in reference to Lord Burghley's handling of his estates, assuring him that "both in this and in all other things, I am to be governed and commanded at your Lordship's good devotion." He continues:

> I would to God your Lordship would let me understand some of your news which here doth ring doubtfully in the ears of every man, of the murder of the Admiral of France, and a number of noblemen and worthy gentlemen, and such as greatly have in their lifetime honoured the Queen's Majesty our Mistress; on whose tragedies we have a number of French aenaeses in this city that tell of their own overthrows with tears falling from their eyes, a piteous thing to hear but a cruel and far more grievous thing must deem it them to see. . . . And sith the world is so full of treasons and vile instruments daily to attempt new and unlooked for things, good my Lord, I shall affectionately and heartily desire your Lordship to be careful both of yourself and of her Majesty, that your friends may long enjoy you and you them. . . . This estate hath depended on you a great while . . . and what shall hap to you I count it hap to myself; or at least I will make myself a voluntary partaker of it. Thus, my Lord, I humbly desire your Lordship to pardon my youth, but to take in good part my zeal and affection towards you, as one on whom I have builded my foundation either to stand or to fall. And,

my good Lord, think not I do this presumptuously as to advise you that am but to take advice of your Lordship, but to admonish you, as one with whom I would spend my blood and life, so much you have made me yours. And I do protest there is nothing desired of me than so to be taken and accounted of you. Thus with my hearty commendations and your daughter's we leave you to the custody of Almighty God.

Your Lordship's affectionate son-in-law,

Edward Oxenford.[26]

This letter is quoted at length to show not only Lord Oxford's good will toward his father-in-law, but also to show his deep distress upon hearing of the Massacre of St. Bartholomew.

His next letter to his father-in-law gives a charming picture of their relationship, and something of the flavor of their life:

My Lord, I received your letters when I rather looked to have seen yourself here than to have heard from you; sith it is so that your Lordship is otherwise affaired with the business of the Commonwealth than to be disposed to recreate yourself, and repose you among your own, yet we do hope after this—you having had so great care of the Queen's Majesty's service—you will begin to have some respect for your own health, and take pleasure to dwell where you have taken pains to build. My wife, whom I thought should have taken her leave of you if your Lordship had come, till you would have otherwise commanded, is departed unto the country this day: and my self as fast as I can get out of town to follow.

Lord Oxford then asks Lord Burghley to see whether he might procure for him some military service abroad, either on land or at sea. Finishing the letter he writes:

Thus remembering myself to your Lordship, I commit you to God; from London this 22nd day of September, by your Lordship to command.

Edward Oxenford.[27]

It was at this time that Lord Oxford suddenly decided to go to the Continent, thereby provoking the Queen's fiery wrath once more. She promptly dispatched his friend, Thomas Bedingfield, to fetch him home. Then Oxford, Bedingfield and Lord Burghley went together to Theobalds to await the Queen's pleasure. The Court was on a progress, but Walsingham, now serving as Principal Secretary, wrote Lord Burghley that he thought her Majesty was inclined to be satisfied with the Earl's return as evidence of his loyalty to her:

> The Earl of Oxford's return has very much qualified her Majesty's displeasure, but she does not mean to wrap up his contempt without some kind of reprehension.[28]

Elizabeth Tudor did not easily forgive.

At the time of Lord Oxford's return from this escapade, there could have been no serious estrangement between the Countess Ann and himself, for her father notes in his diary that they were together visiting at Theobalds for some weeks. Oxford simply acted on impulse in running away to the Continent without the Queen's permission.

Later that year, 1574, the Queen would be in residence at Hampton Court, in anticipation of which Ann wrote to the Lord Chamberlain in charge of arrangements asking for three chambers instead of two, explaining that "the more commodious my lodging is, the willinger I hope the lord my husband will be to come hither."[29] This is the first indication we have that little Ann seems to be aware of her royal rival.

However, the Earl and Countess did go together to Hampton Court and spent the month of October there.

But soon Ann was to learn that her venturesome young husband was desperately eager to take another trip abroad and had already obtained the Queen's permission to go. Sadly the little Countess bade him adieu, and went home to live with her parents.

We can almost see her tears as she watched her lord start off on his travels, with his retinue of eight men as befitting to his station. Lord Burghley notes the retinue in his diary: "two gentlemen, two grooms, one payend, a harbinger, a housekeeper and a trenchman."[30]

Their first destination was Paris. Lord Burghley, perhaps uncertain of the impression his volatile son-in-law might make in that sophisticated capital, had written to the English ambassador there to enquire about him. Lord Burghley's letter has not been kept, but this is the reply of the ambassador:

> I will assure your Lordship unfeignedly my Lord of Oxford used himself as orderly and moderately as might be desired, and with great commendation, nor is there any appearance of the likelihood of any other.[31]

What else could Lord Burghley expect from a de Vere?

Indeed, the English ambassador was greatly taken with the charming young nobleman. He sent this description to Lord Burghley of Oxford's presentation to the French King and Queen:

> I presented my Lord of Oxford also to the King and Queen, who used him honourably. Amongst other talk the King asked whether he was married. I said he had a fair lady. "Il y a donc ce," said the king, "un beau couple."[32]

That letter must have pleased little Ann.

While Lord Oxford was still in Paris he received a letter from his father-in-law telling him that the Countess was expecting a child and suggesting that he might want to come home to be on hand for the birth of his heir.

When the answer to that letter finally came in the Paris post, it must have been a bitter disappointment to Ann. For Lord Oxford told his father-in-law that, while he was delighted to hear the news about his Countess, still he thought that, since his wife was being so well cared for and since there would soon be an heir to the earldom, he had better take this opportunity to go to Italy. He had always wanted to go there and now he was so near. But he softened the blow by sending the Countess a fine pair of horses, and, more precious to her, a beautifully-painted portrait of himself done by a Flemish artist in Paris. It is believed that this was the so-called Welbeck portrait, now in the National Portrait Gallery, London.[33]

How eagerly the little Countess must have watched for the post from the Continent! None of Lord Oxford's letters to his wife at this time have been saved, giving the impression that perhaps there were none. But there are a number of notes addressed to her father. They tell that Lord Edward crossed the Alps and rode on, visiting Padua, Mantua, Verona and Milan, finally coming to Venice. There he received a warm welcome from the Italian noblemen who had been told of his coming by the Venetian Ambassador to London, who had known Lord Oxford at Court. After staying in Venice for a while, he rode on to Siena, Genoa and Rome, even crossing the swirling waters between Scylla and Charybdis to go to Sicily. There is no actual record that he went to Greece, but since there are four months of his travels unaccounted for, it may well have been that he did go to that land of stark mountains and blue seas, whose classics he knew so well.

The letters he wrote to Lord Burghley very often requested more funds. True it is that the money Oxford asked for was his own, derived from what was left of the estates inherited from his father. However, it should be recalled that the inheritance was being greatly depleted, as described in Chapter II. Oxford needed money for travel on the Continent, for his expenses were high and he had a retinue of eight to care for. But it is also true that his nature demanded beautiful things wherever he went, regardless of cost. This may have been because he had been brought up in such luxury when he was a child in Castle Hedingham.

This is one of his letters to Lord Burghley:

> My Lord, whereas I perceive by your Lordship's letters how hardly money is to be gotten, and that my man writes he would fain pay to my creditors some part of that money which I have appointed to be made over to me, good my Lord, let rather my creditors bear with me awhile, and take their days assured according to that order I left, than I so want in a strange country, unknowing yet what need I may have of money myself. My revenue is appointed, with the profits of my lands, to pay them as I may; and if I cannot yet pay them as I would, yet as I can I will, but preferring my own necessity before theirs. . . .
>
> Whereas I understand the greatness of my debt and the greediness of my creditors grows so dishonourable and troublesome to your Lordship, that that land of mine which is in Cornwall I have appointed to be sold.[34]

Whether it was that Lord Burghley thought his son-in-law too extravagant or whether he was trying to save the funds for Ann and her expected child or whether there really was a shortage of money will never be known. But it is known that Lord Burghley was niggardly about sending financial aid, so that Lord Oxford was forced to cut short his trip, albeit he was gone from England a year and a half.

Happily there is a vivid description of the Earl on his travels, by one of his English literary friends. George Chapman gives this stunning tribute to his fellow-dramatist in *The Revenge of Bussy d'Amboise:*

> I overtook, coming from Italy,
> In Germany, a great and famous Earl
> Of England: the most goodly fashion'd man
> I ever saw; from head to foot in form
> Rare and most absolute; he had a face
> Like one of the most ancient honour'd Romans,
> From whence his noblest family was deriv'd;

He was beside of spirit passing great,
Valiant, and learn'd, and liberal as the sun,
Spoke and writ sweetly or of learned subjects,
Or of discipline of public weals;
And 'twas the Earl of Oxford.

What a vivid picture! It is not hard to see why this traveller charmed everybody he met on the way.

Meanwhile back in London Ann's baby was born July 2nd, 1575, and named Elizabeth. What other name could be given to the first grandchild of the Queen's Treasurer of the Realm, as Lord Burghley was at this time!

It must have cheered the new mother to hear the letter that her husband wrote to Lord Burghley, thanking him "for the good news of my wife's delivery." Lord Oxford sent her a Greek Testament with a poem in Latin on the flyleaf. Translated the poem is as follows:

> To the illustrious Lady Ann de Vere, Countess of Oxford, while her noble husband, Edward Vere, Earl of Oxford, was occupied in foreign travel.

After this dedication, the poem proceeds with a series of puns on *truth* in the words *vera, veritas* and *Vere:*

> Words of truth are fitting to a Vere; lies are foreign to the truth, and only true things stand fast, all else is fluctuating and comes to an end. Therefore, since thou, a Vere, art wife and Mother of a Vere daughter, and seeing that thou mayst with good hope look forward to being mother of an heir to the Veres, may thy mind always glow with love of the truth, and may thy motto be *Ever Lover of the Truth*. And that thou mayst the better attain to this, pray to the Author of all Truth, that His Word may teach thee: that His Spirit may nourish thy inner life. So that, thus alleviating the absent longings of thy dear husband,

thou, a Vere, mayst be called the true glory of thy husband.[35]

Meanwhile horrid gossip was whispered about Court regarding this baby; it was said that Lord Oxford was not the father of the child.[36] How the rumor started nobody knows, but soon the whole Court was trying to prove or refute the charge. Lord Henry Howard, Oxford's cousin and brother to the beheaded Duke of Norfolk, was noted for sowing dissension wherever he went. Very likely he started the ugly lie; at least, it was said that he thoroughly enjoyed repeating it widely. He even crossed the Channel to meet Lord Oxford in Paris and tell *him* the cruel gossip.

Edward de Vere, the sensitive, poetic English nobleman, took this news very hard. Not only was it a blow to his pride, but even more it was a blot on his family honor—on that proud and ancient name of de Vere. His first poem is recalled, *The Loss of My Good Name*, which ended:

Help echo that in air doth flee, shrill voices to resound,
To wail this loss of my good name, as of these griefs the ground.[37]

Because he took this news so hard without waiting to check to see if it were true, the whole pattern of Lord Oxford's life was now completely overturned. He really had, it seemed, looked forward to seeing his wife and the new babe and to returning to his family again, when in a moment all this was denied to him.

To cap the climax, on the way home his ship was raided by pirates.

Ann and her father were at the dock to meet him, but he stalked by them without a word and went straight to the Queen. He adamantly refused to see his wife, even forbidding her to come to Court.

At this point Lord Burghley seems to have set his spies on his son-in-law, even as it is known that he had spied upon his own son, Thomas Cecil, when that young man had been a student in Paris. Why he should do this is not clear, but possibly he suspected that Edward de Vere and Henry Howard were becoming too intimate; if so, naturally it was his duty to protect the throne and kingdom.

This letter from Lord Oxford speaks for itself:

> My Lord, this other day your man, Stainner, told me that you sent for Amis, my man, and if he were absent that Lyly[38] should come to you. I sent Amis, for he was in the way. And I think it very strange that your Lordship should enter into that course toward me; whereby I must learn that [which] I knew before, both of your opinion and good will toward me; But I pray, my Lord, leave that course, for I mean not to be your ward nor your child. I serve her Majesty and I am that I am, by alliance near to your Lordship, but free: and scorn to be offered that injury to think that I am so weak of government as to be ruled by servants, or not able to govern myself.[39]

How sad to see the relationship between these two fine men deteriorating! But this letter is intersting for another rason, as proof that Lord Oxford was familiar with his Geneva Bible, which, it will be recalled, he had bought when a young student. The phrase: "I am that I am" is straight out of this Bible, and is found again in *Sonnet 121*, beginning

> 'Tis better to be vile than vile esteem'd....

which may have been written at about this time, for it includes these lines:

> No, I am that I am, and they that level
> At my abuses reckon up their own....

At Court Lord Oxford, heartbroken over the turn his marriage had taken, was trying to console himself. He was writing plays, as

Gilbert Talbot tells his father in a letter, only Talbot fails to say what plays they were.

There is a rather crude little poem in the collection of verse called *A hundreth sundrie Flowres*, which is supposed to have been written by Ann Cecil at this time of her estrangement from her lord. It is signed with the posy: *Spreta tamen Vivunt*, and it plays upon the word *Ver*, this time meaning both spring, the season, and water bubbling from the earth. Here is the poem:

A loving Lady being wounded in the springtime now galded eftsones with the remembrance of the spring doth therefore thus bewail:

The tenth of March when Aries receiv'd
Dame Phoebus rays, into his horned head:
And I myself, by learned lore perceiv'd,
That Ver approached, and frosty winter fled.
I crossed the Thames, to take the cheerful air,
In open fields, the weather was so fair.

And as I rowed, fast by the further shore,
I heard a voice, which seemed to lament:
Whereat I stay'd, and by a stately door,
I left my Boat, and up on land I went.
Till at the last by lasting pain I found,
The woeful wight, which made this doleful sound.

In pleasant garden (placed all alone)
I saw a Dame, who sat in weary wise,
With scalding sighs, she uttered all her moan,
The rueful tears down rained from her eyes;
Her low'ring head, full low on hand she laid,
On knees her arm: and thus this Lady said:

The fragrant flowers, which have not long been seen,
Will flourish now, (ere long) in bravery:
The tender buds, whom cold hath long kept in,
Will spring and sprout, as they do now begin.

The lusty Ver, which whilome might exchange
My griefs to joy, and then my joys increase,
Springs now elsewhere, and shows to me but strange,
My winter's woe, therefore can never cease:
In other coasts, his sun full clear doth shine,
And comfort lends to ev'ry mold but mine.

What plant can spring that feels no force of Ver?
What flower can flourish, where no sun doth shine?
These Bales (quod she) within my breast I hear,
To break my bark, and make my pyth to pine:
Needs must I fall, I fade both root and rind,
My branches bow, at blast of ev'ry wind.

This said: she cast a glance and spied my face,
By sight whereof, Lord how she changed hew!
So that for shame, I turned back a pace
And to my home, myself in haste I drew:
And as I could her woeful words rehearse,
I set them down in this lamenting verse.

Now Ladies, you, that know by whom I sing,
And feel the winter of such frozen wells:
Of courtesy, yet cause this noble spring,
To send his sun, above the highest hills:
And so to shine, upon her fading sprays,
Which now in woe, do wither thus always.

"This noble spring" is obviously a pun on "this noble Vere"—*Vere* having a meaning of *spring* as well as *truth*. The verses doubtless contain many another double entendre.

Meanwhile Ann's father—to please her, no doubt—wrote Lord Oxford this ingratiating letter in December, 1576, in which he requested a meeting to talk things over:

My Lord, My silence and forbearing of speech to your Lordship (now a good time) in a cause of that weight to

> me as concerneth so nearly my dearest beloved daughter, your Lordship's wife, hath hitherto proceeded, partly in hope that after some space of months some change to the better might follow, partly to avoid the offending of you in whom I have seen some change from your old wonted countenance.

Lord Burghley goes on to say that he has been "a long and well-deserving friend toward you," and that "your loving, faithful and dutiful wife [hath] suffered the lack of your love, conversation and company." He then writes:

> specially for my daughter, whose grief is the greater and shall always be inasmuch as her love is most fervent and addicted to you, and because she cannot, or may not, without offence be suffered to come to your presence, as she desireth, to offer the sacrifice of her heart; nor can I find opportunity in open places where we sometimes meet, to reveal my grief's both for my daughter. . . .

Lord Burghley then begs his son-in-law to

> give me answer by this bearer as it shall please you by speech or writing, having made nobody privy with this my letter. Your Lordship's truly affected.
>
> W. Burg.

But "W. Burg." did not receive the answer he had hoped for.

Oxford, meanwhile, was flirting with the Queen in a desultory sort of way, while carrying on the intensely passionate affair with Anne Vavasor.[41]

This was the time when his sister Mary was being so persistently courted by Peregrine Bertie. Although her future mother-in-law, the Duchess of Suffolk, was opposed to the match when it was first broached to her in July of 1577,[42] by December this intrepid lady had come to be so fond of Mary that she sought her help in a most naive scheme to bring together Lord and Lady Oxford, thus rendering a favor to her friend, the all-powerful Lord Treasurer. This is her letter to Lord Burghley outlining her plan:

> On Thursday I went to see my Lady Mary de Vere. After other talk she asked me what I would say to it if my Lord her brother would take his wife again. "Truly," quoth I, "Nothing could comfort me more, for now I wish to your brother as much good as to my own son." "Indeed," quoth she, "he would be very fain to see the child,[43] and is loth to send for her." "Then," quoth I, "an you will keep counsel we will have some sport with him. I will see if I can get the child hither to me, when you shall come hither; and whilst my Lord your brother is with you I will bring the child as though it were some other child of my friend's, and we will see how nature works in him to like it, and tell him it is his own after."[44]

The garrulous old Duchess adds that she hears that Lord Oxford "is about to buy a house in Watling Street, and not to continue a courtier as he had done: but I pray you keep all these things secret or else you may undo those that do take pains to bring it to pass." After sentiments customary at the time, the Duchess signs herself: "Your Lordship's very assured friend,

K. Suffolk."[45]

It is tantalizing that we are not told whether anything ever came of this strategem of the Duchess.

Or perhaps we *are* told, if we turn to the plays, for, it is recalled, "the players tell all."

In *The Winter's Tale* there is an incident very much like this just related, as possibly having happened in the real life of Lord Oxford. King Leontes accuses his Queen, Hermione, of adultery with his best friend. Indeed, in his jealous rage, he persuades himself that the child the Queen is carrying is not his own, and condemns her to prison. There she is delivered of a baby girl. Her faithful woman, Paulina, tries to see the Queen but is prevented by the jailer. Paulina then suggests to another Lady in Waiting that she be allowed to take the babe to Leontes:

> ... Pray you, Emilia,
> Commend my best obedience to the queen:
> I'll show it to the king and undertake to be
> Her advocate to the loud'st. We do not know
> How he may soften at the sight of the child:
> The silence often of pure innocence
> Persuades when speaking fails.[46]
>
> Act II, sc. 2, ll. 35-42

In the play the King remained adamant. But the point is that the plot is unusual, and it is possible that it was suggested to the dramatist by the scheme described in the Duchess of Suffolk's letter to Lord Burghley.

It was nearly eight years before Lord Oxford and his Countess were reconciled, which must have seemed a long, long time to his wistful little wife. It is probable that Edward and Ann were finally brought together by the following letter from Ann herself, through every line of which shines her simple trusting faith and her still great love for her husband:

> My lord, In what misery I may account myself to be that neither can see any end thereof nor yet any hope to diminish it. And now of late having had some hope in my own conceit that your Lordship would have renewed some part of your favour that you began to show me this summer, though you seemed fearful that you began it by open address. Now after long silence of hearing nothing from you, at the length I am informed—but how truly I know not, and yet how uncomfortably I do not seek it—that your Lordship is entered into some misliking of me without any cause in deed or thought. And therefore, my good Lord, I beseech you in the name of that God which

knoweth all my thoughts and love toward you, let me know the cause you are moved to continue me in this misery, and what you would have me to do in my power to recover your constant favour so as your Lordship may not be led still to detain me in calamity without some probable cause, whereof I appeal to God, I am utterly in-ocent.[47]

This letter seems to have touched the heart of the Earl, and he finally returned to the welcoming arms of his wife. The note had been received by him at the very lowest ebb in his career, shortly after he had been wounded painfully in a duel with Sir Thomas Knyvet, and when, to judge from the *Sonnets*, he was in the grip of very serious melancholia. Little Ann at this time would be to him a haven of rest after the tumultuous experience he had just been through.[48]

Now again look at the plays. Ann Cecil appears in many of them, but most recognizably as Desdemona in Othello, the loving wife wrongfully accused. Remembering Ann's last appealling letter to her estranged husband, read Desdemona's speech to Iago in Act IV, sc. 2, beginning at line 148:

O good Iago,
What shall I do to win my lord again?
Good friend, go to him; for, by this light of heaven
I know not how I lost him. Here I kneel.
If e'er my will did trespass 'gainst his love,
Either in discourse of thought or actual deed,
Or that minc cycs, minc cars, or any scnsc
Delighted them in any other form;
Or that I do not yet, and ever did,
And ever will, though he do shake me off
To beggarly divorcement, love him dearly,
Comfort forswear me! Unkindness may do much;
And his unkindness may defeat my life,
But never taint my love.

Gentle little Ann was pitifully happy in the homecoming of her beloved lord and husband. Lord Oxford built for her a fine house near the church of St. Martin's in the Fields, though it might have been more prudent not to have settled so near to Cecil House.

In due time after their reconcilation a child was on the way. Ann knew that if she could give her lord a son her hold on him would be the stronger. The couple even went to Castle Hedingham for the accouchment, so that the expected heir might be born in the ancestral seat, even as Edward himself had been.

But the babe so eagerly awaited was destined not to live. It was a boy, and could have been the heir to the earldom. He was christened in the parish church of St. Nicholas in the little village of Castle Hedingham. Then, most tragically, he died of natural causes when he was only two days old.

The bereaved little mother poured out her heart at the loss of her son in this pathetic attempt at poetry:

> Had with morning the Gods left their will undone,
> They had not so soon herited such a soul:
> Or if the mouth, time, did not glotten up all.
> Nor I, nor this world were deprived of my son.[49]

Three more children were born to the Earl and Countess, but to their disappointment, all three were girls. One child, Frances, died in infancy, but each of the other two will come into this story again. Bridget was born April 6th, 1584, and Susan, May 24th, 1587.

In the interests of truth, which was so important to our hero, it must be reported that Lord Burghley notes in his diary that shortly before Susan was born, he came upon his daughter weeping copiously because her husband had chided her and spoken harshly of her father. Ann may have been overwrought and oversensitive emotionally because of her condition. Or perhaps she was finding, as so many wives have found before and since then, the difficulties of being married to a genius. It is most tragic that Ann, so desperately in love with her lord, seems to have been temperamentally incapable of understanding him.

In a happier vein, it is reported that both the Earl and the Countess of Oxford were back at Court for special occasions. On New Year's Day, 1578, the Earl gave his Queen "a very fair jewel of gold, wherein is a helmet of gold and small diamonds . . .and under the same is five rubies one bigger than the rest."[50] Note Lord Oxford's preoccupation with a *helmet*. It was the *helmet of Athena* which conferred invisibility. There may be significance here in that Lord Oxford was "invisible" as the dramatist of those plays[51] which were already coming to be the popular pastime, both at Court and in the London theatres.

This same holiday the Queen gave Lord Oxford "a basin and ewer, and to the Countess of Oxford a gilt bowl."[52] The basin and ewer were to be used in performing the hereditary duty of the Earls of Oxford serving as Officers of the Ewery to the Sovereign, washing her Majesty's beautiful hands after meals on ceremonial occasions.

On New Year's Day of 1580 Lord Oxford gave the Queen "a fair jewel of gold being a ship garnished with diamonds and a mean pearl pendent," while the Countess on that day gave her Majesty "a pair of bracelets of gold."[53] Again, on New Year's Day, 1581, both the Earl and Countess gave the Queen jewels. Is it surprising that this nobleman was always short of money? But at least he was serving the Queen at Court with his Countess by his side.

After their reconcilation there was only one time that Lord Oxford left his Countess, except perhaps clandestinely. In 1585 he received the military appointment that he, as a de Vere, so craved, a commission as Commander of the Horse in the war in the Low Countries. Perhaps he had identified himself with King Henry the Fifth when that warrior declared:

> I am a soldier, —
> A name that in my thoughts becomes me best.

We know from his letters that Lord Oxford longed for military glory, yet each time that glory seemed to be within his reach, it eluded him.

It was therefore a bitter disappointment when he was recalled from the Netherlands war by the Queen, after only six weeks of service. Contemporary reports indicate that the Earl of Leicester persuaded Queen Elizabeth to undercut Oxford's authority by sending over a civilian in a post of authority. The account is not clear, but it is understood that Leicester himself coveted the commission to go to war, and was responsible for Oxford's recall.

Perhaps there is something more to be learned about the recall from the scene in *Othello,* Act IV, sc. 3. Desdemona is speaking to Othello after *his* recall:

> Why do you weep?
> Am I the motive of these tears, my Lord?
> If haply you my father do suspect
> An instrument of this your calling back,
> Lay not the blame on me.

Is it not conceivable that the dramatist was putting into the mind of Othello words that he himself had said, or even emotions that he had deeply felt?

Lord Oxfod, of course, had had to bear the expense of the Netherlands misadventure for the time that he had been serving. In letters to the Queen after his return he took every opportunity to remind her Majesty of his penurious condition. She frequently hinted at rewards she was considering to give to her one-time favorite, but time went on and, as usual, nothing was done.

Finally, in 1586, she kept her promise of reward by granting to Lord Oxford a particularly gracious honor. This was an annuity of £ 1,000 a year, an enormous amount in those days.[54]

This must have been a source of pride and gratification to both the Earl and the Countess of Oxford, and by reflected glory to Lord Burghley. But even more important to the family than their pride in the recognition was the relief of Lord Oxford's financial situation, always in a precarious state, but strained further by the ill-fated military expedition. Now the Earl was able to indulge his penchant for generosity, and also his own need for expensive luxuries.

However, it was not for long that the little Countess could enjoy these luxuries. She died at the Queen's palace of Greenwich on June 6th, 1588, when only thirty-three. She was buried in state in Westminster Abbey next day, the haste possibly indicating that she had died of one of the contagious fevers then prevalent in England.

A number of biographers of Lord Oxford have made much of the fact that in a description of Ann's funeral in which all the mourners are named, there is no mention of her husband. This question provoked a little extra research, out of which came the interesting fact that in Elizabethan times it was not the custom for the husband to attend his wife's funeral. Doubtless it was considered too great an emotional strain.

A few months later her mother, Lady Burghley, died and was laid by Ann's side in the tomb in the Chapel of St. Nicholas, in the beautiful old Abbey which had been the scene of Ann's festive wedding. The Cecil tomb (see page 40 f) is most elaborate; mother and daughter lying side by side are dressed in red cloaks over gray dresses, and wear little caps on their heads, Ann's showing a wisp of light brown hair. On one side of their effigies kneel the three little girls in light blue gowns, Ann's three daughters: Elizabeth, older than the other two and considerably bigger; then Bridget; and lastly, Susan, the youngest, tiny, as she kneels with little palms together in attitude of prayer. Susan was only a baby when her mother died.

On the other side of the tomb kneels a young man[55] in Court dress, Lady Burghley's only son, Sir Robert Cecil, at this time just beginning to take over the duties of his father to the Queen. The Lord Treasurer himself kneels above them in his robes of state, and he composed the Latin inscription, a resumé of which reads

If anyone asks, who is that aged man on bended knees, venerable from his hoary hairs, in his robes of state, and with the order of the Garter? The answer is, that we see the Great Minister of Elizabeth, his eyes dim with tears for the loss of those who were dearer to him beyond the whole race of womankind.[56]

Except for noting the fact that Ann Cecil was the wife of the Earl of Oxford, no further mention is made of her distinguished husband. No doubt Lord Burghley thought that by inscribing on stone those lines to his beloved women, he was erecting to their memory a monument that would endure forever.

But it is Ann's husband who has created a more lasting monument. *Othello* is the moving drama of a wife wrongfully accused of infidelity and of the dreadful remorse of her husband when he finally learns the truth—too late.

It is our belief that the dramatist must have had Ann Cecil in mind when he drew the character of Desdemona, for he plays upon the name *Vere, truth,* so many times. Emilia, in the terrible scene after *Desdemona*'s death, cries out to *Othello*:

O, she was heavenly true.

Later, *Othello,* trying to explain that he has killed his wife because of her infidelity, blurts out:

It is true indeed.

To which *Gratiano* retorts:

'Tis a strange truth.

Then again *Othello,* after Emilia's death wound plays upon the other connotation of *Vere,* i.e., *honor* and *honesty:*

Why should honor outlive honesty?

Emilia dies, after singing the Willow Song. But before she loses consciousness she whispers: "I speak true." Othello in anguish cries out to Desdemona:

> . . . Cold, cold, my girl?
> Even like thy chastity. . . .
> Whip me, ye devils,
> From the possession of this heavenly sight!
> Blow me about in winds! roast me in sulphur!
> Wash me in steep-down gulfs of liquid fire!
> O Desdemona! Desdemona! dead!
> O! O! O!
>
> (Act V, sc. 2, ll. 275-82)

Finally in the words the dramatist gives to the dying husband he may be speaking from his own heart:

> Soft you! A word or two before you go,
> I have done the state some service, and they know't;
> No more of that. I pray you, in your letters,
> When you shall these unlucky deeds relate,
> Speak of them as they are. Nothing extenuate,
> Nor set down aught in malice. Then must you speak
> Of one that lov'd not wisely but too well:
> Of one not easily jealous, but being wrought,
> Perplex'd in the extreme: of one whose hand
> Like the base Indian threw a pearl away
> Richer than all his tribe; of one whose subdu'd eyes,
> Albeit unused to the melting mood,
> Drop tears as fast as the Arabian trees
> Their med'cinable gum. Set you down this.
>
> ll. 338-51

Notes To Chapter III

1. A. L. Rowse, *The Elizabethans and America.*

2. Lansdowne MS. 104, quoted by B. M. Ward in *The Seventeenth Earl of Oxford.*

3. The Strand was paved in 1532. David Piper, *The Companion Guide to London*, p. 276.

4. Ward, *The Seventeenth Earl of Oxford.*

5. Ibid.

6. E. K. Chambers, ed., *The Oxford Book of Sixteenth Century Verse*, No. 85.

7. A. L. Rowse, *The England of Elizabeth*, p. 383.

8. Ibid., p. 35.

9. Ibid., p. 36

10. Quoted in H. Amphlett, *Who Was Shakespeare?*

11. All quotations from the *Chester Herald*'s accounts are taken from H. Amphlett, *Who Was Shakespeare?*

12. Ward, *The Seventeenth Earl of Oxford.*

13. Ibid.

14. Ibid.

15. Rowse, *The England of Elizabeth.*

16. Emma Marshall Denkinger, *Immortal Sidney.*

17. Martin Hume, *The Great Lord Burghley.*

18. The suggestion of comparing Ann's emotions to Juliet's is taken from Eva Turner Clark, *Hidden Allusions in Shakespeare's Plays.*

19. The Rutland MSS, quoted in Ward, *The Seventeenth Earl of Oxford.*

20. Cal. Rutland MSS, July 28, 1571, ibid.

21. Cal. Rutland MSS, July 28, 1577, ibid.

22. Ibid.

23. Ward, *The Seventeenth Earl of Oxford.*

24. Neville Williams, *Thomas Howard, Fourth Duke of Norfolk.*

25. Ibid.

26. Harleian MSS, 69991. 5.

27. Ibid.

28. From a private notebook.

29. Ibid.

30. Ibid.

31. Ibid.

32. Ibid.

33. Ibid.

33. See Chapter IX.

34. From a private notebook of a de Vere descendant. It would be interesting to know whether "that land of mine which is in Cornwall" might contain the little villages where Lord Oxford's ancestors had lived as refugees during the Wars of the Roses while the Yorkists were in power. See Chapter II. The Earls of Oxford had at one time owned vast grants of land in Cornwall.

35. Quoted from the Hatfield Papers, by a de Vere descendant.

36. One rumor was that Lord Burghley himself had had incestuous relations with his daughter in order to assure an heir to the Earldom. This writer cannot credit such a rumor, knowing a little of Lord Burghley, the ardent, religious statesman. Better proof still is the fact that the Lady Elizabeth de Vere, who was the child concerned, in later life was always known to her contemporaries as a daughter of Lord Oxford. Indeed, she seems to have been a favorite daughter of his, and certainly after her marriage to the Earl of Derby, she became very close to her father and step-mother, the latter being a special friend of hers at Court. See Chapter VI.

37. See Chapter II.

38. John Lyly, Lord Oxford's secretary. He was also a famous writer, and sponsor of "Paul's Boys."

39. Ward, quoting Lansdowne MSS., 42-59, October 30, 1583.

40. This letter is taken by kind permission from a private

notebook of a collateral descendant of Lord Oxford.

41. Chapter V.

42. Chapter II.

43. The child, of course, was Elizabeth de Vere, born while her father was travelling on the Continent.

44. Lansdowne MSS. 2607, quoted in Goff, *A Woman of the Tudor Age.*

45. Ibid.

46. Hermione in *Winter's Tale* is an innocent wife accused of adultery by her husband. Some of Hermione's speeches appear to parallel the phrases of Ann Cecil in this letter. Here are two, both from Act III, sc. 2:

> You, my Lord, best know, —
> Who least will see to do so, —my past life
> Hath been as continent, as chaste as true
> As I am now unhappy.
>
> ll.33-36.

And again:

> To me can life be no commodity:
> The crown and comfort of my life, your favour,
> I do give lost; for I do feel it gone,
> But know not how it went.
>
> ll. 92-98.

47. From a private notebook.

48. See Chapter V.

49. From *Four Epitaphes made by the Countess of Oxenforde after the Death of her young sonne the Lord Bulbecke, etc.*, found in John Sootherne's *Pandora,* quoted by H. Amphlett in *Who Was Shakespeare?* Rendered into modern English by the present writer.

50. Nichol's *Progresses*, II.

51.For a discussion of the significance of the helmet in

denoting invisibility to Lord Oxford, see Charlton and Dorothy Ogburn, *This Star of England.*

52. *Nichol's Progresses,* II.

53. Ibid.

54. Chapter IV.

55. This writer enquired at the muniment room of the Abbey as to the identity of the young man, thinking it might be a statue of the Earl of Oxford. But it is proved by the records that it is Sir Robert Cecil, later Secretary to the Queen, and still later Marquis of Salisbury.

56. From the *Official Guide Book* to Westminster Abbey.

Chapter IV

HIS QUEEN

Thy eye Jove's lightning bears, thy voice his dreadful thunder,
Which, not to anger bent, is music and sweet fire.
Love's Labour's Lost, Act IV, sc. 2

The story of the relationship of the Earl of Oxford with his Queen is the story of his life even to the year before he died. In this brief essay an attempt will be made to disentangle their ever-changing emotions toward one another at crucial moments in the life of each of them.

The Earl like many another man of genius seems to be uncomplicated, direct and somewhat immature emotionally. Although he really had a very complex personality, it may be said that his nature was open, direct, unsuspecting and generous.

Elizabeth Tudor on the other hand was just the opposite. She was scheming, devious, suspicious and self-centered. It is indeed the tragedy of her life that she, who longed for love and to be loved, yet was unable to give the very warmth and loyalty she craved from others.

Her moods were difficult to cope with. Her god-son, Sir John Harington, gave a picture of her when he wrote: "She left no doubtings whose daughter she was." Again he wrote:

> When she smiled, it was pure sunshine that every one did choose to bask in if they could; but anon came a storm from sudden gathering of clouds, and the thunder fell in wondrous manner on all alike.

One is reminded of the background of the portrait of her

Majesty[1] painted for Sir Henry Lee to commemorate her visit to him at Ditchley, Oxfordshire, in which the Queen is represented standing most regally on a map with her dainty foot on Ditchley; in the left background the bright sun shines out of a clear sky, while on the right there are black thunder clouds and jagged streaks of lightning.

The dramatist may have been thinking of her when he drew a picture of another queen:

> Age cannot wither her, nor custom stale
> Her infinite variety.
>
> *Antony and Cleopatra,* Act II, sc. 2

There is no doubt that Queen Elizabeth "woo'd the young Earl of Oxford," as more than one of her contemporaries have reported, even though he was seventeen years her junior. Indeed, she may even have led him to believe that one day she would marry him. Some of his biographers go so far as to suggest that they were married.[2] Yet the Queen did not hesitate to imprison him more than once, to shame him before all the Court, and even to banish him from her sight.

The only emotion on the part of Edward de Vere that a biographer can be sure of is his unfailing loyalty to her Majesty as a subject. No matter how she treated her favorite Courtier, her "Turk," her "Phoebus," his absolute loyalty never wavered. It had been instilled in him from earliest childhood by his father, the Sixteenth Earl.

Lord Oxford had inherited the title of Lord Great Chamberlain of England, and Officer of the Ewery. The Lord Great Chamberlain's function was to attend the sovereign, especially on ceremonial occasions in close proximity to her person. As Officer of the Ewery, on bended knee he held the silver basin of warm water for her to rinse her lovely hands after soiling them eating chops or fowl or venison. This was an important function, because forks had not yet come into common use in England.[3] But the Office of the Ewery was more than that. The ewery was the place where the jugs, or ewers, were kept. Like the buttery, or the pantry, in any of the great households of Tudor England it was under the supervision of a responsible official. In the Queen's household this official was called the Officer of the Ewery.[4]

It seems probable that the young Lord Bolebec had been taken to Whitehall Palace in London to watch while his father performed these duties to his Queen.

When after the death of the Sixteenth Earl, Edward de Vere went to live at Cecil House, he seems to have been a serious little fellow trying hard to do all that was expected of a nobleman of his exalted station.

It will be recalled that misfortune crowded upon him that first year in the city; his mother's hasty marriage, then his step-sister's charge about his parents.

And the Queen—she dares to twit him about the suspicion cast upon his parents' marriage.

"How is our young bastard today?" is the greeting of this insensitive woman to the proud scion of a family older than her own. Indeed, the de Veres had been noble courtiers when Owen Tudor was mere Master of the Horse to King Henry V, barely a hundred years before. The Queen should have known better than to say such a thing to Lord Oxford, since she was constantly berated by the Catholics for being a bastard herself.[5]

The young courtier reacted to the affront by bursting into tears. Then he went home and wrote his first poem, on *The Loss of My Good Name*.[6]

It might have been after an encounter like this that the boy complained that the Queen had the worst voice he had ever heard. He did not speak like that when he grew older.

Early in 1570, shortly after matriculating at Gray's Inn, the Earl was taken very ill while attending Court at Windsor. His bills are recorded in the Chester Herald:

> To Riche, the apothecary, for potions, pills and other drugs, for my Lord's diet in time of Sickness.

Again, a sum was paid

> To William Bishop, for wood and coals and for victuals for my Lord and his men in the time of his said sickness.

And once more the Chester Herald notes payments

> for certain other articles for my Lord during his being sick at Windsor, for rewards to his physicians and others.[7]

The nature of his illness is not known, but it was very debilitating and lasted several months. It must have been not only irksome to the patient, but embarrassing to so active a person as Lord Oxford, a feeling he would have increasingly as he was getting better.

Curiously, although there are such accurate descriptions of mental illnesses in the Shakespeare plays, there is little about physical sickness, although the simile is often used to describe a state of mind.

> More needs she the divine than the physician.
> *Macbeth*, Act V, sc. 1

But here is a most unpleasant description of an apothecary, hopefully not the one at Windsor:

> I do remember an apothecary, —
> And hereabouts he dwells, —which late I noted
> In tatter'd weeds, with overwhelming brows,
> Culling his simples; meagre were his looks,
> Sharp misery had worn him to the bones:
> And in his needy shop a tortoise hung,
> An alligator stuff'd, and other skins,
> Of ill-shaped fishes; and about his shelves
> A beggarly account of empty boxes,

Green earthen pots, bladders and musty seeds,
Remnants of packthread, and old cakes of roses,
Were thinly scatter'd, to make up a show.

Romeo and Juliet, Act V, sc. 1

While Lord Oxford was still convalescing from his illness he wrote to Sir William Cecil requesting a military appointment in the Border War, under his father's old friend, the Earl of Sussex. The de Veres had always longed for military glory, and the young Earl must have thought that this was an opportunity not to be missed. He assured his guardian that in a short time he felt he would be strong enough to serve.

The appointment came through and Lord Oxford did see service in "the Rising in the North." He was only nineteen. There is a portrait of the Earl of Sussex, his commanding officer, in the Tower. Always thin and spare, he became painfully haggard toward the end of his life, finally dying of tuberculosis. It might seem appropriate to imagine him as the prototype of John of Gaunt, that magnificent old man, "time-honour'd Lancaster."

The year 1571 was important in the life of Lord Oxford. In April he came of age, taking his seat in the House of Lords. In December he married. And this year marked another milestone: he contributed the Latin preface to Bartholomew Clarke's translation of Castiglione's *The Courtier,* a literary achievement to which reference will be made again.[8] And he won prizes in two tournaments.

Happily there is preserved a detailed description of the young Earl's entrance into the House of Lords.[9] Since Parliament had not met in five years, the Queen took this opportunity to open the session herself with the ceremony which she felt she owed to her faithful people. She had recently been excommunicated by the Pope, and her throne had been endangered by the plotting Catholics ever anxious to supplant her with a Catholic sovereign.

The day Parliament was to open, the Queen rode over from Whitehall Palace to Westminster Abbey in "a coach drawn by 2 palfreys covered with crimson velvet." Her enthusiastic subjects lining the roadway could see their sovereign lady richly attired and wearing a coronet of gold upon her golden hair. Graciously she smiled and waved her beautiful hand to them first to one side then to the other as they cheered enthusiastically and waved back to her. Queen Elizabeth could be crusty in private but she never failed to be majestic to "her people."

After the blessing in the Abbey, the colorful procession formed again, this time on foot, wending along the old cobbold way[10] to St. Stephen's Palace, where Parliament was to be opened. The Tudor crowd enjoyed this pageantry, seeing their beautiful Queen in her rich robes of state, her train borne by the young and handsome Earl of Oxford on this special day taking precedence over all the other noblemen. Then followed the Courtiers and twenty-four Ladies in Waiting, the younger ones gowned in white in honor of the Virgin Queen.

Was there ever so dramatic an entrance of a young peer into the House of Lords![11]

A measure of the young nobleman's literary reputation is shown in that an older writer, Thomas Bedingfield, son of the Governor of the Tower, asked Lord Oxford to write a preface to his translation of Cardanus' *Comfort.* Oxford not only graciously agreed that he would, but generously offered to publish the translation at his own expense. This book, *Comfort,* has been known as "Hamlet's book," since it contains much of the philosophy of the melancholy Dane. This is Edward de Vere's poem:[12]

Labour and its Reward.
The Earl of Oxford to the Reader of Bedingfield's
translation of Cardanus' *Comfort.*

The labouring man that tills the fertile soil,
And reaps the harvest fruits, hath not indeed
The gain but *pain;* and if for all his toil
He gets the straw, the lord will have the seed.

The manchet fine falls not unto his share:
  On coarsest cheat his hungry stomach feeds;
The landlord doth possess the finest fare;
  He pulls the flowers, he plucks but weeds.

The mason poor that builds the lordly halls,
  Dwells not in them; they are for high degree;
His cottage is compact in paper walls,
  And not with brick or stone, as others be.

The idle drone that labours, not at all,
  Sucks up the sweet of honey from the bee;
Who workest most to their share least doth fall,
  With due desert reward will never be.

The swiftest hare unto the mastive slow
  Oft-times doth fall, to him as for a prey;
The greyhound thereby doth miss his game we know
  For which he made such speedy haste away.

So he that takes the pain to pen the book,
  Reaps not the gifts of goodly golden muse:
But those gain that, who on the work shall look,
  And from the sour the sweet by skill shall choose;
For he that beats the bush the bird not gets,
But who sits still and holdeth fast the nets.

This poem is quoted in full, to show how very modern it is in content. It is indeed a very young man's poem; could it not be by a young man of today? Perhaps it is the influence of Sir Thomas Smith, that makes it seem so modern.

It is after the Earl's return to Court, in 1576, when he was estranged from his wife, that curiosity is aroused about his relations with the Queen. It was at this time that Mary Queen of Scots wrote to her cousin Elizabeth that "the Earl of Oxford dared not become reconciled to his wife for fear of losing the favor that he enjoys through being your lover." And Mary usually knew her gossip!

In 1577 the Queen bestowed upon "our cousin, the Earl of Oxford" a parcel of land worth £250. Why did she do that? And why at this particular time? Elizabeth Tudor was not prodigal with her gifts.

For answer to these questions we turn first to a signed sonnet by "the Earl of Oxenforde," entitled *Love Thy Choice:*

> Who taught thee first to sigh, alas, my heart?
>   Who taught thy tongue the woeful words of plaint?
> Who filled your eyes with tears of bitter smart?
>   Who gave thee grief and made thy joys to faint?
> Who first did paint with colours pale thy face?
>   Who first did break thy sleep of quiet rest?
> Above the rest in court who gave thee grace?
>   Who made thee strive in honour to be best?
> In constant truth to bide so firm and sure,
>   To scorn the world regarding but thy friend?
> With patient mind each passion to endure.
>   In one desire to settle to the end?
> Love then thy choice wherein such choice thou bind,
>   As nought but death shall ever change thy mind.

This again is definitely a young man's poem, the verse of one still trying out his pen. Yet some of its phrases are characteristic of Lord Oxford and will be used by him in better poetry. Note again the phrase: "in constant truth"—another pun on his family name, Vere.

Here is another peom of about the same period. It was published over Lord Oxford's initials, "E. O." in *The Phoenix Nest*, in 1593, but must have been composed much earlier. It is called: *What Cunning Can Express.* We quote here only one stanza:

Fair Cynthia's silver light
  That beats on running streams,
Compares not with her white
  Whose hairs are all sunbeams.
    Her virtues so do shine
    As day unto mine eyene.

It was the custom to address the Queen as *Cynthia*, the moon goddess.

Is there any real evidence to lead us to believe that the Queen had taken more than courtly interest in Lord Oxford? There were those contemporary rumors mentioned above, and the letter of Mary Queen of Scots. And there is a poem, a very pathetic little poem, *By Queen Elizabeth*, showing that she was "but e'en a woman, and commanded by such poor passion as the maid that milks and does the meanest chares."[12] Here is the poem:

By Queen Elizabeth

I grieve; and dare not show my discontent!
  I love; and yet am forc'd to seem to hate!
I do; yet dare not say, I ever meant!
  I seem stark mute; but inwardly do prate!
    I am, and am not; I freeze, and yet am burned;
    Since from myself my other self I turned.

My care is like my shadow in the sun,
  Follows me flying! flies, when I pursue it!
Stands and lies by me! Do'th what I have done!
  This too familiar CARE doth make me rue it!
    No means I find, to rid him from my breast,
    Till, by the end of things, it be supprest.

Some gentler passions slide into my mind;
  For I am soft, and made of melting snow.
O be more cruel, LOVE! and so be kind;

Let me, or float or sink! be high or low,
Or let me live with some more sweet content;
Or die! and so forget what LOVE e'er meant.

It is not often that one thinks of the great Queen as "soft, and made of melting snow." Yet even as she was a fascinating and elusive personality to her own contemporaries, so she has been to every biographer who ever tried to depict her character.

There is reason to believe that the poem above was written during the time when Lord Oxford was uppermost in her affections.

Now turn to the plays. *Love's Labour's Lost* is thought to be one of the earliest, and may have been composed at about this time, in the mid- or late 1570s. We of "the Oxford School" believe that the King's light-hearted courtship of the Princess is a subtle compliment to Queen Elizabeth as she was being courted by himself. In Act IV, sc. 3, l. 230, the King:

My love, her mistress, is a gracious moon.

It will be recalled that Elizabeth Tudor had had her portrait painted as Diana, goddess of the moon. In Elizabethan poetry she is frequenty referred to as *Diana*, or even as *the moon*. That the dramatist was thinking of his Queen while writing this play about the Princess is suggested by a little scene in Act V. In scene 2, beginning at line 45, Rosaline says to the Princess:

O, that your face were not so full of O's!

which could be interpreted as "O, that your face [i.e., your mind?] were not so full of Oxford." Or it could be a reference to the disfigurement by smallpox which the Queen suffered in 1562. The Princess takes the remark in this sense in her retort to Rosaline, which may well have been a rebuke of the Queen to one of her more impudent maids?

A pox o' that jest! And I beshrew all shrows!

These are small tell-tale signs, but they would be readily recognised by the courtly audience watching the play.[13]

Is the young Earl sincere in his poems to the Queen? Probably, in the beginning, before he knew other love, he was. It has been suggested, however, that *Venus and Adonis*, though written long after Lord Oxford's period of service at Court, is in reality the story of the Queen's attempt without shame to possess this young man and of his own revulsion. It is believed that the affair left a lasting scar upon the personality of Edward de Vere. Many years later, in *Sonnet 66*, the poet remembers the afflictions which plagued his youth and writes of

> . . . gilded honour shamfully misplac'd,
> And maiden virtue rudely strumpeted. . . .

Can one visualize the favorite as Elizabeth Tudor knew him at this time? He can be seen as he appeared to two different artists, i.e., in the Welbeck portrait by an unknown Flemish artist, painted when he was twenty-four (see page 40d), and in the Nicholas Hilliard miniature[14] (see frontispiece). The courtier seems to have had a fair complexion, curly auburn hair, a sensitive mouth and those wonderful dark eyes, sometimes mischievous, sometimes grave, sometimes brooding. He was clean-shaven except for the pencil-slim moustache, and he had a high forehead, the shape of his face tending toward round rather than oval. His distinguishing feature, however, seems to have been his aristocratic bearing, a natural hauteur bespeaking his noble birth and lineage. In thinking of his appearance, may we lift the phrases of Ophelia in describing *her* hero, Prince Hamlet? She refers to his "noble mind," then she speaks of

> The courtier's, soldier's, scholar's eye, tongue, sword:
> Th'expectancy and rose of the fair state,
> The glass of fashion and the mould of form,
> Th'observ'd of all observers. . . .
>
> Act II, sc. 1, ll. 159-62

But who can describe Lord Oxford's wit and magnetism? Only by seeing the effect he had upon his friends can one even imagine his delightful charm. Like Falstaff, he was not only witty himself, "but the cause that wit is in other men."[15]

And the Queen? She was now beginning to show her age. Yet she still had the beautiful oval face and pointed chin inherited from her mother, Anne Boleyn, and those dark, sparkling eyes described variously by contemporaries as gray, black, or even green. There is a beautiful portrait of the Queen painted by an unknown artist about 1575[16] (see page 40 e), in which she appears gracious and lovely, her face still unrouged, her hair her own. There is a poise and majesty about her even as she sits for the artist.

Two important events in the life of Edward de Vere occurred in 1576, the year he returned to Court from his travels. He published a group of poems in a small volume called *The Paradyse of Dayntie Deuises.* Some of the poems, as *The Loss of My Good Name,* were signed with his full name, others with his initials, *E. O.*, while again he signed still others with his posy, *Meritum petere grave.*

The other important event of the year was Lord Oxford's secret conversion to the Roman Catholic faith, a step in which the influence of his Howard cousins is apparent.

* * * * *

In July of 1578 Lord Oxford was the recipient of an honor which has special interest for us today. He accompanied the Queen on one of her summer progresses, when the Court stopped at Audley End, near Cambridge. There it was welcomed in Latin verse by Gabriel Harvey.

The Queen had only just heard the news that her "Robin," her first love, the Earl of Leicester, was about to marry Lettice Knollys, widow of the Earl of Essex. This was a bitter blow to Elizabeth Tudor, who had known Dudley and flirted with him since both of them had been imprisoned in the Tower. They had suffered together, and they had loved.[17] But who could blame the aging courtier for marrying somebody else, since Elizabeth gave him no hope that she would ever marry him and make him her consort? Still, his marriage was to her a deep sorrow, a sorrow mingled with a jealous rage, especially since Lettice was a near cousin of hers.

In this sorrow the Queen turned to her present young lover with new warmth. Gabriel Harvey would know that it was wise policy to praise the favorite. Addressing the premier Earl, Lord Oxford, Harvey began in Latin:[18]

> This is my welcome; this is how I have decided to bid All Hail! to thee and to the other Nobles.
>
> . . . .
>
> Thy splendid fame, great Earl, demands even more than in the case of others the services of a poet possessing lofty eloquence. Thy merit doth not creep along the ground, nor can it be confined within the limits of a song. It is a wonder which reaches as far as the heavenly orbs.

Even admitting that Harvey found it expedient to praise the Queen's favorite, his Latin verse was fulsome, honoring Lord Oxford far beyond the other courtiers. He continued:

> O thou great-hearted one, strong in this mind and thy fiery will, thou wilt conquer thyself, thou wilt conquer others; thy glory will spread in all directions beyond the Arctic Ocean; and England will put thee to the test and prove thee to be a native born Achilles. . . .
>
> For a long time past Phoebus Apollo has cultivated thy mind in the arts. English poetical measures have been sung by thee long enough. Let that Courtly Epistle[18]—more polished than the writings of Castiglione himself—witness how greatly thou dost excel in letters. I have seen many Latin verses of thine, yea, even more English verses are extant; thou hast drunk deep draughts not only of the Muses in France and Italy, but hast learned the manners of many men, and the arts of foreign countries.[19]

There is much in this speech to comment upon. Note the reference to *Phoebus Apollo*, the god of arts and learning, whose very name the Queen had given her favorite. The speech also is proof that Lord Oxford had been writing prolifically, both in Latin and in English. Much of this work must have been destroyed, because Harvey refers to "English verses extant," and this could not mean the few juvenile poems we know that were signed by his name. To be sure, Harvey had known Edward de Vere when the latter had been a student at Cambridge when, according to Harvey, Oxford "had bestowed Angels[20] upon me in Christ's College . . . and otherwise vouchsafed me many gracious favours."

The oration given at Audley End is long, and we pause only to listen to the ending:

> In thy breast is noble blood. Courage animates thy brow, Mars lives in thy tongue, Minerva strengthens thy right hand. . . . Within thee burns the fire of Mars. Thine eyes flash fire, thy countenance shakes a speare; who would not swear that Achilles had come to life again.[21]

The attention of the reader is called especially to the phrase: "thy countenance shakes a speare." Lord Oxford held a second title of Viscount Bolebec, whose crest was a lion shaking a broken spear. Obviously Harvey is referring to this crest. And indeed this may be the first public mention of the name by which the dramatist later became known: Shakespeare. This does not appear to be so far-fetched when it is found that in the same speech of welcome Harvey refers to Lord Burghley as Polus, which may well have been a Court nickname for the Principal Secretary to the Queen—if not a nickname as we know the word today, at least the name by which Lord Burghley was known to the other courtiers. Does it not sound something like Polonius? Still another name for Lord Burghley was *Pondus;* the Elizabethans were not particular about their spelling.[22]

To those of us who admire Lord Oxford nearly four hundred

years after he served his Queen on this earth, it is heart-warming to read this praise of him from a contemporary familiar with his writings, and also familiar with his reputation at Court, florid and extravagant though the speech may have been. And how it must have pleased the Queen to know that the unique gifts of her young favorite were so deeply appreciated.

In 1579 occurred the famous tennis court quarrel with Sir Philip Sidney.[23] There is a confusion in the contemporary accounts as to which courtier was playing on the court when the other interrupted. But during the ensuing altercation Oxford impulsively called Sidney: "Puppy!"

Whereupon young Sidney drew himself up with offended dignity, and answered: "Dogs beget puppies. Men beget children."

How this pompous answer would have amused the Queen! Later when Sidney threatened to challenge Lord Oxford to a duel, she forbade it, pointing out to him "the difference in degrees owed to superiors, and how the gentleman's neglect of the nobility taught the peasant to insult both."[24] The Sidneys[25] were mere upstarts in the social scale which acknowledged that the de Veres were an ancient family in France before they even came over to England.[26]

Polonius in *Hamlet* refers to a "falling out at tennis," and even Hamlet himself paraphrases the Queen's rebuke to Sidney when he remarks:

> By the Lord, Horatio . . . the age is grown so picked that the toe of the peasant comes so near the heel of the courtier he galls his kibe.
>
> Act V, sc. 1, ll. 142-5

None of these allusions would have been lost on the courtly audience attending the play.

Meanwhile, Philip Sidney, not yet knighted, was banished from the Court. He retired to his sister's at Wilton. There he wrote for her *The Countess of Pembroke's Arcadia.*

These years, 1578-9, mark the zenith of Lord Oxford's career as a courtier. This was the time when the Queen chose his company above all others, when she wanted him constantly by her side.

It was in 1578 that the Queen granted to him the Manor of Rysing, with its castle and earthworks.

And it was at this time that a contemporary wrote of him: "He is a lord who has a great following in the country." That could not be said about most of the courtiers then gathered about the Queen.

Perhaps it was because there were no further heights to which to aspire that Lord Oxford succumbed to the boredom which is reflected in the *Sonnets*. He was bored with Court life and its insincerities, and he was bored with the Queen, with her moods and tantrums. In a letter to his father-in-law, he wrote:

> For the Queen, she is nothing of her own mind and disposition, as I find so ready to deliver, as speedy to commit, and every little trifle gives her matter for a long delay.[27]

Indeed, the Duchess of Suffolk may have been repeating a well-publicised rumor when she wrote that she heard that the Earl of Oxford was giving up Court life entirely and taking a house in the City on Watling Street.

Then a north country maid came down to London, and once again Lord Oxford's life was drastically changed.[28]

The Queen was beginning to realize that there was a rival in her Court. Since little that went on escaped her eagle eye, her Majesty must have had increasing suspicions that her "Phoebus," her own beloved "Turk," was paying court to this, the youngest and newest of her ladies in waiting. Even as she had allowed herself to care for him with deep passion, so now she was with equal passion profoundly jealous of Anne Vavasor. Still, Elizabeth Tudor had no proof of her lover's faithlessness.

There was a great tournament in honor of Oxford's cousin, Philip Howard, who had recently succeeded to the earldom of Arundel. It was no surprise to the Queen that her favorite was victorious. Graciously she would bestow upon him the prize, a set of scores, or tallies, on which to record the results of games and tournaments. It was a costly thing of gold, studded with diamonds, for nothing was too good for Phoebus Apollo. How gallantly Lord Oxford would have knelt before her as he received from her own hand the prize! She had always admired his courtesy and grace.

Then, ye gods! —though Elizabeth Tudor's oath would have been considerably more scorching than that! The prize she had herself presented to Lord Oxford was found in the possession of this minion, whom she had taken on only to please her Howard cousins! One can imagine the scene of towering rage of the Queen, of the deep humiliation of her Phoebus, and of the fear and trepidation on the part of the new Maid in Waiting, Anne Vavasor.[29]

One is reminded of the anger of another queen, Cleopatra, when she learned of Antony's marriage in Rome, and went into "a paroxysm of unbeautiful rage." Could the playwright have been remembering his own Queen's reaction to his affair with her newest and youngest maid?

The tale just told is fanciful, yet plausible in view of *Sonnet no. 122,* which it is believed Lord Oxford wrote to his Queen in an attempt to excuse himself for having given away to Anne Vavasor the tablet he had won in the tournament:

> Thy gifts, thy tables, are within my brain
> Full character'd with lasting memory,
> Which shall above that idle rank remain,
> Beyond all date, even to eternity:
> Or, at least, so long as brain and heart
> Have faculty by nature to subsist;
> Till each to raz'd oblivion yield his part
> Of thee, thy record never can be miss'd.

That poor retention could not so much hold,
Nor need I tallies thy dear love to score;
Therefore to give them from me was I bold
To trust those tables that receive thee more;
  To keep an adjunct to remember thee
  Were to import forgetfulness in me.

Once more Elizabeth Tudor would grant forgiveness to her "Turk." Perhaps she did not know how far l'affair Vavasor had progressed.

There is a story corresponding to that of the Queen, Lord Oxford and Anne in the first part of *Romeo and Juliet.* Another version is found in John Lyly's *Euphues.* Lyly was Oxford's secretary at the time and thus in a position to know.

Then shortly after the episode of the lost and found tallies, a worse fate was in store for Edward de Vere. The Howards were making trouble again, persistent in their effort to crown Mary Stuart Queen of England as well as Scotland. This time Lord Oxford denounced these treacherous cousins of his, giving Walsingham valuable information on which to act to apprehend the other traitors to the kingdom. Then Lord Oxford renounced the Catholic faith, though all his life he seems to have had leanings toward the doctrines of the old Church. But when he found that adherence meant disloyalty to his Queen, he left the fold, never to return.

The situation at Court caused by the Howards' treachery seems to be unclear; the French ambassador wrote to his king that Lord Oxford was "put to confusion in the presence of his Mistress," and that "he has lost credit and honour by all the ladies of the Court." Indeed, he was even imprisoned in the Tower for one night. But so strong was his hold upon the Queen that she released him, although she left his cousins in prison.

But even further disgrace was to follow. Anne Vavasor "was brought to bed in the Maiden's chamber" at Whitehall, and Edward de Vere was claimed to be the father of the child.

The Queen's first anger was vented upon the unfortunate

Anne, who was ordered from the palace the very night of her baby's birth. The next day mother and child were commmitted to the Tower. This seems rather unnecessary cruelty to the young mother and new-born child, but Elizabeth Tudor was not considering humanitarian treatment just then.

Rumor spread that Anne's "betrayer" had tried to escape from England. If he did, it was to be expected that Walsingham's secret service would see that all ports were closed. It was not long before he was apprehended and committed to the Tower. The following June he was released to his own house though still in custody.

It was not until July that he finally obtained his freedom. Yet what freedom could it have been to the Courtier since he was forbidden to return to Court!

Bitterly he repented his youthful indiscretion. And now he realized that his emotion for Anne had been but a passing fancy, as we believe he tells us in *Sonnet 137,* beginning:

> Thou blind fool, Love, what dost thou to mine eyes. . . .

To add to his troubles, Anne's relatives were out for vengeance against him. There was that "lewed letter," insinuating that his lordship was a coward and would not dare to come out and fight alone. Then there was the determination of Sir Thomas Knyvet to fight with him not only himself, but to set his retainers fighting against Lord Oxford's men, so that the French ambassador wrote to his king that "the streets of London were filled with the Quarrelling clamors of these Montagues and Capulets."

It is interesting that the ambassador refers by indirection to the same play mentioned earlier in this story as being pertinent. *Romeo and Juliet* must have been revised many times, and after the quarrelling retainers' brawls, the dramatist inserted the following scene:

> *Prince Escalus.* Rebellious subjects, enemies of peace,
> Profaners of this neighbor-stained steel—

Will they not hear? What, ho! you men, you beasts,
That quench the fire of your pernicious rage—
On pain of torture, from those bloody hands
Throw your mistemper'd weapons to the ground
And hear the sentence of your moved Prince.

. . . .

Once more on pain of death, all men depart.
(*Exeunt all but Montague, his wife, and Benvolio.*)

Mont. Who set this ancient quarrel new abroach?
Speak, nephew, were you by when it began?

Ben. Here were the servants of your adversary
And yours, close fighting ere I did approach.
I drew to part them. In that instant came
The fiery Tybalt with his sword prepar'd

. . . .

Came more and more, and fought on part and part
Till the Prince came, who parted either part.

Act I, sc. 1, ll. 84-118

The first speech is given to Prince Escalus. But the sentiment is unmistakably that of England's Queen, vexed and annoyed by this brawling in the streets of her capitol city.[30]

Lord Oxford himself did fight twice with Sir Thomas Knyvet, being seriously wounded in the second duel. It is thought, though not recorded, that he sustained a leg wound, which lamed him for life.[31]

But a hurt more poignant than his lameness was that the Queen forbade him to return to Court. Ostensibly she was punishing him for supposed disloyalty to the crown because of his near relationship to the Howards. "Guilt by association" we call it today, and we see that it is nothing new. Actually, Elizabeth Tudor could never forgive her favorite for giving his heart to another woman.

This is the period of the "banishment plays." The Ogburns[32] find that the word *banish* or *banishment* in its various forms occurs frequently in the plays written or revised in the years 1581 to 1583, i.e., the revised *Titus Andronicus, Coriolanus, Romeo and Juliet, Richard II,* and *As You Like It.*[33] The reader may recall others. Our dramatist puts into the mouth of Bolingbroke phrases that spring spontaneously to his mind, as "eating the bitter bread of banishment," *Richard II,* Act III, sc. 1, line 21.

Again:

> Nay rather, every tedious stride I make
> Will but remember me what a deal of world
> I wander from the jewels that I love.
> *Richard II,* Act I, sc. 3, ll. 267-9

And here is the most tell-tale phrase of all: ". . . left me in reputeless banishment," *I Henry IV,* Act III, sc. 2, l. 44. Lord Oxford's pride is deeply wounded, his reputation scarred, that reputation which meant so much to the ancient family of de Vere, with its medieval tradition of chivalry and honor. Doubtless his friends tried to comfort him, even as old John of Gaunt tried to comfort his banished son:

> Teach thy necessity to reason thus;
> There is no virtue like necessity.
> Think not the king did banish thee;
> But thou the king. . . .

For gnarling sorrow hath less power to bite
The man that mocks at it. . . .
Richard II, Act I, sc. 3, ll. 277-80, 292-3

Lord Oxford was banished from Court more than two years, every day of which he must have counted bitterly. Also, his funds, given ever generously not only to his Sovereign and country, but also to his impecunious literary friends, were now alarmingly low.

It was during this period that he became reconciled to his wife, which must have brought him some measure of solace. Both Ann and her father attempted to use influence with the Queen to have him reinstated. Here is a letter dated July 14th, from Walsingham to Lord Burghley:

> I dealt very earnestly with the Queen touching the Earl of Oxford's liberty, putting her in mind of her promise made to your Lordship and to the Lady his wife.

Letters to and from Sir Christopher Hatton and Sir Walter Raleigh show that the Lord Treasurer was working through these Courtiers in an effort to persuade the Queen to reinstate his son-in-law. But that seems strange inasmuch as this was the period of the rise of each of them, when Raleigh had been given Durham House, one of the palatial mansions on the Strand. It would have been to the advantage of each of these gentlemen to keep Lord Oxford away as long as possible.

This is a letter written by the Earl to his father-in-law:

> Robin Christmas did yesterday tell me how honorably you had dealt with Her Majesty as touching my liberty and that this day she had made promise to your Lordship that it shall be. Unless your Lordship shall make some ? to put Her Majesty in ? thereof, I fear in these and other causes of the two Lords she will forget me.

Oxford writes in such a hurry that some of his words are indistinct. He closes his letter:

> But letting these things pass for a while, I must not forget to give your Lordship those thanks which are due to you for this your honourable dealing to Her Majesty on my behalf, which I hope shall not be without effect. The which attending from the Court, I shall take my leave of your Lordship, and rest at your commandment at my house this morning.
>
> Edward Oxenford.[34]

Then quite unexpectedly Lord Oxford was summoned into the royal presence. Roger Manners wrote to the Earl of Rutland a description of the meeting:

> Her Majesty came yesterday to Greenwich from the Lord Treasurer's . . . the day she came away, which was yesterday, the Earl of Oxford came into her presence, and after some bitter words and speeches, in the end all sins are forgiven, and he may repair to the Court at his pleasure. Master Ralley was a great mean herein, whereat Pondus is angry that he could not do so much.[35]

Somebody must have been listening at the keyhold to overhear those "bitter words and speeches." It does not sound like a happy reconciliation. But the correspondence leading up to it is interesting, for it shows that friendly relations had been restored between Lord Oxford and his father-in-law, at least temporarily. However, not until the story is finished can their relationship really be appraised. It is interesting, too, to note Sir Walter Raleigh's generous effort to reinstate his rival.

Just possibly the Queen had been missing her "Phoebus" so badly that she was ready and anxious to summon him to return.

In 1585 her Majesty appointed Oxford Commander of the Horse in the war in the Netherlands. However, after only six weeks she undercut his authority, making his position in the field almost untenable, and he was recalled.[36]

Note a scene in *Othello*, Act IV, sc. 1, in which the hero is reluctant to come home. The scene is doubtless a revision later than 1585, but it recalls the incident:

> *Othello.* I am commanded home. . . .
> . . . Sir, I obey the mandate,
> And will return to Venice.
>
> ll. 269-71

The scene with Desdemona, in which she surmises that Othello blames her father for his recall, has already been quoted.[37]

The disastrous enterprise had been a terrible blow to Lord Oxford's pride, he being a de Vere, all of whom had been great and famous soldiers. And, as other heroes of the land had found, he had had to bear the expense of the campaign himself.

Later his own brother-in-law, Lord Willoughby, was sent over and achieved brilliant success.[38] This, too, must have been galling to Lord Oxford's pride.

He was forced to complain to the Queen about his state of finances, urgently requesting that she appoint him to a post with adequate emolument, instead of to one which was rapidly running him into debt. She seems to have given him some hope of future favor in this respect.

But it was not until June of 1586 that the Queen finally kept her promise. Her Majesty signed a Privy Seal Warrant, which reads:

> Elizabeth, etc. etc., to the Treasurer and Chamberlains of our Exchequer, Greeting. We Will and command you of our treasure being and remaining from time to time within the receipt of our Exchequer, to deliver and pay, or cause to be delivered and paid, unto Our right trusty and well beloved Cousin the Earl of Oxford, or to his assigns

> sufficiently authorized by him, the sum of One Thousand Pounds good and lawful money of England. The same to be yearly delivered and paid unto Our said Cousin at four terms of the year in even portions: And so to be continued unto him during our pleasure, or until such time as he shall be by Us otherwise provided for to be in some manner relieved; at which time Our pleasure is that this payment of One Thousand Pounds yearly to Our said Cousin in manner above specified shall cease. And for the same or any part thereof, Our further will and commandment is that neither the said Earl nor his assigns nor his or their executors nor any of them shall by way of account, imprest, or any other way whatsoever be charged toward Us, Our heirs or successors. And these letters shall be your sufficient warrant and discharge in that behalf. Given under Our Privy Seal at Our Manor of Greenwich, the six and twentieth of June in the twentieth year of Our reign.[39]

This document bears close study. "One Thousand Pounds" was a prodigious sum in Elizabethan days, and moreover the Queen did not give away money carelessly. Indeed, she never gave away anything at all without expecting something in return. The sum could not have been recompense for what Lord Oxford had spent in the campaign in the Low Countries, for that was not mentioned in the Warrant. Moreover, the grant was to be recurrent annually.

Yet how like the capricious Queen to put into the legal document the phrase: "to be continued unto him during Our pleasure"! Actually, the grant was given annually for the rest of Lord Oxford's life, being continued in the reign of King James.

The most interesting aspect of the phrasing of the Warrant is that no accounting of the expenditure is to be made; this was quite emphatic. It indicates that there is a definite reason for the grant; it is to recompense Lord Oxford for some particular service of great value to his country, the service not to be specifically named. What could that service have been?

Here is only one suggestion: This was the time when the history plays began to appear—those plays reminding Englishmen of the grandeur of their past, stirring their hearts into a great frenzy of national pride. Every bit of this fervor would be needed in the next few years to fight for England against the might of Spain.

In 1586 Lord Oxford, the Premier Earl, was one of the judges at the trial of Mary Queen of Scots, proving that his own loyalty was no longer in question.

To digress a moment in connection with the death of the Scottish Queen, there is an interesting coincidence in two of the history plays. In both of them a near relative to the monarch is suspected of being a threat to the throne of England. The Sovereign in each case almost half-heartedly plants in the mind of the nearest Courtier the suggestion that the sudden death of the suspected relative would be welcome news. The relative is murdered, but instead of gratitude and reward, the murdering courtier receives from the monarch only chastisement and contumely.

Turn to the play of *Richard II*. Richard has been deposed and imprisoned in the dungeon of Pomfret Castle; his conqueror has just been crowned at Westminster as King Henry IV. The royal party is at Windsor Castle: Sir Pierce Exton is talking with his servants (*King Richard II*, Act V, sc. 4, ll. 8-11).

Exton.	Didst thou not mark the king, what words he spake: "Have I no friend will rid me of this living fear?" Was it not so?
Serv.	Those were his very words. "Have I no friend:" quoth he; he spake it twice,
Exton.	And urged it twice together, did he not?
Serv.	He did.

Exton. And speaking it, he wistly look'd on me,
As who should say, "I would thou wert the man
That would divorce this terror from my heart,"
Meaning the king at Pomfret. Come, let's go;
I am the king's friend, and will rid his foe.

So they hie them to the dungeon of Pomfret Castle and kill Richard.

This is the scene when they return to Windsor to tell *King Henry* (Act V, sc. 6, ll. 30-43):

Exton. Great king, within this coffin I present
Thy buried fear: therein all breathless lies.

Bolingbroke, King Henry IV. Exton, I thank thee not; for thou hast wrought
A deed of slander with thy fatal hand
Upon my head and all this famous land.

Exton. From your own mouth, my lord, did I this deed.

Bol. They love not poison that do poison need,
Nor do I thee: though I did wish him dead,
I hate the murderer, love him murdered.
The guilt of conscience take thou for thy labour,
But neither my good word nor princely favour:
With Cain go wander through the shades of night,
And never show thy head by day nor night.

King Henry then tells his attending lords that he will make a journey to the Holy Land "to wash this blood off from my guilty hand."

A strikingly similar episode occurs in the play of *King John.* In this drama the near relative is the King's young nephew, the boy, Arthur Plantagenet. Listen as King John begins to plant his devious scheme in the mind of his faithful attendant, Hubert de Burgh (Act III, sc. 3, ll. 20-8):

King John. Come hither, Hubert. O my gentle Hubert,
We owe thee much! . . .
. . . .
Give my thy hand. I had a thing to say,
But I will fit it with some better tune.
By heaven, Hubert, I am almost asham'd
To say what good respect I have of thee.
(ll. 51-66)

King John rambles on, saying how much he loves Hubert.

I would into thy bosom pour my thoughts.
But ah! I will not; yet I love thee well;
And by my troth, I think thou lov'st me well.
Hubert. So well, that what you bid me undertake,
Though that my death were adjunct to my act,
By heaven, I would do it.
King. J. Do not I know thou wouldst?
Good Hubert! Hubert, Hubert! throw thine eye
On yon young boy: I'll tell thee what, my friend,

He is a very serpent in my way:
And wheresoe'er this foot of mine doth tread
He lies before me. Dost thou understand me?
Thou art his keeper.

Hubert. And I'll keep him so
That he shall not offend your majesty.

King J. Death.

Hubert. My lord?

King J. A grave.

Hubert. He shall not live.

King J. Enough.
I could be merry now. Hubert, I love thee;
Well, I'll not say what I intend for thee.

So Hubert de Burgh goes off to murder Arthur. At the last minute, however, he is filled with compassion for the boy, and does not kill him. But he tells the King that he *has* killed him. Here is the scene (Act IV, sc. 2, ll. 205-48).

King John. Thy hand hath murder'd him. I had mighty cause
To wish him dead, but thou hadst none to kill him.

Hubert. No had, my lord? why did you not provoke me?

King J. It is the curse of kings to be attended
By slaves that take their humours for a warrant
To break within the bloody house of life,
And on winking of authority
To understand a law, to know the meaning

Of dangerous majesty, when, perchance, it frowns
More upon humour than advis'd respect.

Hubert. Here is your hand and seal for what I did.

King J. O, when the last accompt 'twixt heaven and earth
Is to be made, then shall this hand and seal
Witness against us to damnation! . . .
. . . .
. . . Hadst not thou been by,
A fellow by the hand of nature mark'd,
Quoted and sign'd to do a deed of shame,
This murther had not come into my mind:
. . . .
I faintly broke with thee of Arthur's death;
And thou, to be endeared to a king,
Made it no conscience to destroy a prince.

Hubert. My lord, —

King J. Hadst thou but shook thy head or made a pause
. . . .
Deep shame had struck me dumb, made me break off
. . . .
But thou didst understand me by my signs
And didst in signs parley with sin;
. . . .
Out of my sight, and never see me more!
. . . .
Hostility and civil tumult reigns
Between my conscience and my cousin's death.

Is it not curious that the scenes in these two plays are so similar? Could it be more than coincidence? Did the dramatist, perhaps, know of a situation like this in real life? If the playwright were a courtier to the Queen, he would have known just this experience.

Elizabeth Tudor had been patient with Mary Stuart for many years. Both Burghley and Walsingham had warned her that the secret service knew that the European Catholics were plotting to seize the throne of England and place Mary upon that exalted seat. To the Catholics, Mary was the rightful heir, being the great-granddaughter of King Henry VII. It will be recalled that Henry VIII had secretly married Anne Boleyn, Elizabeth's mother, while his first wife, Katherine of Aragon, was still living. True, the Pope had granted an annulment of the first marriage, but there were Catholics in England as well as on the Continent who honestly felt that Elizabeth Tudor was illegitimate, and therefore had no right to the throne. Mary Stuart was next in line. It would be of great advantage to Catholicism to place a devout Catholic on the English throne.

Meanwhile in London the climate of fear was exacerbated by a plot against the life of England's Queen revealed in January of 1587. It was only one in a series of plots, but Queen Elizabeth realized that she could hesitate no longer. She tried to persuade Sir Amias Paulet to assassinate the Scottish Queen. When Paulet refused, Elizabeth scoffed at "the niceness of these precise fellows." Clearly she wanted someone else to take the blame for Mary's death.

Finally on February 1st she herself did sign the death warrant for Mary Stuart. Walsingham, her Principal Secretary, being ill, the second secretary, William Davison, was in attendance. Davison, a graduate of Cambridge, had been in office only since September 30th of the year before.

With the warrant in his hand, Davison was beside himself with fear and confusion and anxious to spread the responsibility to Burghley and the other councillors. But at last the sinister document was sealed and sent off to Fotheringay. Mary Queen of Scots was executed February 7th, 1587.

When the news reached London, Queen Elizabeth put on a great show of indignation, whether real or faked, nobody quite knew.[40] She stormed against Davison, declaring that he had acted improperly in showing the warrant to the other councillors. She insisted that she had never meant to sign it in the first place. Indeed, she put on such an act that even Lord Burghley was deceived. He himself got a scorching rebuke for allowing the warrant to be sent.

But the real victim was William Davison. He was tried in the Star Chamber, heavily fined, and sentenced to imprisonment in the Tower during the Queen's pleasure. He remained there eighteen months, not being released until after the victory of the Spanish Armada.

For Americans, especially those of us with New England ancestry, it is interesting to note that Davison's private secretary was a young north country man, recently graduated from Cambridge where, like Davison, he had become infected by the cult of Puritanism. His name was William Brewster. It is tempting to picture this young man going about his duties in Whitehall or Windsor Castle, where he would surely have seen the Premier Earl of the Realm, although never being noticed by that nobleman. This picture is fanciful. But there is record of Brewster visiting Davison every day of that poor man's imprisonment in the Tower—and that at no small danger to himself. Davison appreciated his ministrations so much that he called Brewster his "son," and wanted to adopt him.

Upon release from the Tower, Davison went home to live in obscurity the rest of his life, a broken man, while Brewster was becoming too active in the Puritan cause to stay in London. He went home to Nottinghamshire, where his manor house in Scrooby became the center of Puritanism in the north. Later, when it seemed advisable to leave the country, he led a group of Puritans to Holland, where he taught for two years in the University of Leyden, augmenting his income by taking up the printing trade. But with the persistent persecution of the

Puritans during the reign of James I, Brewster realized that his followers could never return to England to live in peace. He therefore decided to take a little group of a hundred of them to a new land where they could worship their God in freedom. He was instrumental in chartering the ship, *Mayflower*, which in September of 1620 set sail from Plymouth, England, to bring the Pilgrims across the sea to found a new colony, of which he was their Elder.[41]

Though it is most unlikely that the aristocratic Earl of Oxford and the obscure but scholarly private secretary to the Queen's second secretary ever met, there seems to be remarkable evidence in the plays—is there not?—that the Earl, or should one say, the dramatist, whoever *he* was, knew well the story of the death warrant of Mary Queen of Scots and what happened afterward.

Returning now to the story of the distinguished Earl and of his Queen, it will be recalled that the Countess of Oxford died in June of 1588. Once again the life of Edward de Vere was sorely disrupted.[42]

Later that year, anticipating the war with Spain, Lord Oxford fitted out a ship at his own expense, naming it *The Edward Bonaventure* in contrast to Sir Francis Drake's flagship, *The Elizabeth Bonaventure.*

Meanwhile the Queen was doing more than her part demanded. On August 8th, at Tilbury, she reviewed the troops before they set forth to meet the enemy. "Full of princely resolution and more than feminine courage . . . she passed like some Amazonian empress through all her army."

"Lord bless you all," she cried as the men kneeled in her presence.

The following day, mounted on her famous white charger, she witnessed a mimic battle, after which she addressed the troops again at Tilbury in a speech with true Shakespearean ring:[43]

> My loving people, we have been persuaded by some that are careful of our safety, to take heed how we com-

> mit ourselves to armed multitudes, for fear of treachery. But I assure you, I do not desire to live in distrust of my faithful and loving people. Let tyrants fear. I have always so behaved myself that, under God, I have placed my chiefest strength and safeguard in the loyal hearts and good will of my subjects; and therefore I am come amongst you, as you see, at this time, not for my recreation and disport, but being resolved, in the midst and heat of battle, to live or die amongst you all, to lay down for my God, and for my kingdom, and for my people, my honour and my blood, even in the dust. I know I have the body of a weak and feeble woman, but I have the heart and stomach of a king, and of a king of England, too, and think for scorn that Parma or Spain, or any prince of Europe should dare to invade the borders of my realm; to which, rather than any dishonour shall grow by me, I myself will take up arms. I myself will be your general, Judge, and rewarder of every one of your virtues in the field. I know, already for your forwardness you have deserved rewards and crowns; and we do assure you, on the word of a prince, they shall be duly paid you.[44]

The men gave a mighty shout. Next day, upon hearing that Spain was about to invade England, Walsingham wrote in a letter: "This place breedeth courage."

Meanwhile, as captain of his ship, Lord Oxford fought the Spanish Armada under the command of Sir Francis Drake. A poem was written about him which sounds like the enthusiastic expression of an eye-witness, a companion in arms in the battle. It is signed *I. L.*, probably the initials of John Lyly, who sometimes signed himself *Ihon Lyly.* Being Lord Oxford's secretary at the time, he was doubtless on *The Edward Bonaventure* during the fighting. The poem:

> De Vere, whose fame and loyalty hath pearst
> The Tuscan clime, and through Belgike lands

By winged Fame for valour is rehears't.
Like warlike Mars upon the hatches stands
  His tusked Boar 'gan foam for inward ire
  While Pallas filled his breast with warlike fire.[45]

The "tuskéd Boar," of course, refers to Lord Oxford's de Vere crest of the blue boar.

The fighting over, there was a great service of thanksgiving in St. Paul's. In the procession down Fleet Street and up Ludgate Hill, Lord Oxford rode immediately before the Queen. When she alighted from her coach in front of the Cathedral, he and the Earl of Shrewsbury held the golden canopy over their sovereign as she was "brought through the long West Aisle to her travers in the quire, the clergy singing the litany."[46]

Sonnet no. 125 is recalled. It begins:

Were 't aught to me I bore the canopy
With my extern the outward honouring...

A contemporary ballad describes the royal procession from Somerset Place to St. Paul's. Excerpts from it:

The noble Earl of Oxford then High Chamberlain of
  England
Rode right before her Majesty his bonnet in his hand,
And after by two noblemen along the Church was led
With golden canopy carried o'er her head.
. . . .
The Earl of Oxford opening the windows for her grace,
The Children of the Hospital she saw before her face.

Lord Oxford married for his second wife one of her Majesty's young and beautiful Maids of Honor.[47] Surprisingly, the Queen gave her consent; indeed, the wedding could not have taken place without it. But by this time she was growing old, and also her interest had shifted to a much younger man, the Earl of Essex.

In 1592 the long-awaited heir to the earldom of Oxford was born, bringing joy and solace to his father's later years. And only two years after that, his oldest daughter, Elizabeth de Vere, married the Earl of Derby; the Queen was present at the ceremony, and at the reception at Lord Burghley's a day or two later.

Not only did Lord Oxford's human heir appear early in the 1590s, but it is believed that during this decade, 1590-1600, he gave to the world the greatest number of "heirs of his invention." To tell these facts in the conventional way one should say that this decade brought into being the greatest number of Shakespeare plays. Many of them, after being tried out in the Theatre or the Curtain, must have been produced at Court, or possibly some of them were played first at Court. Actually the only *record* of Shakespeare plays being given at Whitehall is *Love's Labour's Lost* on St. Stephen's Night, December 26th, 1598, and *The Merry Wives of Windsor* given there New Year's Day, 1599.[48] Yet it had been said over one hundred performances of Shakespeare's plays were given at Court. They might have been performed at other royal palaces.

Tradition has it that the Queen laughed so hard at the Falstaff plays that she commanded the dramatist to write of the fat knight in love. It is said that he composed *The Merry Wives of Windsor* for her delectation in only ten days. She would have loved that play, especially the setting which had such flavor of Berkshire and the curve of the Thames she knew so well.

There are phrases in the plays which the Queen is reported to have used at about the time of their composition, but whether her Majesty was quoting Shakespeare, or the dramatist quoting the Queen is hard to say. A case in point is the phrase *between Scylla and Charybdis.* It is used only once by the dramatist, in *The Merchant of Venice,* Act III, sc. 5;

> Thus when I shun Scylla, your father, I fall into Charybdis your mother; well you are gone both ways.
>
> ll. 18-20

The Queen is known to have used the phrase in a conversation "being alone in her chamber with Cecil and the Archbishop of York." She was discussing with them the pros and cons of her proposed marriage to the Duc d'Alencon, and she said:

> If I do not marry him, I know not that he will remain friendly with me, and if I do I shall not be able to govern the country with the freedom and security I have hitherto enjoyed. I am between Scylla and Charybdis.[39]

Perhaps the Queen had used the phrase before and Lord Oxford had heard her, or more probably she had heard *him* use it. To Oxford it would have been quite familiar since it is found in two books of the Golding translation of Ovid's *Metamorphoses*, vis. Book VI, beginning at line 88:

> And how Charybdis, utter foe to ships that pass thereby,
> Now sowpeth in, now speweth out the Sea incessantly:
> And ravening Scylla being hemmed with cruel dogs about,
> Amid the gulf of Sicilie doth make a barking out.[50]

In *Book XIII* the poet tells the story of Scylla, beginning at line 865:

> Upon the left side restlessly Charybdis aye doth beat
> them,
> And swalloweth ships and spewes them up as fast as it
> doth eat them.
> And Scylla beateth on their right: which from the navel
> down
> Is patched up with cruel curs: and upward to the crown,
> Doth keep the countenance of a maid.

The poet then gives two pages to the lurid story of Scylla, "sometime a maid right fair of hue," . . . "going to the salt Sea nymphs" and to the dire misfortune which befell her.[51]

It will be remembered, too, that Lord Oxford had actually sailed across the roiling waters between Scylla and Charybdis when on his travels he had crossed from Italy over to Sicily.

It is known that the Queen was familiar with the play of *Richard II*, for once when she thought her throne was in danger of usurpation, she cried out: "I *am* Richard!" Indeed, there were certain scenes in that play which were never given while she lived. The theme of the deposition of an English monarch was too dangerous to enact in those troubled times.

Meanwhile recognition of Lord Oxford's literary achievement was coming to him, guardedly, to be sure, but at least he was now being publicly appreciated as a poet. In 1589 Lord Lumley, a friend and family connection, published his book, *The Arte of English Poesie.* Certain paragraphs from this work have already been quoted in the Introduction, explaining that poets in those days were "despised" and "subject to scorn and derision." Lumley continues that there are "sprung up" a number of "Noblemen and Gentlemen" at Court "who have written excellent well." Then comes that curious conditional clause: "if their doings could be found out and made public." And among these Lord Lumley lists "first that noble gentleman Edward, Earl of Oxford."[52]

It is obvious that Lord Lumley had in mind some reason prohibiting noblemen from acknowledging their own literary work. This might be one explanation why Lord Oxford took a *nom de plume* as a signature for his plays and for his later poetry.

Robert Green in his *Farewell to Folly* shows that it was not unusual for an Elizabethan author to sign another man's name to his own output, though Green is referring to the signing of those scurrilous pamphlets which so frequently appeared in the days of Elizabeth. Still the point is important, and here are Green's own words:

> Others, if they come to write or publish anything in print, . . . Get some other to set his name to the verses.[53]

However, as has been indicated, the most important reason why Lord Oxford dared not sign his name to his literary works after the age of twenty-six is just because he was a courtier to the Queen. To those of us of the twentieth century it is hard to grasp the inhibitions and sense of values of the sixteenth century. Yet this grasp is vital if one is to understand the heroes and heroines of that spacious age.

Toward the end of the last decade of the sixteenth century it was apparent to her people that the Queen was growing old and feeble. A good part of the population of England had known no other sovereign and it must have seemed to them she was immortal. Yet "time's thievish progress to eternity" was evident in her short temper, her ill-considered commands, her extravagant and exaggerated dress, her painted face and ghastly red wig familiar in her portraits, which seem almost a caricature. But still she carried herself with regal splendor, and still she gestured gracefully with her hands, although the fingers were gnarled and the joints swollen, and she wore too many rings. It was said that her teeth turned black.

This is not a pretty picture. Yet her Majesty was loved by her subjects now even more than when she had been young and beautiful. "Good Queen Bess" they called her.

She showed her age and weakened judgment in her conduct of the Essex affair. Because of her emotional involvement with this capricious young man, the decisions were difficult and she came to them after long deliberation. Yet upon learning of his treachery to her throne—to *England*—she never wavered.

It had been necessary to have a trial, though the outcome was a foregone conclusion. Twenty-four Peers of the Realm were chosen to judge the two young Earls, Essex and Southampton, and the premier Peer was the Earl of Oxford. In him the Queen now put her complete trust; there were not many about her of whom that could be said.

Essex was doomed to execution on Tower Hill, while Southampton, perhaps on the intervention of Lord Oxford, was allowed to live, languishing in prison with his cat and his few retainers, until he was set free by King James.

There is a story that on the evening of the day that Essex was to die Lord Oxford and Sir Walter Raleigh were dining with the Queen at Greenwich Palace. According to the anecdote, the Queen was playing on the virginals when news of the execution was brought in. She did not stop playing, which prompted Oxford to nudge Raleigh and whisper:

"When jacks start up, heads go down."

Jacks, of course, referred to the keys of the virginals, as in *Sonnet 128*, in which the poet envied "those jacks that nimble leap. . . .

On this occasion at Greenwich the Queen was particularly gracious to Lord Oxford, promising him the estate of Sir John Danvers, one of the followers of Essex who suffered the same fate as his leader. Unfortunately Sir Charles's affairs were in such a legal tangle that Lord Oxford did not live long enough to enjoy the revenue of those lands.

In 1602 her Majesty appeared in Parliament for the last time. The question of monopolies was to be discussed. This was the way the Queen used to reward her courtiers, but it was becoming increasingly unpopular with her subjects, who felt that the price of living was being raised at their expense. Learning of their discontent, the Queen asked if she might address Parliament in person. This she did, promising to relinquish monopolies since the policy was so displeasing to her people. Then to her kneeling lawmakers she made her last great speech. She began:

> There is no jewel, be it of never so rich a price, which I do prefer before this jewel, I mean your love. For I do more esteem it than any treasure or riches: for that we know how to prize, but love and thanks I count inestimable. And though God hath raised me high, yet this I count the glory of my crown; that I have reigned with your loves. This makes that I do not so much rejoice that God hath made me a Queen, as to be a Queen over so thankful a people.

At this she paused and bade them rise, for she had more to say. As she stood before the Lords and Commons in her gorgeous robes of state, slightly stooped but still queenly, gesturing with her hands, she proceeded:

> To be a King and wear a crown is more glorious to them that see it than it is pleasure to them that wear it. . . . There will never Queen sit in my seat with more zeal to my country, or care to my subjects, that will sooner with willingness yield and venture her life for your good and safety than myself. And though you had, and may have, many princes more mighty and wise sitting in this seat, yet you never had, nor shall have, any that will be more careful and loving.[54]

There was a flourish of trumpets, and with regal dignity the Queen swept out of the room, her Courtiers and Maids of Honor following.

It may have been at this session of Parliament that Lord Oxford saw his Queen for the last time. Or he may have driven in his coach out to Richmond to bid her adieu, for he would have known that she was failing fast.

In the night of March 24th, 1603, she died.

The Queen's funeral was conducted with all the pomp and ceremony she herself had loved. There was a special service in Westminster Abbey before she was interred there, in the chapel of her grandfather, King Henry VII. In the surviving descriptions of the funeral there is curiously no mention of Lord Oxford, but it is fair to assume that he is one of the six earls who walked beside her catafalque, and that later, in the Abbey he bore the canopy over her Majesty for the last time.

To Edward de Vere the passing of the Queen would have been a profound sorrow. In this moment of grief all her moods, procrastinations and harsh words were forgiven. To serve her Majesty had been his life-long career, and now he was bereft. His feeling of loss is beautifully expressed in this letter he wrote to Lord Robert Cecil:

> She hath left [me] either without sail whereby to take advantage of the prosperous gale, or without anchor to ride till the storm be over-past.[55]

It is believed by many of us that Lord Oxford has an even more poignant tribute to his royal mistress in *Sonnet 107*, in which he expresses also his anxiety for what the new reign might bring:

> Not my own fears, nor the prophetic soul
> Of the wide world dreaming on things to come,
> Can yet the lease of my true love control,
> Suppos'd as forfeit to a confin'd doom.
> The mortal moon hath her eclipse endur'd,
> And the sad augurs mock their own presage;
> Incertainties now crown themselves assur'd,
> And peace proclaims olives of endless age.
> Now with the crops of this most balmy time
> My love looks fresh, and Death to me subscribes,
> Since, spite of him, I'll live in this poor rhyme,
> While he insults o'er dull and speechless tribes:
> And thou in this shall find thy monument,
> When tyrants' crests and tombs of brass are spent.

Notes To Chapter IV

1. In the National Portrait Gallery, London.
2. Charlton and Dorothy Ogburn, *This Star of England*.
3. See Introduction.
4. Martin Holmes, formerly director of the London Museum, in a personal letter to the writer.

5. Chapter II.

6. Chapter I.

7. H. Amphlett, *Who Was Shakespeare?*, p. 61.

8. Eva Turner Clark, *Hidden Allusions in Shakespeare's Plays.*

9. At this, his first session in the House of Lords, the new Lord Oxford attended ten meetings, during the eight weeks the House was sitting, and served on a committee "touching matters of religion."

10. This historic cobbold way by the side of Henry VII's chapel is still in use.

11. B. M. Ward, *The Seventeenth Earl of Oxford.*

12. Edward Alber, ed. *The Spencer Anthology*, London, 1901.

13. The linking of this scene from *Love's Labour's Lost* to a contemporary incident at Court is taken from Eva Turner Clark.

14. See Chapter IX.

15. The suggestion is from *This Star of England*, p. 605.

16. In the National Portrait Gallery, London. See page 40 e.

17. It is believed by certain scholars that Queen Elizabeth had a son by Leicester early in her reign. See *This Star of England*, p. 605.

18. Referring to Oxford's Latin preface to Bartholomew Clarke's Translation of Castiglione's *The Courtier. This Star of England*, p. 145-7.

19. Quoted in *The Seventeenth Earl of Oxford.*

20. An angel was a small coin.

21. Quoted in *The Seventeenth Earl of Oxford.*

22. Louis Benezet, *The Six Loves of "Shakespeare."*

23. See Introduction.

24. Another reference to the same idea is found in *King Henry the Fifth*, Act IV, sc. 7. King Henry sees the glove in Fluellen's cap and asks whether Fluellen means to fight the owner. On learning that he does, the King expostulates:

> It may be his enemy is a gentleman of great sort,
> Quite from the answer of his degree.

According to Professor Robert D. French, in the Yale Shakespeare edition of *Henry V*, this means "above answering the challenge of one of his degree."

25. Tresham Lever, *The Herberts of Wilton.*

26. Chapter I.

27. *Lansdowne MSS.*, 33, 6. Quoted in a descendant's notebook.

28. Chapter V.

29. Chapter V.

30. For linking this scene from *Romeo and Juliet* with the contemporary episodes at Court, I am again indebted to Eva Turner Clark.

31. See Chapter VII.

32. Ogburns, *This Star of England*, p. 327.

33. This is an earlier date for these plays than many English scholars would give. It is our contention that the so-called banishment plays were first composed during this period, but revised many times later, sometimes by the dramatist himself, other times by his associates or his executors. Therefore, there is really no conflict in this earlier dating.

34. Ward, pp. 223-4, citing Lansdowne MSS., 33. 6.

35. Ibid. Note the nickname *Pondus* for Lord Burghley, and its suggestion of *Polonius.*

36. Chapter III.

37. Ibid.

38. See Chapter II.

39. Ward, p. 257 and Appendix C, quoting and analyzing the *Book of Privy Warrants.*

40. The courtier, Robert Carey, describing the onset of Queen Elizabeth's last illness, tells that "she fetched . . . forty or fifty great sighs . . . in all her lifetime before I never knew her to fetch a sigh, but when the Queen of Scots was beheaded. Then upon my knowledge she shed many tears and sighs, manifesting her innocence that she never gave consent to the death of that Queen." From the *Memoirs* of the Life of Robert Carey, Baron of Lepington, and Earl of Monmouth, and now published from

an Original Manuscript in the Custody of John Earl of Cork and Orrery, London, 1759.

41. The story of Queen Elizabeth's behavior in connection with the signing of the death warrant of Mary Queen of Scots and the aftermath is taken from Sir John Neale's *Queen Elizabeth*, Chapter Sixteen.

The reference to William Brewster is taken from W. H. Bartlett, *The Pilgrim Fathers*, London, and from Dorothy Brewster, *Elder Brewster*, pp. 29-43.

42. Chapter V.

43. Neale, *Queen Elizabeth*, p. 296.

44. Ibid.

45. H. Amphlett, *Who Was Shakespeare?*

46. Ibid.

47. See Chapter VIII.

48. Ian Dunlop, *The Palaces and Progresses of Queen Elizabeth I.*

49. Clark, *Hidden Allusions in Shakespeare's Plays.*

50. Arthur Golding's *Translation of Ovid's Metamorphoses*, 1567, edited by John Frederick Nims.

51. Ibid., Book XIII, l. 865-75.

52. Quoted in Ward, *The Seventeenth Earl of Oxford.*

53. Ibid.

54. Neale, *Queen Elizabeth.*

55. From a private notebook of a de Vere descendant.

56. In *This Star of England*, Charlton and Dorothy Ogburn, make an excellent case for the theory that Queen Elizabeth actually had a child by the Earl of Oxford. This child, they believe, was quickly spirited away to the Earl and Countess of Southampton and brought up as their own, the Third Earl of Southampton. If this theme could be proved, all the other mysteries fall into line, i.e., the necessity of protecting the name of "the Virgin Queen," by disguising the author of the tell-tale plays, the dedication of the two long poems to the Earl of Southampton, Oxford's own

son, and Lord Burghley's effort to spoil the future reputation of his son-in-law in order to protect the name of the Queen, as well as the name of his daughter, and of his granddaughters.

Chapter V
HIS MISTRESS

. . . thou hast metamorphos'd me;
Made me neglect my studies, lose my time,
War with good counsel, set the world at nought;
Made wit with musing weak, heart sick with thought.
Two Gentlemen of Verona, Act I, sc. 1, ll. 66-9

The story about to be told begins in the year 1580. Historically all too few of the facts are known. But in a careful reading of those plays said to be composed by the actor, Shakespeare, there is found a vivid tale of love, hate, treachery, penury, jealousy, revenge and forgiveness. For the plays "are the abstracts and brief chronicles of the time," the author tells us. This is therefore the story of *Romeo and Juliet,* of *Antony and Cleopatra,* of Edward de Vere and Anne Vavasor.

Who was this hussy who had the presumption to start an *affair du coeur* with the courtier acknowledged to be the favorite of her august Majesty, Queen Elizabeth?

To recapitulate, Lord Oxford, a married man estranged from his wife, had returned to Court from his travels and was now carrying on a most indiscreet flirtation with the Queen. That affair was becoming exceedingly distressing to him, though he needs must continue to write his poetry to her undying beauty and to fulfill her whims as best he could, for her favor meant the very means of his livelihood.

In *Sonnet no. 66,* which is believed to have been composed at this time, the poet is found to be in a mood of bitter disillusionment. Consider the first line:

Tir'd with all these for restful death I cry . . .

In the same sonnet a few lines further on he writes of "maiden virtue rudely strumpeted."

Believing that Lord Oxford is the disillusioned poet, one comes to realize that he was even tempted to suicide: ". . . for restful death I cry."

We may say then, that this was the mood of our hero when out of the north country came a maid,

> A whitely wanton with a velvet brow
> With two pitchballs stuck in her face for eyes.[1]

She doesn't sound like a beauty. Yet this "whitely wanton" seems to have had a seductive attraction to the gentlemen of Queen Elizabeth's Court.

Anne Vavasor was the daughter of Henry Vavasor of Tadcaster, Copmansthorpe, Yorkshire. Her mother, born Margaret Knyvet, was of the cadet branch of the Knyvets of Buckenham, Norfolk. Anne had two sisters, Frances and Margaret.

There had been Knyvets in the royal household since the time of King Henry VIII. Anne's uncle, Thomas Knyvet, was Groom of the Privy Chamber at Queen Elizabeth's Court, while her aunt, Katherine Knyvet, was first Maid of Honor and later Lady of the Bedchamber to the Queen. It was undoubtedly through the Knyvets that Anne and her sister Frances were brought to Court, though the family also had powerful sponsorship in being distantly related to the Howards, who themselves were cousins of the Queen. Like most of the Howards, Anne was a Catholic.

This beguiling lass appeared at Court in 1580 at the age of sixteen. Her appointment was as Gentlewoman of the Bedchamber. From the day of her arrival a goodly number of Courtiers on duty to the Queen were secretly writing verses of more or less amorous content to this, her newest attendant. Edmund Spenser had immortalized her as his *Rosaline*, which may indicate that she had rosy cheeks as well as the coal-black hair and snapping dark eyes we know from her portrait (see page 40 h).

Sir Walter Raleigh wrote her some verses of advice in *Le Prince d'Amour*, which he ends thus:

> For this be sure, the crop being once obtain'd
> Farewell the rest, the soil will be disdain'd.

The aging Earl of Leicester is said to have made improper advances to her, while his illegitimate son, Robert Dudley, was for a brief time engaged to marry her.

But it is her affair with our hero, Edward de Vere, with which we are here concerned. Her cousin, the Earl of Arundel, refers in a letter to a conversation with Lord Oxford after "long speeches in secret between him and my cousin who was the means of our meeting." This rather involved sentence would seem to mean that there had already been secret "long speeches" between Oxford and "my cousin," Anne.

The experience of finding a young woman of infinite charm in the flower of her youth provoked the inevitable response from the lonely and unhappy nobleman estranged from his wife, that little wife whom he had never really loved with passion. Here is the dramatist telling us exactly how he felt, in these scenes from *Romeo and Juliet.* For Romeo, read Oxford; for Juliet, Anne Vavasor; for Rosaline, his past love, read the Queen, the Tudor Rose.

Benvolio describes Romeo arising early in the morning and stealing into a covert of a wood, love-sick for his Rosaline. Montague takes up the story: "Many a morning hath he there been seen with tears augmenting the fresh morning's dew, adding to clouds more clouds with his deep sighs." But then by mid-day he would lock "fair daylight out and make himself an artificial night."

Then Romeo appears and describes his own feelings, somewhat dramatizing his emotions in this beautiful poetry:

> Love is a smoke made with the fume of sighs,
> Being purg'd a fire sparkling in lover's eyes,

Being vex'd a sea nourish'd with loving tears.
What it is else? a madness. . . .

. . . .

Ben. Soft, I will go along,
And if you leave me so you do me wrong.
Rom. Tut, I have left myself, I am not here,
This is not Romeo, he's some otherwhere.
ll. 90-202

Then comes the teasing, which the playwright loves to bring in:

Ben. Tell me in sadness, who is't that you love?
Rom. What! shall I groan and tell thee?
Ben. Groan? why no, but sadly tell me who.
Rom. Bid a sick man in sadness make his will—
(ll. 202-5)

. . . .

In sadness, cousin, I do love a woman.
(ll. 207-215)

Ben. I aim'd so near when I suppos'd you lov'd.
Rom. A right good marksman! and she's fair I love.
Ben. A right fair mark, fair coz, is soonest hit.
Rom. Well, in that hit you miss. She'll not be hit
With Cupid's arrow. She hath Dian's wit,
And in strong proof of chastity well arm'd
From Love's weak childish bow she lives un-
charm'd.
She will not stay the siege of loving terms.

. . . .

She hath forsworn to love, and in that vow
Do I love dead that live to tell it now.
(ll. 226-7)

Is there a better description of the "Virgin Queen"? "She'll not be hit with Cupid's arrow"; that was her policy. And "she hath Dian's wit." Diana, again, the goddess of the moon. "She hath forsworn to love." She could flirt dangerously with her courtiers, but never could she give them hope of anything more. . . .

Benvolio, the well-wisher, tells Romeo that at Capulet's ball he can compare fair Rosaline with all "the'admir'd beauties of Verona. (i.e., the Court.) Compare her face with some that I shall show, and I will make thee think thy swan a crow." To Romeo's stout denial that any other lady could be as fair, Benvolio gently chides him:

> Tut, you saw her fair none else being by . . .
> . . . .
> . . . . .let there be weigh'd
> Your lady's love against some other maid
> That I will show you shining at this feast,
> And she shall scant show well that now seems
>   best.
>
> Act I, sc. 3, ll. 97-102

Then Romeo sees Juliet at the ball, as perhaps Edward de Vere has seen Anne Vavasor the first time. It is love at first sight. . . .

> *Romeo* (*to an attendant standing by*):
> What lady's that which doth enrich the hand
> Of yonder knight.
> *Servant.* I know not, sir.
> *Romeo.* O she doth teach the torches to burn bright.
> It seems she hangs upon the cheek of night
> As a rich jewel in an Ethiop's ear—
> Beauty too rich for use, for earth too dear.
> So shows a snowy dove trooping with crows
> As yonder lady o'er her fellows shows.
> The measure done, I'll watch her place of stand,
> And touching hers make blessed my rude hand.
> Did my heart love till now? forswear it, Sight!
> For I ne'er saw true beauty till this night.
>
> Act I, sc. 4, ll. 157-69

Could the playwright make it clearer? He is telling how he first saw his true love, and how she captivated him from that very moment.

In Act II Romeo's friends, Benvolio and Mercutio, being aware of the sudden change of loyalty in his part, decide to tease him by reminding him of Rosaline's "bright eyes," "her high forehead" (all the portraits of the Queen show this feature), "her scarlet lip," and daringly, "her fine foot, straight leg . . ." Benvolio, always the thoughtful friend, warns that "if he hear thee thou wilt anger him." Edward's friends at Court, perhaps the old Earl of Sussex, may have talked just that way about this, his new infatuation. They knew how dangerous it was to divert amorous attention from the Queen.

The dramatist continues his story with the lovely balcony scene (Act II, sc. 2). It is not unlikely that Edward de Vere stood beneath Anne's balcony at Whitehall Palace, in the cool evening, there in the fruit orchard by the silent river, stealthily watching, sensitive to every leaf that stirred.

Romeo is speaking to himself.

> He jests at scars that never felt a wound.
> But soft, what light through yonder window
> breaks?
> It is the East and Juliet is the sun.
> Arise fair Sun and kill the envious Moon,
> That thou her maid, art far more fair than she.
> Be not her maid, since she is envious,
> Her vestal liv'ry is but sick and green,
> And none but fools wear it, cast it off.
> (11. 43-50)

The brightest object Romeo can think of is the sun—Juliet. And what a picture of the way things are going at Court: —"the envious moon [the Queen], who is already sick and pale with grief that "thou her maid art far more fair than she." He even dares to mention the Tudor "liv'ry"—green! In his present mood, the green looks sick. How bitterly eager he is to have Anne "cast it off," for "only fools" remain as sycophants at Court.

It is almost sacrilegious to attempt to analyze this scene, it is so beautiful. Yet one must eavesdrop on the lovers, "for the players tell all."

Anne in the short time she had been at Court would have learned that the Queen delighted to tantalize her courtiers by lavishing her favor first on one, then when he became too sure of himself, quickly looking to another deliberately in the presence of the one rebuffed. . . . For the sake of our story then, we shall listen

Romeo. Lady, by yonder blessed moon I vow,
That tips with silver all these fruit-tree tops——
Act II, sc. 1, ll. 149-50

But Juliet interrupts with:

O swear not by the moon, th'inconstant moon,
That monthly changes in her circl'd orb,
Lest that thy love prove likewise variable.

Later in this same act the young men friends say:

Ben. Here comes Romeo, here comes Romeo.
Mer. Without his roe, like a dried herring.
sc. 3, ll. 59-60

Of course, *Romeo* without his roe is *me O*, or *me, Oxford.* More likely, the Elizabethans, who delighted in such conceits, would have interpreted it as *E. O.** or *Earl of Oxford.* Edward de Vere has signed a number of poems: *E. O.*[2]

The poet-dramatist has drawn Anne's picture so many times that she would be recognized if she appeared today. He tells of her skin *lac'd with blue of heaven's own tinct.* She loved music and was skilled at playing. Her lover would *envy those jacks that nimble leap to kiss the tender inward* of her playing hand, adding:

> Since saucy jacks so happy are in this,
> Give them thy fingers, me thy lips to kiss.[3]
>
> Sonnet 128, ll. 13-14

Was it the virginals she played? That piano-like instrument with black keys for the scale notes, white only for the half notes, reversing the order of pianos today, so that my lady's hands might show up the better? Or perhaps Anne played the clavichord, that small plucked string instrument that makes the tender, wistful, faraway music so pleasing to the Elizabethan ear.

In two of the *Sonnets* the poet appears to pun upon Anne's name, Vavasor, meaning Master of Vassals. Sonnet 58:

> That god forbid that made me first your slave,
> I should in thought control your times of pleasure,
> Or at your hand the account of hours to crave
> Being your vassal, bound to stay your leisure!
> Or, let me suffer, being at your beck,
> The imprison'd absence of your liberty;
> And patience, tame to sufferance, bide each cheek,
> Without accusing you of injury.
> Be where you list, your charter is so strong
> That you yourself may privilege your time
> To what you will; to you it doth belong
> Yourself to pardon of self-doing crime.
> I am to wait, though waiting so be hell,
> Not blame your pleasure, be it ill or well.

Another passionate sonnet on the same theme is Sonnet 57:

> Being your slave, what should I do but tend
> Upon the hours and times of your desire?
> I have no precious time at all to spend,

Nor services to do, till you require.
Nor dare I chide the world-without-end hour
Whilst I, my sovereign, watch the clock for you,
Nor think the bitterness of absence sour
When you have bid your servant once adieu;
Nor dare I question with my jealous thought
Where you may be, or your affairs suppose,
But, like a sad slave, stay and think of nought,
Save where you are how happy you make those.
  So true a fool is love that in your will,
  Though you do anything, he thinks no ill.

Later when Lord Oxford knew that many of the courtiers were writing sentimental verse to Anne, he must have taken special delight in parodying their efforts—he, who could so far surpass them all in writing sonnets:

My mistress' eyes are nothing like the sun,
Coral is far more red than her lips' red,
If snow be white, why then her breasts are dun,
If hairs be wires, black wires grow on her head.
I have seen roses damask'd, red and white,
But no such roses see I in her cheeks,
And in some perfumes is there more delight
Than in the breath that from my mistress reeks.
I love to hear her speak, yet well I know
That music hath a far more pleasing sound;
I grant I never saw a goddess go;
My mistress when she walks, treads on the ground:
  And yet, by heaven, I think my love as rare
  As any she belied with false compare.

Sonnet 130

Lord Oxford did write poetry to Anne over his own signature. Witness the *Desire poems*. Then there is that young man's effusion *Megliora Spero*, beginning:[4]

Faction that ever dwells in Court where wit excels,
Hath set defiance,
Fortune and Love have sworn that they were never born
Of one alliance.

When he became more bold in admitting his love for Anne, Lord Oxford wrote:

Anne Vavasor's Echo Song.

O heavens! who was the first that bred in me this fever?
Vere.
Who was the first that gave the wound whose fear I wear
for ever? Vere.
What tyrant, Cupid, to my harm usurpt thy golden
quiver? Vere.

Yet who doth most adore this wight, oh hollow caves tell
true. You.
What nymph deserves his liking best, yet doth in sorrow
rue? You.
What makes him not regard good will with some regard
of ruth? Youth.
What makes him show besides this birth, such pride and
such untruth? Youth.

May his favour match with love, if he my love will try.
Ay.
May I requite his birth with faith. Then fearful will I
die. Ay.

And I that knew this lady well,
Said Lord how great a miracle,
To hear how Echo told the truth
As true as Phoebus' oracle.

Note again the harping on *truth*, referring to the Earl of

Oxford's motto, and also his name, *Vere*. Note, too, his reference to himself as *Phoebus*, the nickname the Queen had given him. It was very daring of him to write so openly; he must have been very sure of Anne. And well he might be, for

The following verses were addressed to the Earl of Oxford
(by Anne Vavasor.)

Tho' I seem strange, sweet friend, be thou not so,
Do not accoy thyself with sullen will;
Mine heart hath vowed, although my tongue says no,
To be thine own in friendly liking still.

Thou seest me live amongst the lynx's eyes
That pry into the privy thoughts of mind;
Thou know'st right well what sorrows may arise
If once they chance my settled looks to find.

Content thyelf that once I made an oath
To shield myself in shroud of honest shame,
And when thou list make trial of my troth
So that thou save the honour of my name.

And let my sense although I be not coy
To cloak my sad conceits with smiling cheer;
Let not thy gestures show wherein I joy,
Nor by my looks let not my love appear.

We silly dames that fall suspect do fear
And live within the might of envy's lake,
Must in our hearts a secret meaning bear
Far from the rest which outwardly we make.

So where I like, I list not vaunt my love
Where I desire there must I feign debate,
One hath my hand, another hath my glove,
But one my heart whom I seem most to hate.

Thus, farewell, friend! I will continue strange;
Thou shalt not hear my words or writing ought;
Let it suffice my vow shall never change;
And for the rest I leave it to thy thought.[6]

The playwright tells a little more about Anne Vavasor in *Love's Labour's Lost.* In Act IV, sc. 3, there are these lines:

Berowne. Who sees the heavenly Rosaline,

. . . .

That bows not his vassal head; and, stricken blind,

. . . .

King. What zeal, what fury, hath inspir'd thee now?
My love, her mistress, is a gracious moon,
She, an attending star, scarce seen a light.
ll. 221-31

This time the maiden attendant is given the name, *Rosaline,* the name Spenser gave to Anne in his poem about her. Note again the pun on Vavasor: "Bows not his vassal head." Remember, the audience in the great hall of Whitehall Palace would be much quicker in getting these double entendres than we are.

How Anne must have stood out from the other maids of honor with her black hair, dark eyes, and high color. The beauties in the south of England were usually praised as "fair," the Nordic type, while Queen Elizabeth herself had the fair skin and reddish gold hair of the Welsh.

Johy Lyly, Lord Oxford's secretary, has portrayed the relations of this trio in *Euphues, or The Anatomy of Wit.* He tells of the young hero "who had tarried many a month in Italy." The story concerns an older woman rejected, while the hero falls in love with a young maid.

Meanwhile the affair in real life at the Court of the Virgin Queen was progressing rather faster than the principles in the triangle cared to admit.

On January 22nd, 1581, there was to be a great tournament to celebrate the accession of Philip Howard, Oxford's cousin, to the Earldom of Arundel. Howard was to be the Challenger, and Lord Oxford as "the Knight of the Tree of Gold," the Defender. Here is a contemporary account of the beginning, before the tournament itself got under way.

> By the Tilt stood a stately tent of Orange tawny Taffeta, curiously embroidered with Silver and pendants on the Pinnacles very sightly to behold. From forth this Tent came the noble Earl of Oxenford in rich gilt Armour, and sat down under a great Bay-tree, the whole stock, branches, and leaves whereof, were all gilded over, that nothing but Gold could be discerned. By the Tree stood twelve staves, all which likewise were gilded clean over. After a solemn sound of most sweet Musique, he mounted on his Courser, very richly caparisoned, when his page ascending the stairs where her Highness stood in the window,[7]

and delivered his oration to her.

There is no further description of this particular tournament, but Giles Fletcher has written in Latin verse of Lord Oxford's prowess as a horseman. This is the translation:

> Fearlessly he settles himself in the saddle, gracefully bending his body this way and that. Now he circles round; now with his spurred heel he rouses his charger. The gallant animal with fiery energy collects himself together, and again is pulled up short as the reins control him. Bravo! valiant youth! 'Tis thus that martial spirits pass through their apprenticeship in war . . . glory already ripens thy earliest deed.[8]

Not surprisingly Lord Oxford was victor in the tournament mentioned above. The Queen herself bestowed the prize, the costly jewelled set of tallies.

The descriptions given are the cold facts of history. What follows immediately can only be surmise. Anne Vavasor had written:

> Thou seest me live amongst the lynx's eyes
> That pry into the privy thoughts of mind.

Those "lynx's eyes" had evidently pried into Anne's private life, even into her private apartment, and there discovered the victor's prize. Elizabeth Tudor had suspected an affair between her favorite and this new Maid in Waiting; here was the proof. A dreadful scene must have ensued. Then in desperation the harassed courtier had written Sonnet 122[9] to his Queen. How could her Majesty help forgiving him after reading these beautiful lines!

But worse misfortune was to follow. The Howards tried once more to bring the Catholic Mary Queen of Scots to the English throne.[10] This time Lord Oxford denounced his cousins, confessing all that he knew about their plot. But they insisted upon charging *him* with being their ring leader. We recall the French ambassador's letter to his king, regarding Oxford's disgrace at Court, adding that "he has lost credit and honour by all the ladies of the Court." Does this indicate that Anne Vavasor was a fair-weather friend?

Oxford for a brief time was even imprisoned in the Tower, where his Howard cousin was already incarcerated. But such was his hold upon the Queen that she soon released him.

However, this was to be the year of our hero's greatest misfortunes. On March 23rd, 1581, Mr. Secretary Walsingham who was in charge of the security forces of the kingdom, wrote to the Earl of Huntington:

> On tuesday at night Anne Vavysor was brought to bed of a son in the maiden's chamber. The E. of Oxford is vowed to be the father, who hath withdrawn himself with intent, as it is thought, to pass the seas. The ports are laid for him and therefore if he have any such determination

> it is not likely that he will escape. The Gentlewoman the self-same night she was delivered was conveyed out of the house and the next day committed to the Tower. Others have also been committed to the Tower. Her Majesty is greatly grieved with the accident, and therefore I hope there will be some order taken as the like inconvenience will be avoided.[11]

Did Mr. Secretary really think that he could save human nature from such "inconvenience"? And did the guilty father really try "to pass the seas"? This does not seem characteristic of Edward de Vere. Yet he must have realized that he was in deep, deep trouble and he may have tried to escape to the Continent. If he did, he was apprehended by Walsingham's agents. He was committed to the Tower to remain a prisoner there till June 8th, 1581. Upon release he was confined to his own house a month longer.

But further misfortune was in store for him. Anne's uncle, Sir Thomas Knyvet, took it upon himself to avenge her honor. Not only that, but he set his retainers to fighting Oxford's men, so that the French ambassador wrote his king that the streets of London were full of clamors of the Montagues and Capulets.[12]

During this time that the retainers were fighting each other Lord Oxford received a "lewd letter," from another of Anne's relatives, on the Vavasor side, taunting him with cowardice and demanding that he himself come out and fight instead of sending a second. But nothing more is heard about this demand, or about the relative who sent it.

Sir Thomas Knyvet and Lord Oxford did fight two duels, however. Edward de Vere was supping with his sister and brother-in-law, the Lady Mary and Peregrine Bertie, when the challenge to the second duel came.[13] He left them at once and went out to meet Sir Thomas.

It was a bitter fight this time, both contestants being seriously wounded. Actually the record does not mention the nature of Lord Oxford's wound. But because the author's lameness is mentioned four times in the *Sonnets*, it is thought that it was a leg wound that he suffered, a wound from which he never fully recovered.[14]

These are the four references to lameness in the *Sonnets:*

I, made lame by fortune's dearest spite. Sonnet 37.

Then I am not lame, poor nor despis'd. Again Sonnet 37.

And strength by limping sway disabl'd. Sonnet 66.

Speak of my lameness, and I straight will halt. Sonnet 89.

During all this time the Queen forbade Lord Oxford to return to Court. This was most galling of all to her one-time favorite.

This is the period of the "banishment plays," discussed in the last chapter. And it was also a period of torturing disillusionment to him. Witness Sonnet 137:

Thou blind fool, Love, what dost thou to mine eyes,
That they behold, and see not what they see?
They know what beauty is, see where it lies,
Yet what the best is take the worst to be.
If eyes, corrupt by over-partial looks,
Be anchor'd in the bay where all men ride,
Why of eyes' falsehood hast thou forged hooks,
Whereto the judgment of my heart is tied?
Why should my heart think that a several plot
Which my heart knows the wide world's common place?
Or mine eyes, seeing this, say this is not,
To put fair truth upon so foul a face.
In things right true my heart and eyes have err'd,
And to this false plague are they now transferr'd.

What bitterness shows through these lines! The poet feels that he has not only made a fool of himself, but that he has sinned against the truth—against his own motto, and his proud name, de Vere.

This was the time when Edward de Vere went back to his wife, Ann Cecil.[15] And did he remain faithful to her while she lived? Sonnet 152 would indicate that he did not. It is obviously written to Anne Vavasor, though probably to ease his own conscience rather than to be sent to her:

> In loving thee thou know'st I am forsworn,
> But thou art twice forsworn, to me love swearing
> . . . .
> But why of two oaths' breach do I accuse thee,
> When I break twenty? I am perjur'd most.

After Ann Cecil's death Lord Oxford did definitely return to his mistress, though torturing himself with guilt for doing so. It may be that it was the presence of his charming young son which brought them together. Oxford was strongly tempted to name the lad his legal heir, but while Ann Cecil lived that was impossible. It is thought, then, that it was sometime in the eventful year of 1588 that he returned to Anne Vavasor, and at the same time gave the child his name, Edward Vere.

It is not known when Anne and her babe had been released from prison, or where they went immediately from the Tower, though it is surmised that Anne did not have far to look for a benefactor. How many there were in her long life, only she herself could tell. And she was faithful to none.

At the time Lord Oxford returned to her she was supposedly the wife of one John Finch, a sea captain, whose father seems to have been a humble fishmonger in London. It was convenient having Finch away at sea on long voyages.

And now the "rival poet" appears in the *Sonnets:* who was he? Could he have been the young Earl of Southampton? Or was he George Chapman? Or even Christopher Marlowe? All three have been considered. Here only the mystery can be propounded, as it is presented in Sonnet 144:

Two loves I have of comfort and despair,
Which like two spirits do suggest me still:
The better angel is a man right fair,
The worser spirit is a woman, colour'd ill.
To win me soon to hell, my female evil
Tempteth my better angel from my side,
And would corrupt my saint to be a devil,
Wooing his purity with her foul pride.
And whether that my angel be turn'd fiend
Suspect I may, but not directly tell;
But being both from me, both to each friend,
I guess one angel in another's hell:
  Yet this shall I ne'er know, but live in doubt,
  Till my bad angel fire my good one out.

For Lord Oxford, Anne's next affinity made a less convenient place of rendezvous than Finch's London house had been. Anne went to live in Woodstock with Sir Henry Lee, an aging courtier who had once been the Queen's Champion and very handsome in his heyday. His wife had died, and through family connections, he seems to have found Anne, or possibly it was the other way round. She came to him and stayed. It is hard to tell just when she first appeared in his life, but there is evidence that he had known her in her early years at Court, because her initials are engraved on his armour worn when he was the Queen's Champion. Anne gave Sir Henry a son, also named Henry, and later known both as Henry Vavasor and as Henry Freeman.

It would seem that Lord Oxford reacted vehemently to the fact of his own son's continuing to stay with his mother, who was living "in open adultery" with a man twice her age. In this Sonnet 67, his frustration is expressed:

Ah! wherefore with infection should he live,
And with his presence grace impiety,
That sin by him advantage should achieve,
And lace itself with his society?

Why should false painting imitate his cheek,
And steal dead seeing of his living hue?
Why should poor beauty indirectly seek
Roses of shadow, since his rose is true?
Why should he live, now Nature bankrupt is,
Beggar'd of blood to blush through lively veins?
For she hath no exchequer now but his,
And, proud of many, lives upon his gains.
  O, him she stores, to show what wealth she had
  In days long since, before these last so bad.

Lord Oxford would have taken the child away but the mother refused to part with him. And well she might, for young Edward was becoming a source of riches to her. This is gleaned from the fact that it is known that Lord Oxford was selling off his estates almost recklessly at this time in order, it is believed, to shower luxuries upon his little boy.

The lad must have inherited the combined charm of both his father and his mother. We do not have far to look to find him in the plays, most recognizably in the character of Faulconbridge. The play, *King John*, is based upon an earlier drama in two parts which appeared anonymously in London about 1591, the lengthy title of the first part being: *The Troublesome Raigne of Iohn King of England, with the discouerie of King Richard Cordelions Base sonne (vulgarly named, The Bastard Fawconbridge)*: etc. However, the play we know as Shakespeare's *King John* differs considerably from its predecessor, chiefly in the buildup of the character of Faulconbridge. The dramatist introduced Faulconbridge wherever he could in the later play, giving him the last lines in every act except the third. He has, indeed, drawn the character of The Bastard as strong, spirited, and recognisable. Moreover, the Faulconbridge of *King John* shows a cynical humor and a certain satirical playfulness that is known to be characteristic of Lord Oxford himself. Is it not conceivable that he was drawing a portrait of his son projected into maturity? In the first act he may indeed be repeating some of his son's own words when, for example, Faulconbridge speaks to his mother as perhaps young Edward had been heard to speak to *his* mother, Anne (Act I, sc. 1, ll 260-70)

> Madam, I would not wish a better father.
> Some sins do bear their privilege on earth,
> And so do yours; your fault was not your folly.
> .... Ay, my mother,
> With all my heart I thank thee for my father!

Anne, meanwhile, was receiving from old Sir Henry Lee the devotion she never could inspire in her previous lovers, and which she hardly deserved. Sir Henry seems to have been plagued with either rheumatism or perhaps a stroke, and it was difficult for him to write. But being an Elizabethan, write he did, and copiously, in his letters referring to Anne as his "dearest Deare."

The lad Edward remained with his mother and old Sir Henry at Woodstock until he was fifteen when his father arranged for him to go to the University of Leyden, where he could receive much the same education that he would have had at his father's university, Cambridge. The youth was placed under the guardianship of Lord Oxford's intimate friend and cousin, Sir Francis Vere. This illustrious hero was then commander-in-chief of the English forces still fighting the war with Spain in the Netherlands.

It was not long before the young student left the university to enter the armed services under the command of his guardian. He was appointed a Captain of Pikemen. Then came the news to England that he had been decorated for gallantry in action. A true Vere! How proud his father would have been!

In the following reign Edward Vere was knighted by King James.

To return to the story of his mother, Anne Vavasor, she was taking care of the old man, Sir Henry Lee, who writes that through her "loving care and dilligence I do through God's goodness continue the longer." He invites a friend to come to visit, adding that if he came, "none would be more glad than Mrs. Vavasor."[17]

But even Anne's loving care could not keep the old man alive forever. On February 12th, 1611, Sir Henry died. Leaving no legal heir, he had settled on Anne a sum of £600 a year, "during her life;" and also she was to have life use of the house of Lee's Rest and some land at Spelsburg, this also for her lifetime, only she is told to leave "the house and goods she hath at her death as good as now they are."[18]

Then Sir Henry arranged to leave quite a sum of money for the erection of his own tomb in the chancel of Quarrendon parish church, as well as £ 50 for the burial there of "Mrs. anne Vavasor, alias Finch." He also wished to have a stone engraved with an inscription to the effect that Anne had lived with him in love and "Death could not part them but here they rest within one cell."

But Sir Henry's well-laid plan misfired. The ecclesiastical authorities would not hear of Anne's burial in the chancel of a consecrated church. And furthermore, the testator had not reckoned with Anne, who was very much alive.[19]

Recently there has come to light documentary proof of this story. It happened because Sir Henry left no immediate heir. In the Public Record Office in London there has been found a paper relating to a suit brought by a distant Lee cousin against Anne Vavasor, alleging that she omitted certain items from the Inventory of Sir Henry's estate.[20] In a deposition dated "24 August, 1612," beginning: "Sir Edward Veere, Knight," and signed: "Edward Veere" at the foot of each of its two pages, the deponent's age is given as "32 years or thereabout," which would prove that he was born in 1581, the time of the court scandal. Moreover, he refers to his mother as "the said Anne" and also to Henry Vavasor, Anne's son by Sir Henry, as his brother.

In this deposition, Sir Edward claims to know the parties concerned in the suit on both sides, and he "did know Sir Henry . . . when he lived." Sir Henry had once given him an embroidered cloak, an old one of his own; and later "said Anne," at her own expense, and at the deponent's request, had made it into "furniture" for a bed—now part of the disputed property. Sir Edward tells that once "wanting money to supply some occasion," he had asked his mother for £30, who "not being so well provided at that time spake to the said Sir Henry Lee for the same;" and Sir Henry had sent him the £30 by a servant, which he "refused to take as a gift from the said Sir Henry Lee," but "being then at Sir Henry Lee's house, he offered to repay him in Holland cloth or Rhenish wine from the Low Countries"—"whereto the said Sir Henry Lee answered saying: 'As it pleases you Mr. Vere.' "

Afterward he sent the amount in some form to Sir Henry and he had "heard his mother the said Anne say that it was "accounted in the said Inventory;" but both at that time, and "at other times," he had also sent Holland cloth to the said Anne "for her own use."

He also said that he had been in Woodstock after Sir Henry's death, and remembered that, at the division of his plate, there was one "charger" (a large flat dish) which his brother Henry claimed as having been given to him at his christening by the said Sir Henry. Whereupon it was delivered to him.[21]

Returning once more to Anne herself, the pseudo widow had no intention of being buried in the church chancel with her benefactor—at least, not yet. For in 1613 she married one Sir R. Warburton. She does not appear in history again until 1618. On August 8th of that year, John Chamberlain wrote to Dudley Carleton:

> Mrs. Vavasor, old Sir Henry Lee's woman, is like to be called in question for having two husbands now alive. Young Sir Henry Lee (a cousin of "the old one") the wild oats of Ireland, hath obtained the confiscation of her, if he can prove it without touching her life.

The bigamy case came before the High Commission and

dragged on into a long-drawn-out legal tangle which was not ended till February 1st, 1622, when the judge condemned Anne to pay a fine of £2,000, adding:

> We are inclined to temper the condemnation from public severity of the law with our royal mercy, and grant her dispensation from public penitence or other bodily penalty.

That judge must have come under the influence of Anne's charm.

Anne Vavasor lived on to be over ninety, fascinating, we suppose, even in old age. After the decease of her famous lovers, however, there was little of interest to record about her life.

So exits from our stage the woman who has perhaps the most lasting monument of any courtesan in history: a few precious sonnets now known to the world as Shakespeare's.

Meanwhile, one of the most sympathetic characters in all of the Shakespeare plays is "the Bastard," Faulconbridge, in *King John.*

Sir Edward Vere, like his famous father, became a playwright, the heroes of his dramas, it is interesting to note, being almost always illegitimate sons. Sir Edward was killed in action in the Battle of Bois-le-Duc. His funeral was attended, among others, by Henry Wriothesley, Third Earl of Southampton, and Henry de Vere, Eighteenth Earl of Oxford. Each of these noblemen had had a tenuous relationship with the deceased.

Notes To Chapter V

1. *Love's Labour's Lost,* Act III, sc. 1, ll. 207-8.
2. Charlton and Dorothy Ogburn, *This Star of England.*
3. *Sonnet 128.*
4. Looney, *The Poems of Edward de Vere,* No. VII.

5. Dorothy and Charlton Ogburn, Jr., in *Shakespeare, the Man Behind the Name*, p. 241, quoting the Rawlinson MS. Note the echo metaphor taken straight from Arthur Golding's *Translation of Ovid's Metamorphoses.*

6. Ward, *The 17th Earl of Oxford,* p. 228.

7. The Ogburns, *This Star of England.*

8. *Eclogue, In numtias clarissimi D. Edoardi Vere,* translated by B. M. Ward in *The Seventeenth Earl of Oxford,* p. 60. From Hatfield MSS. Cal. XIII.

9. *Sonnet 122.* After one studies the historical background, this is one poem of whose authorship one can feel reasonably sure.

10. Chapter IV.

11. Ogburn and Ogburn, *This Star of England,* p. 306.

12. *Romeo and Juliet* was revised many times and updated in later years.

13. Cecilie Goff, *Three Generations of a Loyal House.*

14. Chapter IV.

15. Chapter III.

16. Young Edward seems to have inherited the rosy cheeks of his mother.

17. E. K. Chambers, *Sir Henry Lee, An Elizabethan Portrait.*

18. Ibid.

19. Ibid.

20. The scholarly researcher who discovered this document and the contents thereof was the late Charles Wisner Barrell. See Shakespeare Fellowship Newsletter, (Vol. III, No. 3, April, 1942) quoting from Town Depositions, C. 24.379. The story also retold in the *Shakespeare Authorship Review,* No. 15, Spring, 1966.

21. Ibid.

Chapter VI

HIS SECOND WIFE

Let still the woman take
An elder than herself; so wears she to him,
So sways she level in her husband's heart.
Twelfth Night, Act II, sc. 4, ll. 15-17

There must have been much gossip in London social circles as to who might be the lovely Maid in Waiting to the Queen who had captivated the heart of the forty-two-year-old widower, that glamorous man of the world so many noble ladies were eager to ensnare. She was Mistress Elizabeth Trentham, an heiress from Staffordshire. Her father was Sir Thomas Trentham of Rocester, and *his* father had been granted the lands of the Abbey of Rocester by King Henry VIII upon the dissolution of the monasteries. Elizabeth Trentham was beautiful. A gossippy courtier's letter tells that

> Mistress Trentham is as fair, Mistress Edgecumbe as modest, Mistress Radcliffe as comely and Mistress Garrat as jolly as ever.

Her marriage to the Earl of Oxford must have been sanctioned by the Queen; indeed, it could not have taken place without her sanction, as previously noted. But that majestic lady was older now, and softening a little in her attitude toward potential rivals.

At about this time, 1590, Lord Oxford disposed of most of his real estate in London with the exception of "the Gate House" and a few acres in Covent Garden.

From old records it is learned that the bridegroom took his young Countess to live in Stoke Newington, then a suburban village. In the neighborhood were two playhouses closely associated with Shakespeare, i.e., Burbage's, called "the Theatre," and another not far off, called "the Curtain," where "Lord Oxford's Boys" were playing until the year 1588.

In the Parish Register of the little church at Stoke Newington there is record of the birth and christening of Lord and Lady Oxford's son and heir:

> 1593 Henrye, Viscount Bulbecke sonne to the right Honourable Edward Vere Earle of Oxenforde was borne the XXIIII of february 1592 and christened the XXIst day of march in the yere 1593.[1]

Sonnet No. 126 would appear to be Lord Oxford's exuberant tribute to this long-awaited heir:

O thou, my lovely boy, who in thy power
Dost hold Time's fickle glass, his sickle hour;
Who hast by waning grown, and therein show'st
Thy lovers withering as thy sweet self grow'st;
If Nature, sovereign mistress over wrack,
As thou goest onwards, still will pluck thee back
She keeps thee to this purpose, that her skill
May time disgrace and wretched minutes kill.
Yet fear her, O thou minion of her pleasure!
She may detain, but not still keep, her treasure:
  Her audit, though delay'd, answer'd must be,
  And her quietus is to render thee.

Was ever babe so welcomed into this world!

It is on record that in 1596 the Earl and Countess and their small son moved to Hackney, to an estate called King's Place, which had been a royal residence since the time of Henry VIII, and King Henry, King Edward VI and Queen Elizabeth had in turn held Court there. Sometime after 1583 the house passed into the hands of private owners, among them Lord Vaux.[2]

King's Place seems to have had a reputation for harboring Roman Catholic priests who were forbidden by act of Parliament in 1584 to live in England unless they had been ordained there prior to Queen Elizabeth's accession. That King's Place had been such a refuge is proved by a book printed in 1603 called *A Declaration of Egregious Popish Impostures* (published by James Roberts "dwelling in the Barbican"). In this book there is frequent mention of Lord Vaux's place at Hackney, and it is found that Lord Vaux was often prosecuted for not attending the "reformed Church;" indeed, he was more than once imprisoned and sometimes fined. Also local tradition has it that King's Place contained "a priest's hole."

When Lord and Lady Oxford moved into their new home they took in Lord Vaux's widow, Lady Catherine Vaux, as a resident.

The Countess Elizabeth had bought the estate with her Trentham money. It is tempting to give rein to the imagination and try to picture how life went on in this quiet country house behind its high brick wall in suburban London during the last years in the life of the distinguished Earl.

This was the time of the greatest productivity of the Shakespeare plays, many of them having had their premier either in Burbage's Theatre, or in the Curtain, both playhouses nearby Hackney. These were the years of the publication of three editions of *King Richard III;* three editions of *King Richard II;* three editions of *King Henry IV, Part One;* two editions of *Romeo and Juliet;* two editions of *King Henry V;* two editions of *Hamlet;* and single editions of *Love's Labour's Lost; Titus Andronicus; A Midsummer Night's Dream; The Merchant of Venice; King Henry IV, Part II; Much Ado About Nothing;* and *The Merry Wives of Windsor.* This adds up to twenty-two editions, or an average of over three editions every year.

The last was the 1604 *Hamlet,* corrected and enlarged to almost half again as much as in the 1603 edition. *Hamlet!* The story of Lord Oxford himself!

Yet in spite of all his literary work the noble Earl went into London to attend Parliament at Westminster whenever it was expected of him, using his deputy only twice during all the years he lived in Hackney.

In letters written from King's Place to his brother-in-law, Sir Robert Cecil, Lord Oxford twice refers to his "infirmity." The first letter is in regard to his daughter Bridget's marriage. He closes with these words:

> I am sorry that I have not an able body which might have served to attend on her Majesty in the place where she is, being especially there, whither, without any other occasion than to see your lordship I would always willingly go.[3]

In another letter he writes of his inability to do as much as he would like to do:

> By reason of mine infirmity I cannot come among you as often as I wish, and by reason of my house is not so near that at every occasion I can be present as were fit, whether I do not hear at all from you or at least at the latest: as this other day happened to me, receiving a letter at nine of the clock not to fail at eight of the same to be at Whitehall; which being impossible yet I hasted so much as I came to follow you into Ludgate, though through the press of people and horses I could not reach your company as I desired, but followed as I might.[4]

Late mails! Traffic problems! How modern all that sounds, even in Elizabethan language! And what was his "infirmity"? Was it an aggravation of the painful wound Lord Oxford had suffered in the duel with Sir Thomas Knyvet? Or was it more serious trouble due to his advancing years? The letters do not tell. They do show, however, that he seems to be supremely happy writing and living with his young Countess in the country.

There was only one desire unfulfilled: to have more funds at his disposal. Even the annual grant from the Queen did not cover expenses of the luxuries this nobleman felt were necessities. If only he might have one of the honorary posts with large emolument at the Queen's disposal, such as many another courtier was then enjoying! In 1600 he wrote to Sir Robert Cecil of his wish to be appointed governor of the Isle of Jersey. He seems despondent, being doubtful of receiving the appointment:

> Although my bad success in former suits to Her Majesty have given me cause to bury my hopes in the deep abyss and bottom of despair, rather than not to attempt after so many trials made in vain and so many opportunities escaped, the effects of fair words or fruits of golden promises; yet for that I cannot believe but that there hath been always a true correspondence of word and intention in Her Majesty.[5]

But the post he wanted went to Sir Walter Raleigh.

Again Lord Oxford tried for the appointment of President of Wales, reminding the Queen "of my youth, time and fortune spent in her Court, and her favours and promises which drew me on without mistrust the more to presume in my own expenses."[6] But the Queen commissioned someone else. Elizabeth Tudor never quite forgave her "Phoebus" for preferring another woman to herself.[7]

As Premier Earl of the Realm Lord Oxford was the presiding peer at the treason trial of the Earls of Essex and Southampton, which took place on February 18, 1601. This trial must have been a tremendous ordeal for him, for he had known the Earl of Southampton intimately; indeed, for three years and more the younger nobleman had been considered as a husband for Lord Oxford's daughter, Elizabeth.[8] And it is believed that he had dedicated his first long poems, *Venus and Adonis* and *The Rape of Lucrece*, to this young man.[9]

What memories must have raced through his mind as he drove in his coach from the country up Bishopsgate to East Chepe to

Ludgate Hill, passing around St. Paul's, then on to Fleet Street and the Strand where he had lived as a young student. At Charing Cross the coach would turn left into King Street passing between the royal orchards and the tiltyard, and then by the palace buildings of Whitehall where he had spent so much of his youth, and so to Westminster Hall, where the two earls were to be tried.

The trial lasted eleven hours and Essex had been a difficult defendant impudently answering back the learned lawyers. Essex was condemned to death, the only appropriate punishment for his treachery, while Southampton was sentenced to prison for life.[10]

In 1603 the old Queen died. In another chapter has been discussed Lord Oxford's emotional reaction to her passing. It is assumed that he was one of the six earls honored to walk beside her bier in the funeral procession, and that later within the Abbey, by right of heredity he bore the golden canopy above his Queen for the last time.[11] Again what memories would have pressed in upon him as he thought back to those early years at Court when her Majesty had twitted him about being a bastard, and then later when, like all the other courtiers, he had fancied himself in love with her, an affection which she seemed to have returned.[12]

Lord Oxford left Hackney again to attend the coronation of the new king. There is a tradition that he had already met King James at Wilton House,[13] seat of the Earl of Pembroke, when the royal procession had halted there on its way down from Edinburgh to London. At Wilton House on December 2nd, the new King had seen his first Shakespeare play, *As You Like It*.[14]

It is significant that shortly after his accession, King James renewed the annuity of £1,000 to Lord Oxford in exactly the same words that Queen Elizabeth had used in the original grant. This seems to indicate that the payment was to be considered a reward for some exceptional service rendered by the distinguished Earl to benefit the kingdom. The history plays, which in the last decade had been pouring into publication, appear to be the likeliest reason for the annuity.[15] Furthermore, the King granted to Lord Oxford the bailiwick, or custody of the Forest of Essex, and also the keepership of Havering House, both properties which for centuries had pertained to the Earls of Oxford, but which Elizabeth Tudor in her infinite wisdom had seen fit to withhold from him.

To appreciate fully these last happy years of Lord Oxford's life at King's Place, one must turn to his Countess. The noble Earl and his beautiful young wife can be pictured supping by candle light. Since the dining hall at King's Place was small compared to those in the great country houses, it is unlikely that there would have been a head table with other tables at right angles for the retainers. More likely there was just one beautiful carved wooden table in the center of the room. By mellow candlelight the silver service would be gleaming on the white damask cloth, especially the silver fruit dish with the little feet. The meal would have been very specially prepared, for Lord Oxford was a gourmand; the servants quietly efficient. The lovely lady presiding would be wearing one of her black satin gowns with the single rope of pearls about her neck, the pearls a gift from her adoring husband and very precious to her.

The Earl was still handsome in his fifties, his doublet of expert tailoring, for he had always been particular about his apparel.[16] His nobleman's starched lace ruff would set off his aristocratic head and fine features, his auburn hair receding at the temples but only slightly gray. On his left thumb would be the seal ring with the eye, ears, snout and tusk of a boar's head, the cognizance of the Earls of Oxford.[17] His outstanding feature would be those beautiful penetrating dark eyes, sometimes so sad, the next moment teasing and merry.

The Countess rings a little gilt bell to call her servants. After a long day creating dramas and rewriting old ones, how refreshing it would have been to the playwright to sit down thus peacefully at table in the soft light in this setting of quiet luxury, his beautiful Countess across the board from him, so serene, so sympathetic, so eager to help him!

The serenity of the Countess would have been unruffled by the fact that she seems to have had rather troublesome servants. In the Middlesex Session rolls we learn that one Agnes Thomas was "robbed of various garments" while staying at King's Place. The offender was sentenced to hanging. Again, "recognizance is taken by James Freeman of Hackney, gent, servant to the Countess of Oxford, to appear at the next gaol [jail] delivery to witness against Rose Jones committed on suspicion of a felony done to the said Countess. . . ."[18]

Do we know this lady herself? One may say with authority that she was utterly devoted to her husband in spite of his being so many years her senior. She also seems to have been most friendly with her step-daughter, Elizabeth Countess of Derby, who was about her age, a friendship begun while both young ladies were serving in attendance on the Queen. There is record that the two couples, the Oxfords and the Derbys, visited back and forth with one another. And this is important, because the Earl of Derby is one of the dramatists claimed to be the author of the Shakespeare plays. The Earl of Derby in his day did have quite a reputation as a playwright,[19] though unfortunately none of the dramas ascribed to him have been preserved.

Beside her lord and master and her step-daughter it is known that Elizabeth was devoted to her only child, Henry, the young Viscount Bolebec.

She seems to have been a deeply religious lady, this Countess of Oxford, leaning more to the Catholic doctrine than to that of the "reformed Church," even as we have reason to believe her husband did also toward the end of his life. Yet it is recalled that he had formally renounced Catholicism when he realized that such allegiance meant disloyalty to his Queen.[20]

But this Countess loved pretty clothes and jewelry, too, and in picturing her with her husband at King's Place one sees her always with a certain elegance, her gown of finest style and fabric, and everything about her the very best. This would have been one of the reasons why Lord Oxford had been first attracted to her; he, too, always demanded the best.

But these happy days were destined not to last. For in 1604 Lord Oxford contracted one of the dreadful fevers then raging in England. When he realized that he was about to die, he made arrangements to grant custody of the Forest of Essex, that land which had belonged to his ancestors since before the Conquest, to his intimate cousin, Sir Francis Vere, who after campaigning in the Low Countries with his brother, Horace, had now returned to England to settle down. It was understandable that Lord Oxford should donate this property to Sir Francis for it was he who had been guardian to Edward's son by Anne Vavasor, and the dying Earl had many reasons to be grateful to him.[21]

But Sir Francis was to have only half the grant; the other half was to be given to Francis Lord Norris, Lord Oxford's new son-in-law, as part of Bridget's dowry. There is no record of Edward de Vere granting dowries to his other two sons-in-law, but both Lord Derby and Lord Montgomery were extremely affluent noblemen.[22]

How tenderly the young countess would have nursed her husband in this, his last illness! But in spite of her love and care, he died the 24th of June, 1604, and was buried in the parish church at Hackney. He was fifty-four years old.

In 1609 the widowed Countess was forced to sell King's Place and go to live with her son in greatly reduced circumstances in Cannon Row, Westminster, between the old Palace of St. Stephen and the Earl of Derby's residence.[23]

It was while the Countess was living here that young Henry gave his mother the trouble she complains about in her letters. Henry being the only son of a father old enough to be his grandfather, and now the only child of a doting widowed mother, it is not surprising that he seems to have been rather spoiled. He was only eleven when his father died, and doubtless Elizabeth de Vere showered affection upon him to comfort her own grief during these years when she first faced life without her dear lord. As Henry grew into young manhood, he became known as quite a rake. Here is what his mother wrote about him when he was seventeen:

> Under pretence of kindred Hunt insinuated himself into my son's acquaintance, drawing him from his lessons to course with greyhounds; taking him to taverns, plays and bad company; and teaching him swearing, and filthy and ribald talk. He withdrew him from my house in Canon Row to a disorderly life in Essex, hunting in deer parks, and other like disorderly actions. . . . He has . . . borrowed money in my son's name to his dishonour, and lives wholly on my son's purse . . . and causes him to spend all his time in plays at an ordinary in Milford Lane, not coming home until 1 or 2 in the morning.[24]

It was doubtless to get her son away from "Hunt's" influence that Lady Oxford was determined to take Trentham money to finance the repurchase of Castle Hedingham, the ancestral seat of the Earls of Oxford, for her son, now the Eighteenth Earl. Her husband some years before had been forced to sell that estate to his three daughters and their grandfather, Lord Burghley. The Countess would have wanted to take Henry right out of the disreputable life he was living and away from the influence of those who were "teaching him swearing, and filthy and ribald talk." The tiny village of Castle Hedingham would have seemed to her the ideal retreat.

There is a record that Elizabeth's brother, Fraunces Trentham, advanced £10,000 "to clear incumbrances on the Oxford Estates. In consideration whereof, 8 July 1609, by deed inrolled, etc. etc." Lord Oxford's three daughters acting together conveyed Castle Hedingham to their step-mother. She, poor lady, had to get "a private act" to sell "the manner of Bretts, and farm at Plaistow in West Hamm . . ." to help finance the purchase.

If only Edward de Vere could have known that his own son and heir would one day be master of Castle Hedingham!

And how is it that we know so much about this lovely Countess? Ironically, it is from her will,[25] dated February 15th, 1612, proving that it was drawn shortly before her death. One of the executors is her brother mentioned above, who appears to have been her advisor in business affairs.

The will opens with the pious lady commending her soul to her Maker in florid religious prose. She proceeds to record her desire to be buried at Hackney near her husband's tomb. From this and other phrases it is apparent that her heart was there, where she had spent the happiest years of her life with her lord.

Then before any bequests are mentioned, this strict business-like lady lists her debts. Whether these were incurred by her husband and still outstanding after eight years, is not known. It might be kinder to his memory to consider them incidental to his last illness. The Countess lists her creditors: "Namely unto my brother Fraunces Trentham of Rocester in the Countie of Stafford Esquire four hundred pounds." To "Mr. Ferne," two hundred pounds. To "Mr. Prescott, the goldsmith in Cheapside, upon pawn of part of my plate now remaining with him, Two hundred and odd pounds." She asks her executors to clear these debts and any others outstanding, begging "forbearance" of her creditors in accepting one tenth of the amount due "until such time as my said Executors can raise money . . . out of such estates and means as I shall leave unto them for that purpose."

Then comes a touching paragraph.

> Item. I give unto my dear and loving son Henry de Vere Earl of Oxenford to be kept by him as a remembrance of my motherly love unto him my rope of great pearls, my new Jewel, my thirteen diamond buttons, and all those garments, Cloaks, bedding, and household stuff fine diaper and damask linen.

All of these were to be given to Henry when he became twenty-six or when he married, whichever happened first. Henry was twenty in 1612 when the will was drawn up.

Next the Countess remembers her "dear and loving mother," who is to receive "my silver cawdle cup my little gilt bell my silver fruit dish with the feet and my black satin gown cut and laced." Perhaps the silverware had been inherited from her mother's side of the family.

Elizabeth bequeathed to one sister fifteen new pieces of silver, a black velvet gown laced, a black satin gown, and black "taffitie gowne with silver lace," a black and silver "chamblet gowne" [i.e., nightgown], a "crimson velvet petticoat," kirtles of white cloth of silver, and a "collar of cloth of silver."

Another sister fares less well but must make do with "my borders of rubies and diamonds," a white satin gown, a plain black satin gown, a petticoat of cloth of gold and a kirtle of white satin with gold lace.

Then the Countess remembers her god-daughter, Vere Trentham, by "my jewel enamelled with red and diamonds in it." She mentions a young girl she had expected to educate, Marie Trentham, who is to receive "Five Hundred pounds towards her preferment in marriage," but this bequest is to be withheld till all debts are paid, and also all expenses of her funeral.

Another kinswoman, Lady Manwering, is to receive "my gilt standing cup with cover"; "my worthy friend, Sir Edward Moore, my long silver basin with the ewer to it."

To Lady Walter she wills a kirtle of black cloth of gold; to Mrs. Kibbe, a "black gown and kirtle my calimanco gown and my piece of tabyn of about twenty yards."

The Countess then remembers her husband's family with this bequest: "To my loving cousin, John Vere, Esquire, my deep silver bowl." This relative is not identified further, but he seems to be the de Vere in whom she places the greatest confidence. Much of the linen and household goods, not to mention her most precious jewels destined for her son Henry are temporarily stored in John de Vere's house.

In the same sentence with John the testatrix mentions "my nephew Mr. Peregrine Berty," leaving him twenty pounds in gold. This item presents another mystery concerning those last years at Hackney. Why does the Countess leave no treasure to her sister-in-law, Lady Willoughby d'Eresby? The answer suggested is that in those lean years when Lord Willoughby d'Eresby's resources had dwindled in the service of his country, Elizabeth Trentham de Vere may have helped the family financially in the name of her husband. But why should young Peregrine be singled out for a bequest above his brothers? He was only the third son. Of course, he might have been an intimate friend of her son Henry, about his age. Or he may have been the Bertie blessed with that subtle de Vere magnetism which, like the personality of his uncle Edward, endeared him to everyone with whom he came in contact. Young men are like that and the youthful Countess was probably as susceptible as aunts have ever been through the ages.

The next item betrays Elizabeth's anxiety for her son and his estate:

> I give unto my good friend John Wright of Gray's Inn esquire one hundred pounds presuming he will perform his best endeavor to preserve the rights of my son's estate and to assist him with his best endeavor to preserve the rights of my son and to advance his good fortunes and to increase his virtue and honor.

John Wright must have been a staunch friend for the Countess to lean upon, for he is also chosen one of the executors of her will. It should be noted that he is a barrister of Gray's Inn, from which Lord Oxford himself had matriculated. Very likely he had been a special friend of her husband.

The ensuing items tell much about the style of living to which the Countess was accustomed. She mentions certain of her servants with warmth and affection, and it seems that they may have stayed by her from the days of affluence at Hackney through the sad time of her widowhood and financial stress. Here they are with the bequests left to them:

To Margerie Flower, "a waiting woman," a tawny satin gown, five pounds and half of "all my wearing linen about my body."

To Marie, her chambermaid, five pounds and the other half of the underwear.

To her laundress, forty shillings.

To Katherine Three pounds.

To Gallantyne the Frenchman that serveth me, five pounds.

> To Thomas, my tailor dwelling with me, five marks.
> To Thomas my coachman, five marks.
> To John Bill my late servant, five pounds.

And then this thoughtful bequest:

> Item I give to my dumb man yearlie during his life (?) pounds to be paid to him by my Executors quarterly at the four most usual feasts of the year, by even and equal portions.

The Countess leaves bequests to hospitals and prisons, Newgate and Ludgate, respectively, and to the hospitals of Southwark and St. Bartholomews.

Then come these characteristic Elizabethan bequests:

> Item I will that there be distributed on the day of my burial to the poor people of the parish wherein I shall happen to die Ten pounds and to the poor of the said parish of Hackney Twenty pounds. Also I give to the poor of Castle Hedingham (sic) in Essex XX (pounds) to be distributed at the discretion of my Executors.

There follows a most interesting item:

> ... all that the great Parks of Hedingham ad Castrum aforesaid and certain parts and parcels of the Castle Park and the little Park there as also the Site and precinct of the late Priory there and all the lands Tenements and hereditaments to the same late belonging and appertaining And also the Rectory or parsonage of Water Belchampe within the said County of Essex To have and to hold etc. etc. ... from the feast of St. Michael the Archangel now last past until the full end and term of Twenty years from thenceforth next ensuing by and under certain yearly Rentes as in and by the said several deed indented.

In other words, the rent of these lands was to be used to pay the debts of the testatrix. The list is interesting as showing the extent of the hereditary estates of the Earls of Oxford in Essex. Edward de Vere had been forced to sell all this, both land and estates, several years earlier when he was in financial need. Then his Countess when a widow repurchased the lands with her Trentham funds on behalf of her son, the Eighteenth Earl of Oxford, only to be forced to sell them again to satisfy her creditors. This is a commentary on English country life that has been going on for centuries, perhaps never more than in the present day.

The Countess further wishes to have any outstanding sums of rents or other funds bequeathed to her son, Henry, Earl of Oxenford, or to his son, or if he had no children these funds were to be turned over to the Countess Elizabeth's brother, Fraunces.

Later in the will she adds that since she has "given [her son] no allowance for the same," she wills him two hundred marks "of lawful english money and also the sum of two hundred pounds more for a legacy."

This will makes fascinating reading, it is so full of the flavor of Seventeenth Century England and casts considerable light upon the family relations of this clan. Elizabeth Trentham was a good wife for Edward de Vere to have chosen.

But why were there no remembrances for Elizabeth's three step-daughters, at least one of whom was an intimate friend of the Countess? The answer again can be only conjectured. Each of the de Vere daughters had married a wealthy nobleman and each had also inherited quite an estate from her grandfather, Lord Burghley, who died a rich man. Besides, it was not de Vere money to be distributed, but Trentham money. And anyway, this is the affair of the Countess and not of her biographer.

What is learned from the will is that she and the Earl had lived in their mansion of King's Place, Hackney, in quiet elegance and reposeful comfort. In remembrance of those happy days the first item in the will of the countess reads:

> I joyfully commit my body to the earth from whence it was taken, desiring to be buried in the Church of Hackney within the Countie of Middlesex, as near unto the body of my said late dear and noble lord and husband as may be and that to be done with as little pomp and ceremony as possibly may be.

She was. She died in 1612 soon after the will was drawn.

In her last wish do we not hear the echo of Caesar Augustus' words on learning of the death of Cleopatra:

> She shall be buried by her Anthony.

* * *

But the mysteries implicit in the story of this elusive Earl do not perish with his death. The last mystery of all concerns his place of burial.

From the will of his Countess one may say with certainty that Lord Oxford was buried in the parish church of St. Augustine, Hackney. Indeed, from the records, there is every reason to believe that the Earl and Countess were laid side by side in an altar tomb in this church.

Yet Edward de Vere's first cousin, Percivall Golding, son of his beloved uncle and tutor, Arthur Golding, has drawn up a *Table of the honourable progeny of the Earles of Oxenforde*, in which there is this notation:[26]

> Anne, daughter of William Cecil; she lieth buried by her mother Lady Mildred Burghleigh at Westminster.
>
> Edward de Vere; he died at his house at Hackney in the month of June, 1604, and Lieth buried at Westminster.

This is a striking statement, coming from a close relative of Lord Oxford, who must have been sure what he was writing about. Does it mean that Lord Oxford's body was buried in

Hackney and then at some later date re-interred at Westminster Abbey? This possibility no one has yet been able to trace.[27]

Ben Jonson had written of Shakespeare: *Thou art a monument without a Tomb,* which could not apply to William Shakespeare of Stratford, because at the time Jonson penned these words William of Stratford did have a tomb in Holy Trinity Church there.

Another contemporary in a position to know evidently believed that Lord Oxford in the guise of "Shakespeare" was buried in Westminster Abbey. He is one William Basse, a retainer of Lord Wintman of Thame, who was frequently at the home of Bridget de Vere, Lady Norris, and her husband Lord Norris, Earl of Berkshire, also holding the title of Viscount of Thame. William Basse wrote:

> Renowned Spenser lie a thought more nigh
> To learned Beaumont, and Beaumont lie
> A little nearer Chaucer to make room
> For Shakespeare in your threfold fourfold tomb.
> To lodge all four in one bed make shift
> Until Domesday, for hardly will a fifth
> Betwixt this day and that, by fate be slain.[28]

Nothing can be proven in Hackney because the church is now demolished with the exception of its beautiful square stone tower, reminiscent of the tower of the church at Earl's Colne, Essex. So this mystery, perhaps the least of all those pertaining to the Seventeenth Earl of Oxford, must remain, like the others, unsolved.

But Percivall Golding, whose family *Table* first brought up the question of his burial place, has composed a most appropriate epitaph to his cousin, the noble Earl:

> Edward de Vere, only son of John born 12 day[29] of April, 1550, Earl of Oxenford, High chamberlain, Lord Bolebec, Sandford, Badlesmere, Steward to the King's

Majesty that now is. Of whom I will only speak what all men's voices confirm; he was a man in mind and body absolutely accomplished with honourable endowments.[30]

Before leaving this chapter on Lord Oxford and his later years with his beloved wife, it is interesting to follow briefly the career of their only son, Henry, the Eighteenth Earl, who had caused his mother so much anxiety. Somebody, either his uncle, Fraunces Trentham, or John Wright of Gray's Inn, or perhaps his older sisters and their husbands—somebody must have taken Henry in hand, for he grew up to be a fine young man in whom both parents could have taken pride.

Henry took his undergraduate studies and his Master of Arts degree at Oxford and then matriculated at the Inner Temple. It may have been that Oxford was chosen for him instead of Cambridge, and the Inner Temple chosen for his law studies in preference to Gray's Inn, his father's Alma Mater, to distinguish him from his Cecil relatives, who were like Henry's father, Cambridge men and Members of Gray's Inn.

At some point in his career, probably after his university training, Henry went over to the Netherlands to be under the guardianship of Sir Horace Vere,[31] the close friend and cousin of his father, who, it is believed, named after him Prince Hamlet's boon companion, Horatio. Sir Horace had succeeded his brother,[32] Sir Francis Vere, as commander of the English forces in the Low Countries. When the States General granted a pension to the Commander, he made a request that it be continued after his death to his young ward and cousin, Henry. This was done.

And that spoiled young nobleman must have had redeeming features, for on November 15th, 1611, King James created him a Knight of the Bath, and in honor of his father, Keeper of Havering Park.[33] His mother lived just long enough to know of these signal honors conferred upon her heretofore wayward son.

However, Henry de Vere was later to incur the wrath of King James when he gallantly protected a young lady from the rude and unwelcome advances of the royal favorite, the Duke of Buckingham.

In January, 1624, Henry de Vere, now the Eighteenth Earl of Oxford, married the Lady Diana Cecil, who brought him a fortune. This lady was the half first cousin once removed of his step-sisters, being the daughter of the Earl of Exeter and granddaughter of Sir Thomas Cecil, Lord Burghley's older son. However, Henry could not long enjoy married life with his Countess.

Being a true Vere he longed for military service, and volunteered in the English forces still fighting in the Netherlands trying to recover the Palatinate from the Spaniards. This was in reality an effort on the part of the English and European Protestants to try to keep the Catholic Spaniards from becoming too strong.

The English were under the command of Sir Horace Vere. One learns that:

> There is much canvassing for appointments as officers in the new forces and many have flocked to Theobalds [now the King's residence], but the King has not vouchsafed to see them. The Earls of Oxford, Essex and Southampton are three of the Colonels, the fourth place is being contested for by Lord Willoughby and two other noblemen. Men of unusual rank seek to be officers in order to raise volunteer companies by their credit.[34]

Lord Willoughby was chosen—Robert Bertie, Baron Willoughby d'Eresby, the oldest son of the Lady Mary de Vere.[35] From the Countess of Oxford's will it is learned that Edward de Vere's family and his sister's were on friendly terms. It might have been pleasant for Henry de Vere and Robert Bertie to meet again over in the Low Countries.

The Earl of Southampton had once been a suitor for the hand of the Lady Elizabeth de Vere, Lord Oxford's oldest daughter.[36] He had also been an intimate friend of the Seventeenth Earl.

Upon the accession of King James he was released from the Tower, where he had been imprisoned by Queen Elizabeth because of his implication in the Essex Rebellion. Southampton was allowed to return to his family and thereafter lived the life of a soldier first, and later not only a patron of the arts, but also of the Virginia Company.[37]

In the British Museum there is an interesting old engraving of the young Earl of Oxford and the older Earl of Southampton, fiery soldiers in battle dress astride their rearing steeds. The juxtaposition is significant to those who recall their story.

There had been another Vere fighting under the command of Sir Horace: Sir Edward Vere, Lord Oxford's illegitimate son by Anne Vavasor.[38] The brothers, Edward and Henry, must have known one another somewhere, either in London or in the war zone, because there is a record that Henry was present at the funeral of Sir Edward Vere.

The fighting force in which Henry volunteered embarked from the mouth of the Thames in July, 1618, fearful that "the Dunkirkers" who had been active hereabouts, might harass them. However, they had a quiet uneventful crossing and arrived safely in Holland. This is a description of them:

> This spring gave birth to four brave regiments of foot (a new apparition in English history), 1,500 in each regiment, which were transported and trained in Holland under four gallant Colonels: being well-armed and exercised in Holland, they were ready to be marched into the field.[39]

This sounds more like a propaganda news release than a true record of the facts, for it completely ignores the terrible privations endured by the troops in the early part of the campaign. For two months they were encamped on damp low ground, their numbers dwindling daily from disease.

A more realistic account gave the true picture:

> Such a rabble of poor raw recruits were never seen, and they go so unwillingly that they must be rather driven than led.[40]

These privations took their toll of the strength of Elizabeth Trentham de Vere's son, so recently married to the Cecil heiress, and so eager for military glory. He was taken ill with one of the virulent fevers prevalent in the battle zone and died at the Hague in the autumn of 1625 before he was thirty-two years old. Unfortunately he left no children to carry on the famous name.

* * * * *

In 1626 Lord Willoughby d'Eresby sought to claim the title of Earl of Oxford by right of descent of his mother, who had been the daughter of the Sixteenth Earl. But the claim was disallowed, the title and earldom passing to another Vere cousin.

However, Robert Bertie was proclaimed Hereditary Lord Great Chamberlain, the wording of his appointment by the King being as follows:

> In consideration of the merits of Robert, Lord Willoughby, Beke, and Eresby, that he be Lord Great Chamberlain of England: and that he is the brave son of a brave, most noble father, and of great Loyalty to us. And also how much he merited by those services in the United Provinces, where he behaved as a valiant Knight, fit for command, and crowned his high birth, virtue, and wisdom by sweetness of behavior. . . .[41]

Also, because none but an Earl had ever held this high office, he was created Earl of Lindsey.

Since Edward, the Seventeenth Earl of Oxford, had left no de Vere grandson, it might have pleased him that his sister Mary's son would carry on the duties to the Sovereign for him.

Notes To Chapter VI

1. J. T. Looney, *The Seventeenth Earl of Oxford.*

2. The father of Lord Vaux, Thomas, Second Baron Vaux (1510-1556), was one of the minor Tudor poets. In Tottel's *Miscellany*, published in 1557, there is a poem of his entitled *The Aged Lover Renounces Love.* Three verses of this song somewhat garbled, are sung by the First Gravedigger in Hamlet. (Act V, sc. 1). The Earl of Oxford and Lord Vaux were near neighbors when the de Veres were living in Stoke Newington. It would have been natural that Lord Vaux would have shown the younger nobleman his father's poem. The MS. copy preserved in the British Museum has fourteen verses, all slightly ribald. We quote the three stanzas later "corrupted" by the First Gravedigger:

I loth that I did love,
In youth that I thought sweet,
As time requires: for my behove
Methinks they are not mete.

For Age with stealing steps
Hath clawed me with his crowch
And lusty "Youth" away he leaps,
As there had been none such.

A pickax and a spade,
And eke a shrouding sheet,
A house of clay for to be made
For such a guest most mete.

These verses are taken from the complete poem in *Reliques of Ancient English Poetry*, vol. I. The Preface notes that this was a popular song for ballad-singers of Shakespeare's time, "greatly altered and disguised" each time it was sung.

3. Hatfield MSS. Quoted by Looney, in *The Seventeenth Earl of Oxford.*

4. Ibid.

5. Ibid.

6. Ibid.

7. Chapter V.

8. Chapter VII.

9. Ibid.

10. Chapter VII.

11. Chapter IV.

12. Ibid.

13. The only authority for this statement appears to be a letter now lost mentioning that "the man Shakespeare" was at Wilton House during King James's first visit. A. L. Rowse, *William Shakespeare, A Biography*, p. 358. Inasmuch as Lord Oxford was a personal friend of the Earl and Countess of Pembroke, it seems reasonable to suppose that "the man Shakespeare" refers to him.

14. A. L. Rowse, *William Shakespeare.*

15. Chapter IV.

16. Chapter II.

17. This description taken from the Ashbourne Portrait. See Chapter IX.

18. Ward, *The Seventeenth Earl of Oxford.*

19. Chapter VII.

20. Chapter IV.

21. Chapter V.

22. Chapter VII.

23. In Elizabethan days the name of the street was spelled *Canon*, being the site of the houses of the Canons of St. Margaret's Westminster.

24. Looney.

25. Ibid., quoting State Papers, Elizabeth, Domestic.

26. H. Amphlett, *Who Was Shakespeare?*

27. The present writer questioned the Assistant Keeper of the Muniments in Westminster Abbey as to whether he had any

record of the reburial of the famous Earl in the Abbey. This gentleman courteously spent some time consulting ancient records, but could find no proof of the reinterment. Unfortunately the burial records of the Abbey do not reach as far back as 1613.

28. Quoted in Amphlett, *Who Was Shakespeare?*

29. According to the old calendar before the Gregorian Calendar was adopted. After that the date was known as April 23rd.

30. From the conclusion of Golding's *Table of Progeny*, quoted in Amphlett, *Who Was Shakespeare?*

31. We know Sir Horace, later Baron Vere of Tilbury, from his magnificent tomb in the North Transept of Westminster Abbey. His brother Francis lies in the same tomb. It is of marble, surrounded by four very handsome, very life-like soldiers, kneeling to hold up the black marble slab on which rests the armour of Sir Horace.

32. A point of interest to our story is that Myles Standish, the soldier who came over to America on the *Mayflower*, had seen military action in the Netherlands under Sir Horace Vere. A. L. Rowse, *The Elizabethans and America*, pp. 135-6.

33. Havering Park, Essex, had once been part of the estates of the Earls of Oxford. By the time of Edward, the Seventeenth Earl, it had reverted to the crown and was a favorite hideaway for Queen Elizabeth.

34. Fortesque Papers: Camden Society (new series) quoted in a private notebook.

35. Chapter II.

36. Chapter VII.

37. A. L. Rowse, *Shakespeare's Southampton*, p. 199.

38. Chapter V.

39. Quoted in War, *The Seventeenth Earl of Oxford*.

40. Ibid.

41. Goff, *Three Generations of a Loyal House*, p. 108.

Chapter VII
HIS DAUGHTERS

. . . all the daughters of my father's house.
Twelfth Night, Act II, sc. 4, l. 122

All three daughters of Edward de Vere and Ann Cecil led such interesting lives and married such interesting husbands that it is decidedly worthwhile to study them. There are, unfortunately, no portraits of any of these ladies, except possibly the effigies of the little girls praying on their mother's tomb in Westminster Abbey, though these are hardly likenesses. Therefore the only way one can come to know the young girls is to see the reactions of other people to them, and very occasionally to see their own responses.

The Lady Elizabeth de Vere

Elizabeth, the oldest of the three daughters, was the child born while her father was travelling on the Continent, and it was this little girl whose paternity was questioned. The fact that this daughter appears to be the closest to her father in his later years would seem to still that ugly rumor forever.[1]

The next story about Elizabeth is contained in the letter the Duchess of Suffolk wrote to her prospective daughter-in-law, the Lady Mary de Vere, suggesting that Mary's little niece be taken "to some neutral place" where her father could be with her yet not know who she was.[2] The Duchess was quite sure that if Lord Oxford could only see the little girl and see how beguiling she was, he would immediately wish to be reconciled with her mother. This shows that even as a small child Elizabeth was a real little personality, and blessed, no doubt, with the de Vere charm.

Lord Oxford, it is recalled, did finally return to his wife, Ann, so Elizabeth was to know a complete and natural home life at last, even to the joy of having two small sisters to play with. However, life in the home of the Earl and Countess may not have been entirely peaceful, for there is evidence of tension which the little girl would have felt even if she didn't understand the cause. Lord Oxford might have been difficult to live with; what genius is not? Also, as indicated, it is feared that both of the elder Cecils were interfering grandparents.[3]

As the Lady Elizabeth approached marriageable age (they married young in Elizabethan days!), there were a number of noble suitors for her hand. Lord Burghley was taking charge of the marriage negotiations. He tried to arrange a match for Elizabeth with the duke of Northumberland, as a letter to the Duchess of Rutland tells:

> Lord Burghley has tried to marry Elizabeth Vere to Lord Northumberland.... She cannot fancy him.[4]

This sounds as though Elizabeth, like her father, had a will of her own.

Next, her hand was sought for the handsome Earl of Southampton, Henry Wriothesley. Like so many other sons of Elizabethan nobility, Wriothesley had been brought up as a Royal Ward at Cecil House, and Elizabeth de Vere would have known him, even as her mother had known the Royal Ward, Edward Earl of Oxford. Southampton was a personable young man; he had blue eyes and wore his brown hair in a long curl hanging down over his left shoulder. He must have had a rather insidious charm, for both men and women were attracted to him; yet this is hard to understand, because his numerous portraits show only a good-looking but rather effeminate young man with a somewhat disdainful expression. He was the heir to a large fortune, and he was the right age for Elizabeth de Vere, being two years older than she. Moreover, the young man and her father had much in common, both being interested in literature. Southampton had been a munificent patron of poets and other writers including Nashe, Markham, Barnebe Barnes and John Florio, the latter becoming a member of his household and teaching him Italian.

It was Lord Burghley who suggested his granddaughter as the bride of this eligible bachelor. Southampton's mother, the Dowager Countess, was eager for the connection not only with the Lord Treasurer, the most powerful courtier in the land, but also because Elizabeth's father, Lord Oxford, bore title to the oldest earldom in England. Edward de Vere was the Seventeenth Earl of Oxford, whereas Henry Wriothesley was only the Third Earl of Southampton. Moreover, Lord Oxford was known to have been a favorite of the Queen—all of which to this ambitious lady would have been valuable assets in a daughter-in-law.

For nearly four years the negotiations continued, pressed by Lord Burghley in a number of letters still preserved among the Hatfield papers. We believe that this match was pressed also by the Lady Elizabeth's father, who in a series of beautiful sonnets, urged the youth to marry and carry on the name of Wriothesley and the Southampton title. Here is *Sonnet 1:*

From fairest creatures we desire increase,
That thereby beauty's rose might never die,
But the riper should by time decease,
His tender heir might bear his memory:
But thou, contracted to thine own bright eyes,
Feed'st thy light's flame with self-substantial fuel,
Making a famine where abundance lies,
Thyself thy foe, to thy sweet self too cruel.
Thou that art now the world's fresh ornament
And only herald to the gaudy spring,
Within thine own bud buriest thy content
And, tender churl, mak'st waste in niggarding.
  Pity the world, or else this glutton be,
  To eat the world's due, by the grave and thee.

Lord Oxford was forty in 1590 when these negotiations began, the Earl of Southampton twenty-two years younger. This is the second Sonnet:

When forty winters shall besiege thy brow,
And dig deep trenches in thy beauty's field,
Thy youth's proud livery, so gaz'd on now,
Will be a tatter'd weed, of small worth held:
Then being ask'd where all thy beauty lies,
Where all the treasure of thy lusty days,
To say, within thine own deep-sunken eyes,
Were an all-eating shame and thriftless praise.
How much more praise deserv'd thy beauty's use,
If thou couldst answer, 'This fair child of mine
Shall sum my count, and make my old excuse,'
Proving his beauty by succession thine!
This were to be new made when thou art old,
And see thy blood warm when thou feel'st it cold.

There were seventeen of these poems. But the young man remained uninterested, because another young lady, Elizabeth Vernon, had caught his fancy.

However, in 1592 Elizabeth's father, we believe, published a long poem, *Venus and Adonis*, which he dedicated to the nobleman he still hoped might be his son-in-law. Here is the dedication in characteristically humble though florid Elizabethan prose:

'Vilia miretur vulgus; mihi flavus Apollo
Pocula Castalia plena ministret aqua.'[5]

TO THE RIGHT HONOURABLE HENRY WRIOTHESLEY
Earl of Southampton, and Baron of Tichfield.

Right Honourable,

I know not how I shall offend in dedicating my unpolished lines to your lordship, nor how the world will censure me for choosing so strong a prop to support so weak a burthen: only, if your honour seem but pleased, I account myself highly praised, and vow to take advantage of all idle hours, till I have honoured you with some graver labour. But if the first heir of my invention prove deformed, I shall be sorry it have so noble a godfather, and never after ear so barren a land, for fear it yield me still so bad a harvest. I leave it to your honourable survey, and your honour to your heart's content; which I wish may always answer your own wish and the world's hopeful expectation.

Your honour's in all duty,

And what is the name here signed? *William Shakespeare.* This name had never before been seen in print; that it should appear now is one of the many mysteries in the story of Edward de Vere. All that one can say with assurance is that *Venus and Adonis* came out during the period of negotiations in regard to the marriage of Lord Oxford's daughter and the young Earl of Southampton, to whom the poem is dedicated.

Two years later a second poem twice as long as the first was published and again dedicated to the Earl of Southampton. This was *The Rape of Lucrece*, and again the poet's name is given as *William Shakespeare.* This time the dedication is warmer and more intimate, even as the sonnets written persumably at the same time to the same young man are also warmer and more personal.

These two amorous poems may tell far more than one can guess—one of the lust of an older woman for a younger man, the other the lust of a man for a pure and innocent woman. For example, in the light of what is known of the relationship of Lord Oxford and the Queen, *Venus and Adonis* appears to be the story of that affair and of the young man's disgust with the persistent pleadings of the older woman, goddess of love though she may have been.[6] If this be so it is obvious that it would be disastrous for the author if his identity were discovered by the public, though doubtless there were courtiers who were well aware of the whole story.

Given this hypothesis, it is clear that the poet must find for himself a name which would disguise his own identity to all but a few close friends. He therefore chose the name by which he may have been known to them: "the spear shaker," a nickname to which Gabriel Harvey had alluded so long before, in the ceremony at Audley End.[7]

Some scholars think that the poet took the name of an obscure young actor recently come to town, who may possibly have been a distant cousin through the Trussells.[8]

It seems more plausible that Lord Oxford took for his nom de plume a name suggested by the coat of arms of one of his own titles, Viscount Bolebec, which shows a lion shaking a broken spear. It may well be, as suggested above, that he was known to his special friends by this name, even as he was recognized at Court as *Phoebus*, or *the Turk*, nicknames the Queen herself had given him.

Returning to the story of Henry Wriothesley and Elizabeth de Vere, neither of them showed the slightest interest in the proposed marriage. The Earl subsequently married Mistress Elizabeth Vernon, a maid of honor to the Queen, who had lost *her* honor to him some months before. Consequently it had to be a hurried wedding and brought little happiness to either of them.

The Lord Treasurer tried again to marry his granddaughter Elizabeth to a bridegroom of his choice. But Elizabeth (a very modern young woman!) was holding out for a husband of *her* choice. She had fallen in love with William Stanley, a nobleman who returned her love most ardently. These young people must have known one another for some time, since Stanley belonged to the circle of rising young dramatists in Lord Oxford's group, the so-called *Euphuists*. However, as Elizabeth's father would one day write, "the course of true love never did run smooth."

Unfortunately Stanley, who was only the second son of the Earl of Derby, could not be considered as a suitor for the hand of Elizabeth, an Earl's daughter, as long as his father and elder brother were alive. But fate was kind to the young couple; the old Earl of Derby died. Yet still William Stanley was one removed from the earldom as the title descended to his brother, Ferdinando, Lord Strange, the nobleman who will be recognised as the patron of the company of actors to which young Will Shakespeare of Stratford belonged.

Then quite suddenly Ferdinando died, leaving the title of Earl of Derby at last to William Stanley. Now he was able to negotiate for the hand of his beloved Elizabeth, assuring her family that her social position would not be demeaned by marrying him, Stanley also inherited the Derby fortune, said to be one of the largest in the kingdom.

The wedding took place on January 26th, 1595, in the Queen's Palace at Greenwich, the reception being held four days later at Lord Burghley's spacious mansion on the Strand.

The church wardens of St. Martin's in the Fields duly recorded:

> Item paid the XXXth of January for ringing [the bells] at her Majesty's coming to ye Lord Treasurer's to ye Earl of Darbie's wedding And at her Departure from thence ye sixth of february ijs.[9]

Lord Burghley would have spared no expense in planning the wedding of his favorite daughter's oldest child. The festivities lasted for ten days during London's cold winter weather. As part of the celebration *A Midsummer Night's Dream* was presented, and was said to have been composed especially for this occasion. The evidence is, however, that the dramatist had taken one of his own earlier plays as the basis for this final production.[10] It is possible that Elizabeth de Vere's father was giving the bride a handsomer wedding present than even her wealthy grandfather could have given.

The new Earl and Countess went to live on Cannon Row, Westminster, about where Derby Gate is today. This was conveniently near to Whitehall Palace, where each of them was in attendance on the Queen.

Here Lord Oxford visited them and wrote this significant letter upon leaving:

> On my coming to Byfleet from Cannon Row the Earl of Derby was very earnest that he might assure £ 1,000 a year for my daughter, and marvelled that Sir Robert Cecil, her uncle, and I her father, were so slack to call upon it; so I desire some thing to be done herein.[11]

This letter is characteristic of Edward de Vere. He would have known that his new son-in-law was probably the richest nobleman in the kingdom, yet he had made no attempt to secure any of those riches for his beloved child. Lord Oxford, although frequently in need of funds himself, was nevertheless beyond coveting the riches of another man.

Lord Derby did settle the £ 1,000 a year on his bride, an impressive sum, being the same amount that the Queen had granted annually to Lord Oxford himself.

Lord Oxford and his young Countess and Lord Derby and his bride seem to have been especially congenial, visiting back and forth in the next few years. Edward de Vere and presumably his young wife were entertained by the Derbys in September of 1596. Later it is learned that Lady Oxford was visiting at Islesworth, one of the Derby country estates, apparently without her husband, and that her host accompanied her home to Hackney. Again, in November of 1599 the Earl and Countess of Derby were visiting Lady Derby's father and step-mother at King's Place. As reported earlier, Elizabeth Trentham de Vere was about the age of the Countess of Derby, and had been her close friend at Court before either of them were married.

The Earl of Derby attended the House of Lords only fourteen times in its first sitting after his elevation to the peerage. This caused some comment: a contemporary wrote of him:

> The Earl of Derby is busied only in penning commedies for the common players.[12]

Here again there is a mystery, for no plays signed with his name have been preserved. However, some scholars have thought that *Love's Labour's Lost*, that early play, is largely from his pen. This may be so, though the play was included in the *First Folio* of dramas attributed to *William Shakespeare.*

Love's Labour's Lost was presented in the great hall of the Royal Palace of Whitehall on January 26th, 1599.[13] This was not its first presentation, but it is on record that *this* play was given at Whitehall on *that* particular date. Could it have been in celebration of the fourth wedding anniversary of the Earl and Countess of Derby, a graceful gesture to its co-author?

The Lady Bridget de Vere

After Ann Cecil's death the relations between Lord Oxford and Lord Burghley, strained since his desertion of Burghley's favorite daughter, became decidedly worse. This was indeed a bitterly unhappy.time in the life of the widowed Earl. He took a house called *Fisher's Folly* in the city, where Devonshire Square is now. The estate was a little back from Bishopsgate and near the two playhouses, the Theatre and the Curtain. Also, it was not very far from London Stone, struck by Jack Cade in *King Henry VI, Part II.*[14] This was 'way downtown from the fashionable neighborhood where the Cecils lived, on the Strand.

Since Lord Oxford was at this time in close asociation with his literary friends, whom Lord Burghley had once referred to as "my son-in-law's lewd companions," it is not surprising that the Lord Treasurer felt this atmosphere unsuitable for the granddaughters, Elizabeth, Bridget and Susan. Therefore he took the three sisters into Cecil House to be properly brought up.

The young girls must have found their grandfather rather old and formal and not nearly as much fun as their own father. This is conjecture only, judging from the portrait of the Lord Treasurer in the National Portrait Gallery, in which he appears in his black robes of state, his white staff in his hand, a thoughtful, careworn expression on his face. By comparison the portraits of Lord Oxford always show him in a handsome doublet, "the glass of fashion and the mould of form." And even when he looks sad there is a gleam in his eyes.

Little is known about the de Vere girls at this time, until the curtain of mystery parts when the Lady Elizabeth reaches marriageable age. The other two girls born after their parents' reconciliation, were much younger.

Their grandfather died in 1598, after which the marriage negotiations of the young ladies were carried on by their uncle, Sir Robert Cecil, rather than by their father, who had married again early in 1590 and was living in the suburbs.

Late in the 1590s a marriage was being considered between the Lady Bridget de Vere and Lord William Herbert, older son of the Earl and Countess of Pembroke. The match must have seemed eminently suitable, for the Herberts were brought up in an atmosphere of aristocratic splendor and renaissance culture comparable to that of the de Veres. Furthermore, a great bond between them would have been that each family had a passion for plays and play-acting. Quite a few of the contemporary plays had had a premier performance at Wilton House, the Earl of Pembroke's country seat. Tradition tells that Lord Oxford himself acted there in one of his own plays, though most unfortunately, the gossip does not tell which one. The Pembrokes' Town House was Baynard's Castle, that gaunt old structure on the Thames which had once belonged to royalty, far down river from the newer residences on the Strand.

Mary Countess of Pembroke is known from her portrait at Wilton House, as a lovely, gracious lady.[15] She was the sister of Sir Philip Sidney, whose *Arcadia* was composed for her enjoyment and dedicated to her. Although Sir Philip and Lord Oxford were not particularly friendly, being of completely different temperaments, his sister, Mary Herbert, is thought to have been one of the group of literary and witty friends gathered about the Earl, all of whom were creative and any one of whom may have had a hand in some of the famous plays.

It was the Earl and Countess of Pembroke who first offered their son and heir as a bridegroom for the Lady Bridget de Vere. Her father seems to be delighted with this prospective son-in-law, to judge from this letter dated from Hackney September 8th, 1597. addressed to Sir Robert Cecil:

> I am pleased that my Lord and Lady persevere for Bridget's sake. I know no reason for delay. I always wished her a good husband. If it is a thing aggreeable to your love and care to my daughter I know no reason for delay.
>
> I hope all parties will receive comfort as the young Gentleman has been well brought up, and has good parts.
>
> I refer all to your wisdom.[16]

It is not known why this prospective marriage which seemed so ideal to the parents of the young people concerned, never took place. Perhaps Bridget, like her sister Elizabeth, had a mind of her own.

It should perhaps be mentioned that young William Herbert was coming to have a reputation for being a little wild. Sir Robert may have thought that the family had had enough of unstable young men of literary bent.

If this were his train of thought, he was soon to find that the next suitor decided upon for Bridget was quite as unstable as the first. He was Francis, Lord Norris, who later became the Earl of Berkshire. He must have endeared himself to his father-in-law, though, because just six days before Lord Oxford died he granted custody of the Forest of Essex, that land which had belonged to his ancestors since before the Conquest, to be divided between his cousin, Sir Francis Vere, and Francis Lord Norris.[17] Undoubtedly this was to be a part of Bridget's dowry, but Lord Oxford would not have decided to do this unless he had some special feeling toward Francis. Was he just another charming young nobleman? Or was he chosen for some other now unknown reason? We do not know. The husbands of the other two sisters are not so honored.

Unfortunately Lord Norris turned out to be a rather choleric young man. He had a long and loud dispute with Robert Bertie, young Lord Willoughby, as they were entering Parliament together one day, a dispute for which he had to be severely reprimanded. Whether this dishonor preyed upon his mind, or whether he was a neurotic anyway, is not recorded. But he shot himself not long afterward.

The Lady Susan de Vere

The Herberts and the de Veres and the Cecils must have been happy when finally the youngest de Vere daughter, Susan, married the younger Herbert son, Philip, who later became Earl of Montgomery.[18] Philip Herbert was named by his mother for her beloved brother, Sir Philip Sidney.[19]

The wedding took place on December 27th, 1604. This was only six months after the death of the bride's father, yet because of the prominence of the two families, there was a round of gaieties culminating in a great ball. December, that darkest month of the year, was a favorite among the Elizabethans and early Stuarts for fashionable festivities.

This bride and her groom must have been favorites at Court, because it is noted in a letter by Sir Dudley Carleton that "they were lodged in the council chamber, where the King gave them *reveille matin* before they were up."[20] That was an old English custom, awaking a bride and groom with music the morning after their wedding night.

It is particularly interesting to find a record telling that as part of the wedding festivities of Susan de Vere a masque was performed. This was a form of drama new in the reign of King James, in which the cast often represented allegorical characters. There is a masque within the play of *The Tempest.* In the particular masque presented in connection with Susan de Vere's wedding, it is noted that her bridegroom's brother, William

Herbert, played an important part. We shall have occasion to refer to this masque again in the next chapter.

We are just beginning to learn about the bride at the time of her wedding. We know that her husband and his brother were later to become known redundantly as "the Incomparable Paire of Brethren."

It may be noted, then, that each of these charming young ladies, the de Vere sisters, had married a nobleman of distinction according to the social standards of the time. Two, the Countess of Derby and the Countess of Montgomery, were to be ladies of great wealth. All three of the Countesses were Ladies in Waiting at the Court of the new King, James, and his Queen, Anne.

Notes To Chapter VII

1. Chapter III.
2. Chapter V.
3. Ibid.
4. From a private notebook of a de Vere descendant, quoting a contemporary source.
5. A. L. Rowse in *William Shakespeare: A Biography*, p. 149, translates these lines from *Ovid* thus:

> Let the populace admire base things, but for him let the god minister cups filled with water from the purest Castalian spring.

Or, as Ben Jonson translated it:

> Kneel hinds to trash: me let bright Phoebus swell,
> With cups full flowing from the Muses' well.

6. Chapter VI. The suggestion is taken from Charlton and Dorothy Ogburn, *This Star of England.*

7. Chapter VI.

8. Introduction.

9. From a private notebook of a de Vere descendant, quoting a contemporary source.

10. A similar play was mentioned by Francis Meres in *Paladis Tamia,* published in 1598. See *Notes* to *Midsummer Night's Dream,* by William Higley Durham, in the Yale edition of the play.

11. From the notebook of a de Vere descendant, quoting a letter from Lord Oxford.

12. Quoted in B. M. Ward, in *The Seventeenth Earl of Oxford.*

13. Introduction.

14. Chapter II.

15. Ben Jonson composed a famous epitaph for this lovely Countess of Pembroke:

> Underneath this sable hearse
> Lies the subject of all verse,
> Sidney's sister, Pembroke's mother;
> Death, ere thou hast slain another
> Learn'd and fair and good as she,
> Time shall throw a dart at thee.

16. Ward, *The Seventeenth Earl of Oxford.*

17. Chapter VI. .

18. Much later, after the death of his brother William, Philip Herbert succeeded to the earldom of Pembroke.

19. F. Denkinger, *Life of Sir Philip Sidney,* p. 257.

20. Sir Dudley Carleton in a letter to a "Mr. Winwood."

Chapter VIII
THE FIRST FOLIO

Thou art aliue still, while thy Booke doth liue,
And we have wits to read, and prayse to giue.

Lines taken from Ben Jonson's tribute: "To the memory of my beloued, The Author." In the *First Folio.*

Passing on quickly to the year 1623, it is found that the eternally beautiful plays of Shakespeare had finally been gathered together and were about to be published in the large volume that was to be known as the *First Folio*. The play scripts were collected from prompter's copies, from actors' memories and from the printed copies of those "stolne" or pirated editions which had been appearing surreptitiously from time to time. And then there were to be included eighteen plays which had never before been in print, making thirty-six plays in all.[1]

It was now nineteen years after the death of the Earl of Oxford, whom we believe to have been the author of these dramas, or at least the presiding genius over their composition. Yet in the *First Folio* the playwright's name is given as *William Shakespeare.*

If there were mysteries in the story of Edward de Vere before this, when we come to study the *First Folio* it seems that those mysteries are compounded. Consider a few of the questions which have plagued English literature scholars for more than three centuries. First, who decided to bring together all the known plays attributed to Shakespeare?[2] Who found those eighteen plays that had as yet been unpublished? And where had they been all these years? And finally, who paid the cost of printing and editing this collection? That would have been an expensive undertaking. It is believed that the *First Folio* was set by hand, a project begun several years before, certainly as early as 1619. The cost of this enterprise has been estimated variously at between three and six thousand pounds, a great deal of money for those days. Over a thousand copies were printed and were priced at one pound each. But since only six hundred copies were actually sold, somebody must have taken an enormous loss.[3]

And then there was the mystery about the author's name, *Shakespeare*. The actor known as William Shakespeare had gone to his home in Stratford-on-Avon long before, and had died there in 1616. But he never had taken the slightest interest either in publishing or in preserving the plays attributed to him. One must look further.

The *First Folio* had a dedication written by Ben Jonson, a dramatist in high favor in the 1620s, being Master of the Revels and author of many of the masques currently popular at Court. However, before this Ben Jonson had made it plain that he thought the dramas of Shakespeare lacked "art." This sounds like the envious commentary of a less successful playwright, but Jonson's criticism went deeper than that due to his different interpretation of *art*. Indeed, Jonson had been pretty caustic, writing in one of his notebooks:

> I remember the players have often mentioned it as an honor to Shakespeare that in the writing (whatsoever he penned) he never blotted a line. My answer hath been, Would he had blotted a thousand.[4]

A little further on in the same paragraph Ben Jonson wrote:

> He flowed with that facility that sometimes it was necessary he should be stopped.
> *Sufflaminandus erat.* [He needed a brake.] as *Augustus* said of *Haterius*. His wit was in his own power; would that the rule of it had been so, too. Many times he fell into those things, could not escape laughter, as when he said

> in the person of Caesar, one speaking to him, "Caesar, thou dost me wrong," he replied: "Caesar did never wrong but with just cause,"[5] and such like; which was ridiculous.[6]

Jonson wrote apparently in haste and in a state of pique, for he left out words and punctuation recklessly. However he generously added;

> But he redeemed his vices with his virtues.
> There was ever more in him to be praised, than to be pardoned.[7]

These added lines seem to indicate that Ben Jonson had really known the Earl of Oxford. He must have known that Oxford was the true author of the plays now being brought together. Every one who had come in contact with that gracious nobleman "prays'd him," even those who disapproved of him or of his work. And so Jonson in the Preface to the *First Folio* refers to the playwright as "the applause, delight and wonder of our Stage.. (l. 18).

He writes:

> To the memory of my beloued
> The AUTHOR
> Mr. William Shakespeare:
>
> To draw no envy (*Shakespeare*) on thy name,
> Am I thus ample to thy Book and Fame:
> While I confess thy writings to be such,
> As neither *Man*, nor *Muse* can praise too much.
>
> (l. 1-4)

Jonson's poem is so long that only excerpts from it can be quoted here. This is an interesting bit:

> Thou art a monument, without a tomb.
>
> (l.22)

This could not apply to William Shakespeare of Stratford, because he had both a monument and a tomb in Holy Trinity Church there.

Jonson proceeds to tell how far the playwright of the *Folio* outshines the English poets and dramatists, Lyly and Marlowe and the rest, and he says that the author can be compared only with the ancient Greek writers,

> . . . thund'ring Aeschylus,
> Euripides, and Sophocles.
>
> (ll. 33-34)

Then in a burst of rhetoric he exclaims:

> Triumph, my Britain, thou hast one to show,
> To whom all scenes of *Europe* homage owe.
> He was not of an age, but for all time!
>
> (ll. 41-3)

Jonson ends this long panegyric:

> Shine forth, thou *Star* of Poets, and with rage,
> Or influence, chide or cheer the drooping Stage;
> Which, since thy flight from hence, hath mourn'd like
> night,
> And despairs day, but for thy Volume's light.
>
> Ben: Ionson.

How can this man Jonson now write such extravagant praise of the dramatist when he had heretofore been so disparaging of his work? And why does he do it?

Perhaps the answer is to be found within the dedication of the *First Folio*. And to whom does Ben Jonson dedicate this great volume? *To The most noble and incomparable paire of brethren.* These are the Herbert brothers, now the Earl of Pembroke and the Earl of Montgomery, foremost patrons of literature in the reign of King James. The Earl of Pembroke was at this time Lord

Chamberlain,[8] and it would have been through his influence that Ben Jonson had been appointed to the office of Master of the Revels. Moreover, he had had Jonson's stipend increased to £200 a year. Jonson had told his friend Drummond that "every first day of the new year he had twenty pounds sent him from the Earl of Pembroke to buy books."[9]

It would seem to have been this Earl who had commissioned Jonson to write the Preface to the *First Folio*, and also the *Lines to the great variety of readers*, signed by the actors Heminges and Condell.[10] These actors apparently made pretensions to a larger responsibility than was actually theirs, the general consensus of scholars being that Ben Jonson composed both of these pieces.

Look again at the dedication of the volume. This is the beginning:

> To the most noble and incomparable paire of brethren, William Earl of Pembroke, & c. Lord Chamberlain to the Kings Most Excellent Maiestie, and Philip, Earl of Montgomery, & c. Gentleman of his Maiesties Bed-chamber. Both Knights of the most Noble Order of the Garter and our singular good Lords.

Jonson continues his dedication in the flowery prose of the day, mentioning that the two Earls had known the "Author living," and deprecating the fact that, the plays "outliving him," the dramatist was unable to see the final collection through publication himself. These are Jonson's words:

> But since your lordships have been pleas'd to think these trifles something heretofore; and have prosecuted both them, and their Author living, with so much favour, we hope that (they outliving him, and he not having the fate, common to some, to be executor to his own writings)
> (Dedication, ll. 8-12)

It is obvious that each of these noble Earls would have known the "Author living," because the Earl of Oxford was not only known to them through their mother, Mary Countess of Pembroke, who was his friend, but also through Lord Oxford's daughters.[11] The Earl of Pembroke, it will be remembered, had once been a suitor for the hand of the Lady Bridget de Vere, while his brother, the Earl of Montgomery, was married to the Lady Susan.

Let us consider Susan de Vere, now the sprightly Countess of Montgomery. It is recorded that she was not only "a lady of strict piety and virtue," but also that she loved the theatre.[12] It will be recalled also that as part of her wedding festivities there had been a masque presented in which Sir William Herbert, now the Earl of Pembroke, had performed. The record is in the Revels Accounts for the years 1604-5, quoted by F. G. Fleeay.[13] In the same "accounts" there is a list of all the ladies at Court who had acted in masques between the years 1605 and 1611. Twenty-nine ladies are mentioned, but only three of them performed in *all* the masques presented. Susan, Countess of Montgomery, is one of these three ladies. Like her father, she seems to have been stage-struck.

Ben Jonson as Master of the Revels would have come to know his players well, in rehearsals as well as in actual performances. His *Epigrammes*, which he himself characterized as "the ripest of my studies," are dedicated to the Earl of Pembroke, while one of the loveliest of them is addressed to Susan:

To Susan, Countess of Montgomery.

Were they that named you prophets? Did they see
Even in the dew of Grace what you would be?
Or did our times require it to behold
A new SUSANNA equal to the old?
Or, because some scarce think that story true—
To make those faithful did the Fates send you?
And to your Scene lent no less dignity

Of birth, of match, of form, of chastity?
Or more than born for the comparison
Of former age, or glory of your own
Were you advanced past those times to be
The Light and mark unto posterity?
Judge they that can; Here I have raised to show
A picture, which the world for yours must know:
And like it too; if they look equally:
If not, 'tis fit for you, some should envy.[15]

Not only is this a charming and complimentary poem to Susan, but Jonson proves that he knows her well. He puns on her maiden name, *Vere:* "because some scarce think that story *true. . . .*" Also, he uses the word "scene" instead of "your time," playing up to Susan's love of the theatre and play-acting.

He refers to her noble birth, her equally noble consort, and her own beauty, or "form." Perhaps "chastity" was a rare virtue among Court ladies in the reign of King James.

Then he goes on:

. . . . more than born for the comparison
Of former age.

The "comparison" could mean not only comparison to Biblical times, but to those of the last reign, for even as soon after as the time of the Stuarts, people had begun to look back with awe and admiration upon the golden age of Queen Elizabeth, which both Jonson and the Countess could have remembered well.

The epigram to Susan resembles Ben Jonson's poem *To The Reader* (on the second page of the First Folio) in reference to the Droeshout engraving of Shakespeare:

This Figure, that thou here seest put,
It was for gentle Shakespeare cut.

Jonson does not say that this is a portrait of Shakespeare, any more than that his poem to Susan is a *picture of her.* He says quite definitely:

> Here I have rais'd to show
> A picture *which the world for yours must know.*
> (italics mine)

From the foregoing, it is deduced that the Earl of Pembroke, the Earl and Countess of Montgomery, and the Master of the Court of Revels, Ben Jonson, were friendly and apparently in close touch during the opening of the second decade of the Seventeenth Century.

Those questions are still plaguing us: Who were the "Grand Possessors" of these priceless manuscripts about to be published, and especially, who had possessed those plays that had never before been seen in print?

Would it not have been likely that Lord Oxford as he was growing older would have consigned his plays, both those finished and those unfinished, to a literary executor? And who would this be but his playwright son-in-law and collaborator, William Stanley, Earl of Derby, who had been his friend even before he became a son-in-law?[16] It is recorded in letters that the Earl and Countess of Oxford and the Earl and Countess of Derby were visiting back and forth in the years between 1594 and 1600.

Also it is learned from existing letters and documents that the de Vere sisters were in frequent contact with one another after their marriages. They would have seen each other at Court, where all three of them were in attendance on the new queen. It is known, too, that they banded together to sell Castle Hedingham to their step-mother for the benefit of their step-brother, young Henry de Vere.[17] He, too, as the years wore on, seems to have been in touch with his sisters, for in the year after publication of the *First Folio* he married their cousin.[18] The brothers-in-law, the Earls of Derby and Montgomery, were Courtiers at this time, and as noted, the Earl of Pembroke held an important post, Lord Chamberlain, in the Court of King James.

Would it not be natural that the four children of Lord Oxford should wish to preserve and publish all their father's plays, using as a nucleus those still unpublished dramas in their possession?

Therefore, considering the close relationship of the three de Vere sisters and their husbands and their young brother, the fact that Lord Derby himself was an acknowledged dramatist, and that the Herbert brothers were the foremost patrons of playwrights and other literary men, may it not be boldly declared that "the Grand Possessors" in all probability were: the Earl and Countess of Derby; the Countess of Berkshire, whose husband had committed suicide;[19] the Earl and Countess of Montgomery; this Earl's brother, the Earl of Pembroke; and Henry de Vere, his father's heir, now the Eighteenth Earl of Oxford—these seven, with the Earl of Derby as acknowledged Executor? It would have been this group, we believe, which decided to gather together the plays of the late Earl of Oxford whom each of them, with the possible exception of the Earl of Pembroke, had known intimately. Even the Earl of Pembroke might have known the famous dramatist during the years when his parents were negotiating on his behalf for the hand of the Lady Bridget de Vere.[20] And Lord Pembroke would have been well aware that Oxford had been the true author of the so-called Shakespeare plays.

The cost of bringing together, editing and publishing these plays for the *First Folio* was borne, we believe, by the Earls of Derby, Pembroke and Montgomery, the most affluent noblemen in the kingdom. Any one of them could well afford the tremendous price of the enterprise; indeed, each of them had a deep personal interest in seeing that the beautiful dramas were preserved for posterity. And it would have been these three Earls who were willing to take the large financial loss when only six hundred copies of the *Folio* were sold; the loss of even two hundred pounds a piece would not have been more than any one of them would have wished to contribute to so worthy a project.

In arranging the plays for publication the editors seem to have deliberately placed first one of the unpublished dramas, *The Tempest*, hoping no doubt to attract the attention of the hesitant buyer leafing through the volume in the book stall. This play has been edited with care, stage directions given with precision and the play is complete with locale of scenes and names of characters. In some of the other plays in the *Folio* the editors neglected to write stage directions at all, and frequently omitted names of cast and locale. Even proofreading was careless. Jaggard the printer had been inexcusably remiss in numbering pages; for instance, in *Hamlet*, page 156 is followed by page 257. But evidently somebody had taken a little extra care in preparing *The Tempest* for publication.

In this connection it may be interesting to note that an eminent French Shakespearean scholar[21] has made a strong case to prove that the Earl of Derby is the author of *The Tempest*, and not his father-in-law. True, *The Tempest* is more closely akin to the masques that Ben Jonson was composing for the pleasure of the courtiers of Queen Anne and King James, than it is to the plays of Shakespeare created for the entertainment and stimulation of the Elizabethans, be they courtiers or cockneys. Lord Oxford wrote not only for the worldly noblemen and noblewomen at Court, but he also delighted in writing plays for the amusement of the citizens of Whitechapel, Southwark and the City, giving his dramas exciting plots and interesting characters who behaved like the people of London whom they knew and recognised.

But not the Earl of Derby, nor Kit Marlowe, nor Francis Bacon, nor the Countess of Pembroke could have composed the poetry in the speech given to *Prospero* when he casts away his magic wand.

It is tempting to imagine Lord Oxford in his last days at Hackney, nursing his "infirmity" and very likely in pain. Musing upon his early life as older people sometimes do, his thoughts would hark back to his childhood days in Essex and to the lovely countryside around Castle Hedingham where he had played with his sister Mary. Phrases from his uncle Arthur Golding's translation of the *Metamorphoses* stray into his mind, especially Medea's speech in Book VII. These haunting lines come back to him:

> Ye ayres and windes, ye elves of hilles,
> or brooks or woods alone...
>
> l. 265

And thus inspired he would write down the poetry as the images crowd into his mind. He had always been exhilarated by bold promontories along the seacoast, which he had known well, especially the rocky cliffs of Dover. He had described such a height in King Lear:

> There is a cliff, whose high and bending head
> Looks fearfully on the confined deep.
> Act IV, sc. 1, ll. 73-4

He remembers a storm there . . . once again his Muse seizes him: words pour forth in a torrent. . . . He writes on furiously . . . the speech of Prospero as he abjures his magic and casts away his potent staff. . . . These may be the last lines ever composed by the greatest poet-dramatist in the English language. How fortunate that this precious fragment was found after his own hand had been stilled.

Prospero's speech:

> Ye elves of hills, brooks, standing lakes, and groves:
> And ye, that on the sands with printless foot
> Do chase the ebbing Neptune, and do fly him
> When he comes back; you demi-puppets, that
> By moonshine do the green sour ringlets make,
> Whereof the ewe not bites; and you, whose pastime
> Is to make midnight mushrooms; that rejoice

To hear the solemn curfew; by whose aid, —
Weak masters though ye be—I have bedimm'd
The noontide sun, call'd forth the mutinous winds,
And 'twixt the green sea and the azur'd vault
Set roaring war: to the dread rattling thunder
Have I given fire and rifted Jove's stout oak
With his own bolt: the strong-bas'd promontory
Have I made shake; and by the spurs pluck'd up
The pine and cedar: graves at my command
Have wak'd their sleepers, op'd, and let them forth
By my so potent art. But this rough magic
I here abjure; and, when I have requir'd
Some heavenly music, —which even now I do—
To work mine end upon their senses that
This airy charm is for, I'll break my staff,
Bury it certain fathoms in the earth,
And, deeper than did ever plummet sound,
I'll drown my book.

(Solemn music.)
Act V, sc. 1, ll. 34-57

Notes To Chapter VIII

1. Material in this paragraph is taken from Sir E. K. Chambers, *William Shakespeare.*

2. Of the plays attributed to Shakespeare, *Pericles, Prince of Tyre* was the only one left out of the *First Folio.*

3. F. E. Halliday, ed., *The Shakespeare Companion.*

4. Ben Jonson in his Conversations with Drummond.

5. Ibid. Jonson has either misquoted *Julius Caesar*, or has taken Caesar's speech from an earlier version. The lines to which he apparently referred now read:

Know, Caesar doth no wrong, nor without cause
Will he be satisfied.

Caesar speaks the lines in response to the humble petition of Metellus Cimber.

6. Jonson, "Conversations with Henry Drummond.'

7. Ibid.

8. The title, Lord Chamberlain, must not be confused with the title of Lord Great Chamberlain. According to the Oxford Dictionary, the Lord Chamberlain was the chief officer of the royal household, sharing with the Lord Steward, Master of the Horse, and Mistress of the Robes, the oversight of all servants in the royal palace. This included "Control of actors, and the Licensing of plays." Polonius was Lord Chamberlain to King Claudius (see *Hamlet*, Act II, sc. 2). The title of Lord Great Chamberlain was of higher technical status, and also higher social degree. This was the hereditary prerogative of the Earls of Oxford. The duties of the Lord Great Chamberlain were "to attire the sovereign" for coronation, to be in attendance on state occasions, especially at the time of the creation of peers and bishops. The Lord Great Chamberlain also had oversight of certain of the royal palaces and edifices, including Westminster Hall.

9. Marchette Chute, *Ben Jonson of Westminster*, p. 153.

10. James Boswell, father of the biographer, was the first to recognize the hand of Ben Jonson in the *Lines to the great variety of readers*. However, scholars disagree, some believing the lines to have been composed by Edward Blount, Marlowe's friend, who did have something to do with seeing the volume through the press.

11. Chapter VII.

12. Sir Sidney Lee, *Life of Shakespeare*, p. 687.

13. Rev. F. G. Fleeay, *Accounts of the Revels, 1559-1640.*

14. W. Gifford, Esq., Notes to Ben Jonson's *Epigrammes*, London, 1816.

15. Ben Jonson's *Epigrammes*. No. CIIII, Vol. VIII of Percy

and Simpson, *Prose and Poems of Ben Jonson*, p. 67.

16. In mentioning William Stanley, Lord Derby, it is interesting to note that some people believe that he is the author of the "Will Sonnets," nos. 135 and 136, that he filed them away with those of his father-in-law, and somehow they got published together. Other scholars believe that *Will* was used as a nickname for *poet* in Elizabethan times. Sir Philip Sidney is referred to as *Will* and *Willy* by his biographer, Sir Fulke Greville. Scholars of the so-called orthodox school are assured that William Shakespeare is the poet of the Sonnets to which his name is signed, giving these two sonnets as part of their proof. How ironic it would be if the unwitting mistake of Lord Oxford's beloved son-in-law should give these professors one of their most convincing arguments!

17. Chapter VI.

18. Ibid.

19. Ibid.

20. Ibid.

21. Professor Le Franc, in *Sous Le Masque*, quoted in Ward, *The Seventeenth Earl of Oxford.*

22. Ibid.

Chapter IX
THE PORTRAITS

Look here, upon this picture, and on this,
The counterfeit presentiment. . . .
See what a grace was seated on this brow;
Hyperion's curls, the front of Jove himself
. . . .
Where every god did seem to set his seal,
To give the world assurance of a man.
Hamlet, Act III, sc. 4, ll. 53-62

Of all the nine ladies who were so closely associated with the Earl of Oxford, one can see today the portraits of only two of them, and curiously these two are of ladies at the extremes of the social scale: the Queen of England, and her Woman of the Bedchamber, Anne Vavasor. There are many portraits of the Queen; indeed, she would undoubtedly be recognised if she came to life today, even as her portraits are recognised before the label is consulted.

The portrait of Queen Elizabeth on page 40 e was painted by an unknown artist about 1575. It is said by Dr. David Piper, former director of the National Portrait Gallery, London, to be one of the finest pictures of her Majesty, and almost certainly one of the rare portraits of her painted from life. So this is how she looked when the young courtier, Lord Oxford, fell in love with her.

There is today only one portrait of Anne Vavasor (see page 40 h); yet there are those priceless character portraits of her in the Shakespeare plays.

And now, how about our hero himself, Edward de Vere, that illustrious and glamorous Seventeenth Earl of Oxford? The understanding of this writer is that there are today seven known portrait likenesses of the Earl, and two engravings showing him bearing the Sword of State before the Queen. There is also an engraving of the Earl with three other noblemen attending the Queen at the opening of Parliament. And there is an interesting old engraving of the trial of Mary Queen of Scots, in which Lord Oxford was one of the judges, but the figures of the noble peers are too small to distinguish their features. And then there is that engraving of Queen Elizabeth's funeral procession showing six Earls walking beside her bier, but since they are not identified, one cannot be sure which is the Earl of Oxford. Indeed, if truth must be told, it is not recorded that he *was* one of those six Earls.

There is a painting called *Queen Elizabeth in Procession*, in the collection of the Hon. Simon Wingfeld Digby, M. P. (see page 401), in which there is a dashing young courtier in graceful pose wearing an impeccable doublet, immediately in front of the Queen's litter. He seems to stand out from the other courtiers by his style and noble bearing. It has been suggested that this aristocrat might be the Earl of Oxford, since he is bearing the Sword of State, while the gorgeous lady in the wheel farthingale might well be his sister, Mary. Let it be emphasized that there is no historical proof of these identifications.

Now consider some of the portraits known as likenesses of the Seventeenth Earl of Oxford. The only one which can be said with certainty to be authentic is the Welbeck portrait[2] now in the National Portrait Gallery, on loan from his Grace, the Duke of Portland. And even this may be a copy[3] of the original for which Lord Oxford sat in Paris to be painted by an unknown Flemish artist, and which he thoughtfully sent home to his wife when he learned that she was pregnant. He was then twenty four years old.

In the upper righthand corner of this portrait can be read:

> Edward Vere, Earle of Oxford, Lord High Chamberlaine of Eng., married 1st Ann daughter to Wm. Cecil Lord Burghley, 2nd the Daughter to Sir Thos. Trentham of Rocester in Coun. . . . and died 26 of June 1604.

Obviously, this inscription which is now nearly obliterated, must have been painted in sometime after the death of the Earl. But in the upper lefthand corner one finds after some undecipherable words, quite clearly the date: *1575*.

This portrait shows the nobleman in a jaunty black velvet cap with feather, worn at a rakish angle, showing a little of his auburn hair. He is dressed in a tight olive-green tunic with yellow stripes across, buttoned down the front, topped by a beautifully painted, starched white lace ruff framing his face. His right arm seems to be on his hip, and the picture shows part of his nobleman's gauntlet.

In this portrait of Lord Oxford his face is that of a charming and aristocratic young nobleman turning slightly to his left. He has a long straight nose, thin lips and a pencil-thin moustache barely discernible. He has a high forehead, and the shape of his face is more rounded than oval, in which respect he resembles the portrait of his cousin, Sir Horace Vere, Baron Tilbury, also in the National Portrait Gallery. In the Welbeck portrait it is the eyes that are the arresting feature, for they look straight into the eyes of the person admiring the picture. They are beautiful eyes, dark, penetrating, and seeming to say so much. Sometimes they look inexpressibly sad, other times merry and mischievous. This portrait reflects the style which was very important to this Earl. It is remarkably life-like, and if one can be sure of only one likeness of him, it is well that it is this one.

The picture known as the St. Albans portrait in the possession of his Grace, the Duke of St. Albans, could well be the same nobleman as depicted in the Welbeck, in middle age. It is painted by Marcus Gheeraedts, who painted the Armada portrait of the Queen. An inscription across the top of the canvas appears to read:

Ed^{w} De Vere
17th Earl of Oxford.

This portrait has always been known as a likeness of the

Seventeenth Earl of Oxford, yet truthfully, there are gaps in the history of its recorded ownership, so that authenticity cannot be proven.

The St. Albans portrait shows a nobleman with longer face than in the Welbeck, slightly turning to his left, even as in the earlier painting, and with a thick dark auburn moustache and beard on the lower part of the chin. Remarkably, this portrait also features the dark eyes which here are almond-shaped and infinitely sad and brooding. Lord Oxford had lived to know much grief by the time this portrait was done. The hair appears to be dark, but with a decided auburn tinge.

The Earl is dressed in a light-colored tunic with high collar bound in a dark lace ruff. About his neck is a twisted ribbon from which hangs a pendant in the shape of a boar, which it will be recalled, was one of the devices of the Earls of Oxford. This pendant alone would seem to authenticate the portrait.

The St. Albans has one interesting feature lacking in the Welbeck portrait; it shows the subject's hand, the left hand, fingering the boar pendant. The fingers are long and shapely; this is the hand of an aristocrat. The middle finger wears a ring above the knuckle, instead of at the bottom of the finger where one would expect to find it. The elongated thumb is noticeable; this could, of course, be the artist's error, though Marcus Gheeraedts was famous for his likenesses, being one of the Flemish painters brought over to London to paint the Queen. He would not have been apt to make a mistake in measurement.[4]

The frontispiece to this volume is a photograph of the miniature of Lord Oxford by Nicholas Hilliard, now in the possession of his Grace, the Duke of Buccleuch. This shows a somewhat younger man than the St. Albans, and quite truthfully there are experts who doubt that the subject was the same nobleman as painted in the Welbeck and St. Albans portraits. This writer, however, believes that he is that nobleman, our hero. True, his face is rounder, but in the engravings of Lord Oxford attending the Queen his face is rounder than hers. Remembering the shape of the face of the beautifully painted portrait of Sir

Horace Vere, who was Lord Oxford's first cousin, one may say, perhaps, that this rounded face contour was a de Vere characteristic. The curly auburn hair seems to be a shade darker here than in the other two portraits. However, this is the way Lord Oxford looked to the famous miniaturist, Nicholas Hilliard. Hilliard's miniature of the Queen is quite different from other portraits of her, yet entirely recognizable.

In a biography of the great Dutch artist, Cornelius Ketel, who was second only to Rembrandt as a portrait painter in Holland, there is a record of a portrait he painted of the Earl of Oxford. But where is that portrait today? A likeness of so eminent a nobleman and scholar, not to mention a painting by Ketel, could hardly vanish away. Yet this portrait seems to have disappeared completely.

In the Folger Library, Washington, D.C., there is a portrait of William Shakespeare known as the Ashbourne. It is a three-quarter-length painting showing a handsome middle-aged gentleman wearing a black silk tunic belted, and with a flimsy ruff about his neck and narrower ruffs at the wrists. He stands beside a table, on which there is a skull, leaning his right arm upon the skull. In this hand he holds a book, with finger between the pages as though to mark the place where he had stopped reading to pose for the artist. As in the Welbeck portrait of Lord Oxford, he turns slightly to his left, but again the eyes look straight into the eyes of the viewer. They are dark eyes, very beautiful, but sad and thoughtful. The subject has a high forehead, bald head, a sandy-colored moustache and a well-trimmed Van Dyke beard. From his left hand dangles a nobleman's gauntlet, and here again we are struck with the unusually long left thumb. On his thumb he wears a ring.

The only inscription is painted in the upper left hand corner, reading:

AETATIS SUAE 47
A^{D} 1611.

The date and age would be appropriate to William Shakespeare, who was born in 1564. Obviously, they would not apply to the Earl of Oxford, who would have been forty-seven in 1597, and we remember that he died in 1604.

However, there was something about the eyes and the pose that arrested the attention of an American scholar; Charles Wisner Barrell, Secretary-Treasurer of the Shakespeare Fellowship, which is the American equivalent of the English Shakespeare Authorship Society, both groups commited to establishing the authorship credit to the Seventeenth Earl of Oxford. After months of negotiation, Mr. Barrell obtained permission to X-ray this portrait.

This is what the infra-red plate revealed:

1. A wide courtier's ruff under the flimsy bourgeois ruff, of the style that a courtier to Queen Elizabeth would have worn, but not found in portraits dating from the time of the early Stuarts, i.e., the date, 1611, painted on the picture.
2. A shock of thick curly hair under the painted bald head.
3. The seal ring, which in the portrait showed only as a blurred face, seems to show under X-ray the eye, ears, snout and tusk of a boar's head.
4. Under the date, "1611," a hole in the canvas, showing that another date had been erased with vigor before the "1611" date had been painted in.
5. Below the date, a coat of arms surmounted by a griffin's head, supported on one side by a large cat-like beast; on the other by a griffin. On the shield were three beaked heads, torn off instead of being cut straight across, two side by side, the third below, all facing left.
6. Below the coat of arms there is a monogram, which is probably the artist's signature. The letters are "C" and "K" overlapping a little, with the "C" slightly to the left and above the "K."
7. The gold of the book cover held by the gentleman, and the gold of the ring on his thumb, was originally a true lemon

gold, instead of the orange gold to be seen today.

The revealing of the nobleman's ruff of an earlier date proved that the date now on the painting, 1611, is wrong. Indeed, the ruff is a bad give-away, for it matches the lace on the cuffs in the picture as it is today. Historic costume experts remark that if a gentleman of 1611 were to sit for his portrait, he would not have worn an old ruff with the Tudor rose in the lace, but the lace would show the Scottish thistle of King James.

Furthermore, the thumb ring was worn *only* by a noble Englishman of high degree, proving that the portrait could not have been the likeness of the actor from Warwickshire, who was very much a man of the people, his father having been a butcher and glove maker in Stratford-on-Avon.

Indeed, the signet ring showing the boar's tusk practically proves the portrait to have been a painting of the Earl of Oxford, the boar's head being his crest.

But the coat of arms was a matter of considerable anxiety on the part of Mr. Barrell and the scholars interested, since it was not the coat of arms of the de Veres, as might have been expected.

It was the College of Heralds in London who finally identified the crest of the three griffins as the badge of two prominent Staffordshire families, i.e., the Sneyds of Keep Hill, and the Trenthams of Rocester Abbey. Research on the family of Elizabeth Trentham, Lord Oxford's second wife,[5] revealed that she was descended from both of these families, so the coat of arms of each belonged to her through both lines of descent.

Then Mr. Barrell consulted a book on *The Bearing of Coat Armour By Ladies*, and learned that originally there was no provision for women to bear arms at all, since they bore no armour. But, said the book, if the lady were an heiress, or owned considerable property, her husband bore her coat of arms for her.

In the play of *King Henry IV, Part II*, there is an example of this usage: Richard Neville, the "King Maker," carried the Beauchamp arms of his mother on his great seal, instead of his own coat of arms.

Subsequently, the signature, "C. K." was recognised as the monogram of the great Cornelius Ketel, mentioned earlier in this discussion. In a book, *La Nouvelle Biographie Generale* it is recorded that

> La reine Elizabeth, le comte d'Oxford, les Principaux seigneurs et dames de la cour lui firent executer leurs portraits.

"Lui" in this instance refers back to Ketel, and it will be seen that Shakespeare is not even mentioned as having sat for a portrait by this Dutchman, whereas the noble "comte d'Oxford" is.

Here is another interesting note: The Dutch painter, Karel Van Mander, wrote a book called *Lives of the Most Celebrated Painters*, which was published in 1604. In this book one reads:

> Ketel also made a portrait of the Duke of Oxford (Edward de Vere), the High Chancellor (Sir Christopher Hatton), and of many other important members of the nobility. Some of these portraits were life sized and full length.

Comparing Ketel's portrait of Sir Christopher Hatton with the Ashbourne portrait of Shakespeare, a marked resemblance is found in pose and in the actual painting. Still closer examination of the Ashbourne reveals that it has been cut off, indicating that this may well have been one of the "life sized and full length" portraits referred to by Van Mander. Could there have been some detail on the lower part of the portrait which might have betrayed the original subject? Sir Christopher Hatton's portrait bears his name on a light-colored background in the lower part of the canvas; it is possible that the Ashbourne portrait showed a similar inscription bearing Lord Oxford's name and/or coat of arms. It would have been easier to cut it off than to try to paint it over.

Mr. Barrell compared the Ashbourne portrait of Shakespeare

with the Welbeck and the St. Albans portraits of Lord Oxford. The high forehead and bald head were the most marked differences, but the X-ray had proved these features to have been painted in at a later date. Curiously, the Ashbourne resembled each of the two portraits of the Earl much more than they resembled each other.

There remained only to try to find out the pedigree of the Ashbourne portrait. It can be traced back to the Ashbourne Grammar School in Staffordshire, where it had been hanging on the wall since the seller could remember. It may be added that when it was sold by the Ashbourne school master to Mr. Eustace Conway in 1847, it was learned that the schoolmaster was an amateur artist.

Now the village of Ashbourne is only five miles from Rocester Abbey, seat of the Trentham family. At the time of the death of the Countess of Oxford, Rocester Abbey was the home of her brother, Sir Faunces Trentham, the executor of her will. Sir Fraunces had frequently helped his sister, both financially and in other ways, particularly after her husband's death, and in the repurchase of Castle Hedingham for her son.[6]

Sir Fraunces Trentham's daughter, another Elizabeth Trentham, lost the estate to a relative, Sir Christopher Trentham, but regained it again after considerable legal difficulties in 1651.

The Ashbourne Grammar School was founded in 1585. A descendant of the founder, Brian, Second Viscount Cullen, married an Elizabeth Trentham of Rocester Abbey, a famous beauty in her day , whose portrait was painted by Sir Peter Lely.

It does not seem too far-fetched to reconstruct the history of the Ashbourne portrait. It is almost certainly the famous lost portrait of Lord Oxford painted by Cornelius Ketel, and mentioned in *La Nouvelle Biographie Generale,* and again by Van Mander in his book on *The Most Celebrated Modern Paintings.*[7]

It seems reasonable to believe that it had belonged to Lord Oxford's wife, Elizabeth Trentham de Vere, and that it had at some time been taken by her brother, Sir Fraunces, to his own country house, Rocester Abbey, most likely at the time when the Countess was forced to break up her home at King's Place, Hackney. Possibly Sir Fraunces took the portrait to keep it for his nephew, Henry de Vere, still a minor. But Henry died young, leaving no children.[8] Again, the Countess being badly in need of funds, may have had to sell the cherished portrait to her brother in order to raise money to pay for the repurchase of Castle Hedingham. As a painting by Ketel it would have had considerable value, though today the value is not so much due to the artist as to the fact that it may very likely be the best likeness we have of that wonderful author of the famous plays and poems.

Assume then, that the Ashbourne portrait of Lord Oxford was hanging in Rocester Abbey, the Trentham country seat, until that later Elizabeth Trentham married the Second Viscount Cullen. At this time the bride could have taken it with her to Ashbourne Hall, her new home. There it hung until Lord Cullen, or possibly one of his descendants, transferred it to the Ashbourne Grammar School, in which he would have had an interest, since it had been founded by an ancestor of his. Sometime later, possibly in the eighteenth century, or even as late as the nineteenth, it was torn off and painted over to make it represent the dramatist, William Shakespeare.

Mr. Barrel has also X-rayed two other portraits known as Shakespeare's, i.e., the Janssen portrait also in the Folger Library, and the Hampton Court portrait, until recently hanging on the wall in Hampton Court Palace and owned by the Royal Family. In each portrait the X-ray revealed that the picture had been tampered with, and that underneath the outer coat of paint was the likeness of an unmistakable nobleman of the Elizabethan period.

Would it not be ironic if it were ever proved that the best likeness of the Earl of Oxford had been for four centuries underneath layers of paint representing a portrait of William Shakespeare of Stratford![9]

Notes To Chapter IX

1. Gwynneth Bowen, Hon. Secretary of the Shakespeare Authorship Society.

2. According to Dr. David Piper, former director of the National Portrait Gallery, London, and now curator of the Fitz William in Cambridge.

3. Ibid.

4. This writer, through the courtesy of the Duke of St. Albans, has studied this portrait by Gheeraedts, and is thoroughly convinced that it does represent the Earl of Oxford in middle age.

5. Chapter VI.

6. Chapter VI.

7. The story of the revelation of the X-ray is taken from the charming book of Professor Louis P. Benezet, *The Six Loves of "Shakespeare,"* p. 113-26.

8. Chapter VI.

9. Two more notes might be added to this chapter:

   a. That as recently as ten years ago this writer saw the portrait at Hampton Court proudly shown as Shakespeare's. But in the summer of 1971 an enquiry about the portrait, of one of the guards, produced the answer that "there never was a picture of Shakespeare at Hampton Court."

   b. In the spring of 1966, the Flower Portrait of Shakespeare which until then had hung on the wall in the birthplace of the dramatist, was X-rayed by the Courtauld Institute of Art in London. The infra-red plate proved that this portrait was an Eighteenth Century fake, the picture of the Italian Madonna underneath being far more valuable than the portrait of Shakespeare. Yet this portrait had for years been in a place of honor in the Shakespeare birthplace, and had frequently been reproduced as a frontispiece for editions of the Sonnets and Plays. This news story is taken from *The London Times*, May, 1966.

BIBLIOGRAPHY

Acheson, Arthur. *Shakespeare and the Rival Poet.* London, 1903.

Acheson, Arthur. *Shakespeare, Chapman and "Sir Thomas More."* London, 1904.

Adams, George Burton. *Constitutional History of England.* Rev. by Schuyler, Robert L., New York: Henry Holt, 1951.

Alber, Edward, Ed. *The Spenser Anthology.* London, 1901.

Allen, Percy. *The Case for Edward De Vere, Seventeenth Earl of Oxford as "Shakespeare."* London: Cecil Palmer, 1930.

Allen, Percy. *The Life Story of Edward De Vere, as "William Shakespeare."* London: Cecil Palmer, 1932.

Amphlett, H. *Who Was Shakespeare?* William Heinemann, 1955.

Anderson, John L. Comp. *A Fifteenth Century Cookry Boke.* New York: Charles Scribner's Sons, 1962.

Anthony, Irvin. *Ralegh and His World.* New York: Charles Scribner's Sons, 1934.

Ashley, Robert and Moseley, Edwin M., eds. *Elizabethan Fiction.* New York: Holt, Rinehart and Winston, 1964.

Aubrey, John. *Brief Lives.* Edited by Andrew Clark. Two Vols. London, 1898.

Bacon, Francis. *The Works of Francis Bacon*, edited by James Spedding, R. E. Ellis, Douglas D. Heath. vol. 11, 12, 13, 14. Boston: 1840.

Bartlett, Rev. W. H. *The Pilgrim Fathers, or The Founders of New England in the Reign of James the First.* London, 1853.

Beckingsale, B. W. *Burghley, Tudor Statesman. 1520-1598.* New York: Macmillan, 1967.

Bedford, John, Duke of. *A Silver-Plated Spoon.* London: Cassel, 1959.

Baedeker, Karl. *London and Its Environs.* Leipzig: Karl Baedeker, 1905.

Benezet, Louis F. *The Six Loves of "Shakespeare."* New York: Pageant Press, 1958.

Bevington, David. *Tudor Drama and Politics, A Critical Approach to Topical Meaning.* Cambridge: Harvard University Press, 1968.

Bindoff, S. T. *Tudor England.* Pelican History of England, no. 5, Harmondsworth, Middlesex, England: Penguin Books, 1964.

Bowen, Catherine Drinker. *Frances Bacon, The Temper of the Man.* London: Hamish Hamilton, 1963.

Bowen, G., Articles in the Shakespeare Authorship Review, and many enlightening personal conversations.

Braff, E. *A Memorial Presented to Queen Elizabeth by William Cecil, Lord Burghleigh, then Lord High-Treasurer of England, to prevent Her Majesty's being engross'd by any one Favorite.* London, 1706.

Brewster, Dorothy. *William Brewster of the Mayflower: Portrait of a Pilgrim.* New York: New York University Press, 1970.

Brown, Ivor. *Shakespeare, A Biography and an Interpretation.* New York: Doubleday, 1949.

Brown, John Russell. *Shakespeare's Dramatic Style.* London: Heineman, 1970.

Burlington Fine Arts Club. *Catalogue of a Collection of Early Drawings and Pictures of London.* London, 1920.

Butler, Ewan. *The Cecils.* London: Frederick Muller, 1964.

Buxton, John. *Sir Philip Sidney and the English Renaissance.* New York: Macmillan, 1954.

Buxton, John. *Elizabethan Taste.* New York: Macmillan, 1965.

Byrne, M. St. Clare. *Elizabethan Life in Town and Country.* London: Methuen, 1950.

Camden, William. *The History of the Most Renowned and Victorious Princess Elizabeth, Late Queen of England.* Ed. with an introduction by Wallace T. MacCaffray. Chicago and London: University of Chicago Press, 1970.

Cantor, Norman F. and Werthman, Michael S. eds. *The English Tradition.* New York: Macmillan, 1967.

Chambers, E. K. *The Elizabethan Stage.* 3 vols. Oxford, 1923.

Chambers, E. K. *William Shakespeare.* 2 Vols. Oxford: Oxford University Press, 1930.
Chambers, E. K. *Sir Henry Lee, An Elizabethan Portrait.* Oxford: Clarendon Press, 1934.
Chambers, E. K. *Shakespeare Gleanings.* Oxford: Oxford University Press, 1944.
Chambers, E. K. ed. *The Oxford Book of Sixteenth Century Verse.* Oxford: Clarendon Press, 1961.
Chapman George. *The Shadow of Night.* London, 1594.
Charlton, H. B. *Shakespearean Tragedy.* Cambridge University Press, 1971.
Charlton, William Henry. *Burghley.* Stamford, England, 1847.
Chute, Marchette. *Shakespeare of London.* New York: E. P. Dutton, 1949.
Chute, Marchette. *Ben Jonson of Westminster.* New York: E. P. Dutton, 1953.
Clark, Eva Turner *Axiophilus,* New York: Knickerbocker Press, 1926.
Clark, Eva Turner *Shakespeare's Plays in the Order of Their Writing.* London, 1930.
Clark, Eva Turner *Hidden Allusions in Shakespeare's Plays.* New York, 1931.
Clark, George, ed. *The Reign of Elizabeth.* 2d ed. History of England Series. Oxford: Oxford University Press, 1959.
Clark, George, ed. *English History, A Survey.* Oxford: Clarendon Press, 1971.
Constant, G., *The Reformation in England*, Harper Torchbooks, 1966.
Copeman, W. S. G. *Doctors and Diseas in Tudor Times.* London: Dawson's of Pall Mall, 1960.
Creighton, Mandell. *Queen Elizabeth.* London: Longmans, Green & Co., 1920.
Davenport, Milia. *The Book of Costume.* Vol. I.
Dean and Chapter of Westminster. *Westminster Abbey.* Official Guide. Rev. ed. Norwich, England: Jarrold & Sons, 1971.
Dean, Leonard, F. ed. *Shakespeare: Modern Essays in Criticism.*

Rev. ed. Oxford: Oxford University Press, 1967.
De Montaigne, Michael. *Essays.* Translated by John Florio. London, 1603.
Denkinger, Emma Marshall. *Immortal Sidney.* Brentano's, 1931.
Dewar, Mary, ed. *A Discourse of the Commonweal of This Realm of England.* Attributed to Sir Thomas Smith. The Folger Shakespeare Library. Charlottesville, Virginia: University Press of Virginia, 1969.
Dodd, A. H. *Life in Elizabethan England.* English Life Series. B. T. Batsford, Publishers, 1961.
Douglas, Montagu. *Lord Oxford and the Shakespeare Group.* Oxford: Alden Press, 1952.
Dugdale, George S., M.A. *Whitehall Through the Centuries.* London, 1950.
Dunlop, Ian. *The Palaces and Progresses of Elizabeth I.* London, 1962.
Egger, Katherine E. *Shakespeare in His True Colours.* London, 1951.
Elizabeth I. *The Letters of Queen Elizabeth I.* Edited by G. B. Harrison. New York: Funk & Wagnals, 1968.
Encyclopaedia Brittanica. 9th and 11th eds. S. V. "Edward de Vere, Seventeenth Earl of Oxford.
Evans, A. J. *Shakespeare's Magic Circle.* London, 1956.
Fellowes, Edmund H. *The English Madrigal.* Oxford: Oxford University Press, 1935.
Fleeay, F. G. *The Shakespeare Manuel.* New York: Macmillan, 1876.
Fluchère, Henri. *Shakespeare and the Elizabethans.* New York: Hill & Wang, 1964.
Forbes, Thomas Rogers. *Chronicle from Aldgate, Life and Death in Shakespeare's London.* New Haven: Yale University Press, 1971.
Franklyn, Julian. *Heraldry.* New York: A. S. Barnes & Co., 1970.
Frisbee, George. *Edward de Vere, A Great Elizabethan.* London: Cecil Palmer, 1931.

Froude, James Anthony. *History of England.* Vol. IV. New York: Charles Scribner, 1867.

Galloway, David, ed. *The Elizabethan Theatre, II.* Papers given at the International Conference on Elizabethan Theatre held at the University of Waterloo, Ontario, in July, 1969. Canada: Macmillan, 1970.

Garrett, George. *Death of the Fox.* Doubleday, 1971.

Gascoigne, George, ed. *A hundreth sundrie Flowres.* London, 1573.

Gascoigne, George, ed. *A Gorgeous Gallery of Gallant Inventions.* London, 1577-78.

Gibson. H. N. *The Shakespeare Claimants.* London: Methuen, 1962.

Goff, Cecilie. *A Woman of the Tudor Age.* London: John Murray, 1924.

Goff, Cecilie. *Three Generations of a Loyal House.* London: Privately printed under the care of The Rampant Lion Press, 1957.

Golding, Arthur. *Translation of Ovid's Metamorphoses,* edited with an Introduction and Notes by John Frederick Nims. New York: Macmillan, 1965.

Golding, Louis Thorn. *An Elizabethan Puritan.* New York, 1937.

Granville-Barker, H., and Harrison, G. B. eds. *A Companion to Shakespeare Studies.* New York: Macmillan, 1934.

Green, John Richard. *History of the English People.* Vol. II. New York: Harper & Brothers.

Hadfield, John, ed. *Elizabethan Love Lyrics.* London: Studio Vista, 1958.

Halliday, F. E., ed. *A Shakespeare Companion. 1550-1950.* New York: Funk & Wagnals, 1952.

Halliday, F. E., ed. *Shakespeare, A Pictorial Biography.* 400th Anniversary edition. New York: Viking Press, 1964.

Hare, Augustus, F. C. *Walks in London.* 2 vols. New York: George M. Routledge and Sons, 1878.

Harris, Frank. *The Women of Shakespeare.* New York: Mitchell Kenerley, 1912.

Harrison, G. B., comp. *The Elizabethan Journals.* 2 Vols. George Routledge & Sons, 1938.

Harrison, G. B., comp. *A Last Elizabethan Journal.* London: Constable, 1938.

Haydn, Hiram, ed. *The Portable Elizabethan Reader.* New York, 1946.

Hazlitt, William. *Lectures on the Dramatic Literature of the Age of Elizabeth.* New York: Wiley & Putnam, 1845.

Hibbert, Christopher. *London, the Biography of a City.* New York: William Morrow & Co., 1970.

Hind, Arthur M. *Wenceslaus Holler, His Views of London and Windsor in the 17th Century.* London, 1922.

History and Treasures of Hatfield House. Official Guide.

Holland, H. H., C. B. *Shakespeare, Oxford and Elizabethan Times.* London, 1933.

Holmes, M. R., *The London of Elizabeth I.* The London Museum, 1959.

Holmes, M. R. *Shakespeare's Public.* London: John Murray, 1960.

Home, Gordon. *Mediaeval London.* Ernest Benn, 1927.

Hotson. J. Leslie. *The First Night of Twelfth Night.* London: Mercury Books, 1961.

Hume, Martin, A. S. *The Great Lord Burghley.* Longmans, Green & Co., 1898.

Hunter G. K. *John Lyly, The Humanist as Courtier.* London: Routledge & Kegan Paul, 1962.

Hurstfield, Joel. *The Elizabethan Nation.* New York: Harper Torchbooks, 1967.

Huston, Craig. *The Shakespeare Authorship Question. Evidence for Edward De Vere, Seventeenth Earl of Oxford.* Philadelphia: Dorrance & Company, 1971.

Irving, Washington. *Westminster Abbey.* Literary Mosaics. New York: George M. Allen Company, 1893.

Ben Jonson. Prose and Poems. Ed. by C. H. Herford Percy and Evelyn Simpson. Oxford University Press, 1947. Vol. VIII. *Epigrammes,* and *Timber, or Discoveries made upon men and matter: as they have flow'd out of his daily Readings; or had their refluxe to his peculiar notions of the Times.* (This volume published in 1947.)

Jonson, Ben. *Epigrammes,* and *Timber, or Discoveries made upon men and matter: as they have flow'd out of his daily Readings; or had their refluxe to his peculiar notions of the Times.* Of Prose and Poems of Ben Jonson, vol. VIII. Edited by E. H. Herford, Percy, and Evelyn Simpson. Oxford: Oxford UniversityPress, 1947.

Jonson, Ben. *The Complete Poetry of Ben Jonson.* Edited by William B. Hunter, Jr. Anchor Books, Doubleday & Co., New York.

Jonson, Ben. *Five Plays.* Oxford: Oxford University Press, 1964.

Jonson, Ben. *Epigrammes,* The Works of Ben Jonson. Edited by W.Gifford. London, 1816.

Joseph, Sister Miriam. *Rhetoric in Shakespeare's Time.* 1962. Harcourt, Brace & World.

Judges, A. V., ed. *The Elizabethan Underworld.* George Routledge & Sons, 1930.

Johannes, J. G. *Shakespeare's Mysterious W. H. and Dark Mistress Revealed.* Batavia, 1928.

Kelly, Henry Ansgar *Divine Providence in the England of Shakespeare's Histories.* Cambridge: Harvard University Press, 1970.

Kent, William et al. *Edward de Vere, Seventeenth Earl of Oxford, The Real Shakespeare.* The Shakespeare Fellowship, 2nd ed., 1957.

Kittle, William. *Edward de Vere, 17th Earl of Oxford as Shakespeare.* Baltimore, 1942.

Lacey, Robert. *Robert, Earl of Essex, an Elizabethan Icarus.* London: Weidenfeld and Nicolson, 1971.

Laughlin, Clara E. *So You're Going to England!* Boston: Houghton Mifflin, 1926.

Lee, Sidney. *Life of Shakespeare.* New York: Macmillan, 1916.

Le Riche, Kathleen. *Shakespeare in Essex.* Reprinted from *The Essex Review,* vol. LXI, October, 1952.

Lever, Tresham. *The Herberts of Wilton.* London: John Murray, 1967.

Levy, F. J. *Tudor Historical Thought.* Huntington Library, 1967.

Lewis, Hilda. *I Am Mary Tudor.* New York: David McKay Company, 1972.

London Society, Journal of, No. 192, February, 1934.

Looney, J. Thomas. *"Shakespeare" Identified as the Seventeenth Earl of Oxford.* London, 1920.

Looney, J. Thomas. *The Poems of Edward de Vere.* London, 1921.

Luke, Mary M. *A Crown for Elizabeth.* New York: Coward-McCann, 1970.

Lunt, W. E. *History of England.* 4th ed. New York: Harper Brothers, 1957.

Lyly, John. *The Descent of Euphues, Euphues, Pandosto, Piers Plainness.* Edited by James Winny, Cambridge University Press, 1957.

Maitland, F. W. *Constitutional History of England.* Cambridge University Press, 1948.

Majendie, Severne A. Ashurst. *Some Account of the Family of de Vere, the Earls of Oxford and of Hedingham Castle.* Chelmsford, England: Tindall & Jarrold, 1904.

Markham, Gervase. *The Fighting Veres.* London, 1888.

Marlowe, Christopher. *Complete Plays.* The World's Classics. Oxford: Oxford University Press, 1964.

Marlowe, Christopher. *Plays & Poems.* Everyman's Library, no. 383. Edited by M. R. Ricley, 1965.

Mason, H. A. *Shakespeare's Tragedies of Love.* London: Chatto & Windus, 1970.

Mattingly, Garrett. *The Spanish Armada.* Boston: Houghton Mifflin, 1959.

McCollum, John I., Jr., ed. *The Age of Elizabeth.* Houghton Mifflin Research Series, no. 1. Boston: Houghton Mifflin, 1960.

McGrath, Patrick. *Papists and Puritans Under Elizabeth I.* New York: Walker & Company, 1967.

McIlwraith, A. K., ed. *Five Elizabethan Tragedies.* Oxford: Oxford University Press, 1963.
McIlwaith, A. K., ed. *Five Elizabethan Comedies.* Oxford: Oxford University Press, 1965.
Mees, Arthur. *Essex, London's North Sea Neighbor.* London: Hodder and Stoughton, 1956.
Mellanby, Ruth. *Cambridge in Brief.* Cambridge: W. Heffer and Sons, 1955.
A Memoir of Peregrine Bertie, Eleventh Lord Willoughby d'Eresby. London: John Murray, 1838.
Morton, H. V. *In Search of London.* New York: Dodd, Mead & Co., 1951.
Muir, Kenneth, and Schoenbaun, S., eds. *A New Companion to Shakespeare Studies.* Cambridge University Press, 1971.
Munday, Anthony, et al. *The Book of Sir Thomas More.*
Neale, John E. *Queen Elizabeth.* New York: Harcourt, Brace, 1934.
Neale, John E. *The Elizabethan House of Commons.* New York: Jonathan Cape, 1949.
Neale, John E. *The London of Elizabeth I.* New York: Jonathan Cape, 1959.
Nicoll, Allardyce. *Shakespeare.* London: Methuen & Co., 1952.
Nicoll, Allardyce. *The Elizabethans.* Cambridge University Press, 1957.
Ogburn, Dorothy and Charlton. *This Star of England.* New York: Coward-McCann, 1950.
Ogburn, Dorothy and Charlton, Jr. *Shake-speare, the Man Behind the Name.* New York: Morrow & Co., 1962.
Ogburn, Charlton, Jr. *Shakespeare and the Men of Stratford.* Washington: The Shakespeare Oxford Society, 1964.
The Paradyse of Daynty Deuises. London: H. Dis Le, 1578.
Piper, David. *The Companion Guide to London.* New York: Harper & Row, 1965.
Proctor, Thomas, ed. *A Gorgeous Gallery of Gallant Inventions, 1578.* Edited by H. E. Rollins. Cambridge: Harvard University Press, 1926.

Purcell, James M. *Sidney's Stella.* Oxford: Oxford University Press, 1934.
Quennell, Peter. *Shakespeare, a Biography.* World Publishing Co., 1963.
Quiller-Couch, Arthur, Chooser. *The Oxford Book of English Verse.* Oxford: Clarendon Press, 1910.
Read, Conyers. *The Tudors.* New York: Henry Holt, 1936.
Read, Conyers. *Lord Burghley and Queen Elizabeth.* London: Jonathan Cape, 1960.
Read, Evelyn. *Catherine, Duchess of Suffolk.* London: Jonathan Cape, 1962.
Reliques of Ancient English Poetry. 6th ed. 4 vols. Grocer's Hall Court, The Poultry, London: Samuel Richard & Co., 1823.
Rendall, Gerald H. *Ben Jonson and The First Folio Edition of Shakespeare's Plays.* Colchester, Essex, England, 1939.
Ribner, Irving. *William Shakespeare, An Introduction To His Life, Times, and Theatre.* Waltham, Mass.: Blaisdell Publishing Company, 1969.
Rolfe, William J. *A Life of William Shakespeare.* New York: Harper & Brothers, 1904.
Rowse, A. L. *The England of Elizabeth.* London: Macmillan, 1950.
Rowse, A. L. *The Expansion of Elizabethan England.* New York: Harper & Row, 1955.
Rowse, A. L. *The Elizabethans and America.* New York: Harper & Row, 1959.
Rowse, A. L. *William Shakespeare.* New York: Harper & Row, 1963.
Rowse, A. L. *Christopher Marlowe.* New York: Harper & Row, 1964.
Rowse, A. L. *Shakespeare's Southampton.* New York: Harper & Row, 1969.
Rowse, A. L. *Tudor Cornwall.* London: Macmillan, 1969.
Rowse, A. L. *The Cornish in America.* London: Macmillan, 1969.
Sackville-West, Victoria. *Knole and the Sackvilles.* London: Ernest Benn, 1958.

Salzman, L. F. *Edward I.* London: Constable, 1968.
Saxo Grammaticus. *Amleth.* Translated by Oliver Elton. *The Sources of Hamlet.* Edited by Israel Gollancz. Oxford: Oxford University Press, 1926.
Shakespeare, William. *Comedies, Histories, and Tragedies. First Folio*, London, 1623. *The life and death of King John*, pp. 1-22.
Sheppard, Edgar. *The Old Royal Palace of Whitehall.* London, 1902.
Sidney, Sir Philip. *The Countess of Pembrokes Arcadia, Astrophel and Stella, The Ladie of May and other poems.* Edited by Albert Feuillerat. Cambridge University Press, 1922.
Sitwell, Edith. *The Queens and the Hive.* Boston: Little Brown, 1962.
Smith, A. Murray, and Lady Birchenough. *The Westminster Abbey Guide.* 34th ed. 1959.
Smith, Lacey Baldwin. *This Realm of England, 1399-1688.* A History of England Series, vol. II. Lexington, Massachusetts: D. C. Heath and Company, 1966.
Smith, Lacey Baldwin. *The Horizon Book of The Elizabethan World.* New York: American Heritage Publishing Company, 1967.
Smith, Lacey Baldwin. *Henry VIII, The Mask of Royalty.* Boston: Houghton, Mifflin, 1971.
Spenser, Edmund. *Complete Works.* Edited by Francis J. Child. Boston: Fields, Osgood & Co., 1871.
Spurgeon, Caroline F. E. *Shakespeare's Imagery and What It Tells Us.* Cambridge University Press, 1935.
Stephenson, Carl, and Marcham, Frederick George. *Sources of English Constitutional History.* New York: Harper & Brothers, 1937.
Stow, John. *The Survey of London*, with additions by Anthony Munday. London: George Purslowe, 1618.
Stow, John. *The Survey of London.* Edited by H. Morley. London: George Routledge Sons, 1890.
Strachey, Lytton. *Elizabeth and Essex, a Tragic History.* New York: Harcourt, Brace, 1928.

Sturt, Mary. *Francis Bacon.* New York: Morrow & Co., 1932.
Sullivan, Mary. *Court Masques of James I.* New York: G. P. Putnam, 1913.
Thomson, Elizabeth McClure. *The Chamberlain Letters.* New York: G. P. Putnam, 1965.
Thorndike, Ashley, ed. *Minor Elizabethan Drama.* Pre-Shakespearean Tragedies, vol. I. Everyman's Library. New York: Dutton & Co., 1964.
Tillyard, E. M. W. *The Elizabeth World Picture.* Penguin Books.
The Tower of London. Ministry of Works Guide book. 1962.
Toynbee, Arnold J. *A Study of History.* Abridgement by D. C. Somervell. 2 vols. Oxford: Oxford University Press, 1957.
Trevelyan, George Macaulay. *History of England.* London: Longmans, Green & Co., 1927.
Waldman, Milton. *England's Elizabeth.* Boston: Houghton Mifflin, 1933.
Waldman, Milton. *Elizabeth and Leicester.* Boston: Houghton Mifflin, 1945.
Ward, B. M., ed. *A Hundreth Sundrie Flowres.* London. 1926.
Ward, B. M. *The Seventeenth Earl of Oxford.* London, 1928.
Ward, B. R. *The Mystery of "Mr. W. H."* London, 1923.
Weiss, Theodore. *The Breath of Clowns and Kings, Shakespeare's Early Comedies and Histories.* London: Chatto & Windus, 1971.
Wheatley, Henry B. *London, Past and Present.* London, 1891.
Willison, George F. *Saints and Strangers.* New York: Reynal & Hitchcock, 1945.
Williams, Neville. *Thomas Howard, Fourth Duke of Norfolk.* New York: E. P. Dutton & Co., 1965.
Wilson, John Dover. *The Essential Shakespeare.* Cambridge University Press, 1960.
Wilson, Violet A. *Society Women of Shakespeare's Time.* New York: E. P. Dutton, 1925.
Winny, James. *Elizabethan Prose Translations.* Cambridge University Press, 1960.

The Yale Shakespeare is used in quotations from the plays. It is edited by members of the English faculty, Yale University. University.

Special material is taken from the *Sonnets* in this same Series; the *Sonnets* are edited by Edward Bliss Reed. New Haven: Yale University Press, 1956.

INDEX

Plays quoted in text.

Sonnets.